MOTHER OF THE SECRET

To
Sandy
God Bless you

Fr. Peter

MOTHER OF THE SECRET

**FROM EUCHARISTIC MIRACLES TO MARIAN APPA-
RITIONS, HEAVEN HAS SOUGHT TO ILLUMINATE
AND DEFEND WHAT WAS ONCE THE CHURCH'S
GREATEST SECRET.**

by Dr. Thomas W. Petrisko

Queenship
PUBLISHING COMPANY
P.O. Box 220, Goleta, CA 93116
(800) 647-9882 • (805) 692-0043 • Fax: (805) 967-5843

CONSECRATION AND DEDICATION

This book is consecrated to the Most Holy Trinity. It is dedicated to Fr. Richard Foley, whose indomitable love for Our Lord in the Eucharist is an example to all the members of the Mystical Body of Christ on Earth

Library of Congress #: 97-68889

Published by:
Queenship Publishing
P.O. Box 220
Goleta, CA 93116
(800) 647-9882 • (805) 692-0043 • Fax: (805) 967-5843

Printed in the United States of America

ISBN: 1-57918-003-5

ACKNOWLEDGMENTS

I am indebted to many people. Most significantly, Bridgette Hooker and *Come Alive Communications*. Under a heavy cross, Bridgette edited this work and offered it to God. I also want to thank some who were especially helpful with this work: Therese Swango, Dr. Frank Novasack,Jr., Robert and Kim Petrisko, Joan Smith, Sister Agnes McCormick, Carole McElwain, Karen Seisek, Bud MacFarlane, Stan and Marge Karminski, Father Richard Foley and Mary Lou Sokol. A special thank you to Bob Schaefer and Queenship Publishing for their tremendous support.

I am grateful to many others who helped me by their encouragement and support, especially Father Robert Herrmann, Father John O'Shea, Jan and Ed Connell, Patty and George Pietripola, Georgette Faniel, John Haffert, Anatol Kaszczuk, George Malouf, the staff at Family Chropractic Center, the Pittsburgh Center for Peace prayer group and the Ambridge Holy Trinity prayer group, Amanda Ree, Jim Petrilena, Linda and Audrey Santo, Dominic and Joan Laitteri, and Joe and Gerry Simboli (cover design).

Once again, a big thank you to my mother and father, Mary and Andrew Petrisko and my uncle Sam. Last but not least to my precious wife, Emily, and my children Maria, Sarah, Joshua and Natasha.

ABOUT THE AUTHOR

Dr. Thomas W. Petrisko is the President of the Pittsburgh Center for Peace. From 1990 to 1997, he served as editor of the Center's four newspapers, which featured the apparitions and revelations of the Virgin Mary and were published in many millions throughout the world. He is the author of *The Fatima Prophecies-At the Doorstep of the World, For the Soul of the Family- The Story of the Apparitions of the Virgin Mary to Estela Ruiz, The Sorrow, the Sacrifice and the Triumph - the Visions, Apparitions and Prophecies of Christina Gallagher, Call of the Ages, The Last Crusade, Pray For Me Little Audrey, the Miraculous Story of Audrey Santo, False Prophets of Today* and *The Prophecy of Daniel.*

Along with his wife Emily, they have two daughters, Maria and Sarah, a son, Joshua, and expect their fourth child in May, 1997.

If you wish to have Dr. Petrisko or someone from his staff speak at your church or to your organization, you may write to:

St. Andrews Productions
6111 Steubenville Pike
McKees Rocks, PA 15136

or call (412) 787-9735

(Please submit all letters or faxes in a typed format.)

CONTENTS

FOREWORD
BY: Richard Foley, SJ.

This book comes as much from Dr. Thomas Petrisko's heart as from his head. For he is known to be generously devoted both to the Lord of the Eucharist and His Mother.

What we are given in these pages is an overview of Eucharistic devotion down the centuries, with particular reference to Mary's prominent role in promoting it. Indeed, Mother of the Blessed Sacrament is one of her proudest titles. It is also one of the most significant. Pope St. Pius X rated this Marian title as *"the most theological"* after the Mother of God.

The author presents us in chapter after chapter with a wealth of information about the Eucharistic mysteries, all the way from Roman-catacomb days (they were then protected by the so-called *"discipline of the secret"*) down to modern times. In the process we are taken on a veritable tour de monde as the spotlight focuses on events such as Marian apparitions, Eucharistic miracles and mystical phenomena, which took place in localities spread right across the globe. The Holy Father once referred to this widespread distribution as *"the geography"* of supernatural interventions.

Thus, a whole galaxy of place-names feature in Dr. Petrisko's survey - it could be called a panorama - of heavenly visitations past and present. To take a random selection: Lanciano in Italy; Paray-le-Monial, Lourdes and La Salette in France; Knock in Ireland; Fatima in Portugal; Medjugorje in Bosnia; Turzovka in Czechoslovakia; Konnersreuth in Germany; Cracow in Poland; Damascus in Syria; Betania in Venezuela; Naju in South Korea; Akita in Japan; Guadalupe in Mexico; the Tabor Islands in New Guinea... The complete list would fill several pages.

What, then, is the bottom line, so to call it, in all these heavenly manifestations? What is their common denominator? Quite simply it is this: the Mother of God is principally concerned therein with promoting faith in her Son's True Presence and our due adoration and reparation.

Of very special interest and importance in this context is Fatima. Besides reinforcing our belief in the Eucharistic Presence and exhorting us to adore and make reparation, the Portuguese shrine acts as a beacon for contemporary humanity as it gropes its way through this benighted century to the fast-approaching third millennium and the dawning of an era of peace.

Indeed, that coming era is really Our Lady of Fatima's crowning prophecy and promise: her Immaculate Heart will finally triumph, and her Eucharistic Son will be adored and honored as never before.

St. John Bosco pointed in the same direction in his famous prophetic dream of 1862. Before the year 2000, we learn from that source, Mary Help of Christians will achieve a major victory over those seeking to destroy the Church. And this victory will be brought about through the Church's faithfulness to God's Mother and to the tabernacle Presence of the Word-made-flesh.

What Dr. Petrisko's book really amounts to is a feast of facts and lessons relating to Mary in her role as Mother of the Blessed Sacrament. Readers will find here, among other things, all they ever wanted to know about the altogether astonishing Eucharistic miracles, both past and present, that have taken place in different part of the world.

Particularly striking among the contemporary miracles are the dozen or so associated with Naju in South Korea. One of these reportedly actually took place while the visionary Julia Kim was attending Mass said by the Holy Father in his private chapel. After she had received Holy communion a strong fragrance of roses as well as the scent of blood filled the chapel. The sacred Host then became larger in Julia's mouth, and she saw a bright light descend upon the Holy Father. That was in late 1995.

The previous year an even more astounding miracle took place in Naju itself. It was witnessed by no less a person that the Vatican archbishop who was Apostolic Pronuncio in Korea; moreover, he had earlier made it clear that he was visiting Naju not merely as a private pilgrim but as the official representative of the Holy See.

In a chapel a large Host was brought by the Archangel Michael and placed in Julia's hand; she in turn placed its halves in the hands of the visiting papal diplomat and her spiritual director. Though they proceeded to give Holy Communion to a good number of people with portions of this single Host, it more that sufficed for everyone present. Subsequently the same Host was preserved in a pyx for exposition and adoration.

To end on a somber and somewhat sad note. Those who would stand to benefit most by this book are, the least likely to read it. Here I particularly have in mind a fair number of my fellow-priests. Having been infected with liberal theological views, some of which are downright heretical, they tend to affect a superior and disdainful attitude towards such phenomena as Marian apparitions and Eucharistic miracles.

The basic problem underlying theological liberalism is lack, or even loss, of faith. And this negative state of mind reaches rockbottom when it denies or doubts what is the mystery of faith par excellence: the all-sacred presence of Jesus, as Priest, Victim and Food, in the most holy Sacrament of the Altar.

Readers of Dr. Petrisko's book are urged to pray for all priests that their lives may be oriented more and more towards the Blessed Sacrament. Let us never forget either that the Mother of that all-holy Sacrament - she is also the Mother of Priests - is unceasingly present, as adorer and advocate alike, within the ambience of the tabernacle.

Fr. Richard Foley SJ.
London, England
June 24, 1997

Mother of the Secret

INTRODUCTION

It will be stunning. It will also be unique and vast. For according to numerous visionaries, mystics, prophets and seers, the world is going to experience a wondrous change.

Visionaries foretell that mankind will move from a secular, agnostic, practically atheistic realm into a world which basks in the reality of God and belief in the presence of the supernatural. The prophets say that mankind will then thrive on secure faith and confidence in this reality, for true peace will rule and the Church will reign supreme.

Most notably, many Catholic visionaries insist that the world will at last come to deeply understand the power, the mercy and the grace which is available in the miraculous True Presence of Jesus Christ in the Sacrament of Holy Eucharist.

Unbelievable?

Indeed, based upon an objective assessment of the current world around us, God will truly have to take drastic measures in order to alter our present course. To say the least, a major undertaking is in order if we are to arrive at a future comparable to that foretold by the prophets. As much of the world today wishes to have little to with God and belief in the miraculous. In fact, the overall effort by the secular media to create doubt about the reality of God is ever mounting.

On April 10, 1995, *Time* magazine's cover boldly asked the question: "CAN WE STILL BELIEVE IN MIRACLES?" With a painting of the Resurrected Christ on its cover, *Time* methodically documented testimonies from reportedly acknowledged "Biblical scholars" who debunked, ridiculed and doubted that anything supernatural has ever occurred in history. This included Christ's Resurrection. To emphasize the essence of the argument, the Roman orator Cicero was quoted in boldface typeset, "WHAT WAS IN-CAPABLE OF HAPPENING NEVER HAPPENED, AND WHAT WAS CAPABLE OF HAPPENING IS NOT A MIRACLE ... CON-SEQUENTLY, THERE ARE NO MIRACLES."

One year later, *Time*, *Newsweek* and *U.S. News* and *World Report*, America's three largest weekly news magazines, all ran Easter week (April 8, 1996) cover stories which again challenged the validity of Christ's Resurrection.

For followers of Marian apparitions and revelations, these reports should not be surprising, because the Virgin Mary has described in her prophetic messages the chronological unfolding of events that must occur before the new era will begin. These events, Mary says, will continually reveal the great apostasy of faith which will come upon the world as she has foretold for centuries.

In fact, as the new era draws nearer, the world will move farther and farther away from God and especially, Mary emphasizes, away from her Son, Jesus Christ, and the teachings of His Church.

Indeed, the Blessed Mother's revelations specifically foretell that, before God's coming victory over evil and the dawn of true peace the world must be on the threshold of total denial of Jesus Christ's divinity.

While strongly confirming Mary's prophetic words, the April 4, 1994 cover article in *Newsweek* magazine, entitled "The Death of Jesus" defines our times quite accurately.

After researching the teachings of contemporary seminaries concerning the life of Jesus Christ, *Newsweek* wrote the following in an article titled "A Lesser God":

> *Outside the mainstream of Christian Bible study, iconoclastic scholars are piecing together the portrait of a Jesus no one ever encountered in Sunday school. These experts believe that the Biblical Jesus was a myth created by church-building Christians decades after the Crucifixion. The real Jesus, many of them say, was no more the child of God than anyone else.*

But while the alleged Biblical experts and scholars are expressing doubts, it seems the general public still wants to believe in

God. Polls repeatedly show that over 90% of Americans say that they believe in God. In 1995 *Time* magazine conducted a poll that asked the question of whether or not people believe in miracles. Of those polled, 69% said "yes".

Furthermore, *Time* reported that the fastest growing churches in America, the Charismatic and Pentecostal congregations, are churches where worship is centered around miraculous "signs and wonders".

Time also cited the huge throngs at Conyers, Georgia and Lubbock, Texas where apparitions of the Virgin Mary have reportedly occurred. The irony, noted *Time*, was *"just when the faithful are so eager to embrace the possibility of miracles in everyday life, prominent American theologians are working furiously to disprove the miracles in the Bible."*

For Catholics, the belief in miracles is a teaching of the Church. One of the great documents of Vatican I was the Dogmatic Constitution on the Catholic Faith (*Dei Filius*). This document had chapters dealing with God the Creator, faith, revelation, and faith and reason. These chapters were followed by certain rules, or canons, as the Church calls them. The third chapter, "On Faith" states that God gives external signs as arguments on behalf of revelation. Among the canons of this chapter, we find this statement in support of miracles:

> *If anyone should say that there can be no miracles, and that all accounts of them, even those contained in Sacred Scripture, are to be thought of as fables or myths; or that miracles cannot be certainly known; or that they can never be rightly used to prove origin of the Christian religions, let them be anathema.*

Vatican I also emphasized three things about miracles:

1. Accounts of miracles, particularly Biblical accounts, are not to be dismissed as fables or myths.
2. Miracles can be known with certainty.
3. Miracles are proof of the divine origin of Christianity.

While the early Fathers of the Catholic Church had much to say about miracles, they did not formally define them. It is believed that St. Augustine was the first to attempt a definition. *"I call a miracle,"* wrote St. Augustine, *"any difficult or uncustomary thing which appears, exceeding the hope and expectation of the onlookers."*

Centuries later, St. Thomas Aquinas, in his *Summa Theologiæ*, wrote:

> *I reply that the word miracle comes from wonder, but wonder arises when the result is manifest and the cause obscure, as one might wonder when he sees an eclipse of the sun, not knowing its cause, as Aristotle says at the outset of the Metaphysics. The cause of an effect can be known to some yet unknown to others, so something can be a wonder to one and not to another, as the eclipse is a wonder to the uninstructed but not to the astronomer. Miracle suggests something full of wonder, whose cause is unknown simply and absolutely. This cause is God. Hence what God does outside of causes known to us are called miracles.****

St. Thomas Aquinas also established different grades of miracles, with some being greater than others. His view was that those miracles which exceed nature to the greatest degree are of the highest level; such as, the sun moving east rather than west. Miracles of the lowest level are the ones that exceed nature only in the timing of the event; such as, someone being cured in Christ's name rather than by normal rest or the active powers of nature.

But for Catholics, the greatest miracle is one that is not even subject to appraisal by the mind and senses as determined by St. Thomas' grading system. It is a miracle that is recognized and defined by faith alone and requires contemplation of the stupendous might and power of God. Indeed, the Church asks the faithful to believe in the mysteries of the Eucharist by *"detaching, as much as possible, their mind and understanding from the dominion of the senses."* (Council of Trent)

Indeed, the Church's teachings on miracles invite the faithful *"to believe"* after being confronted mentally and through their senses with the possibility of divine assistance. Yet specifically concerning the Eucharist, the Council of Trent states that after *"consulting the sight, the touch, the smell, the taste, and finding nothing but the appearance of bread and wine, the faithful will naturally judge that this Sacrament contains nothing more than bread and wine"*.

There is even more to the Church's specific teaching regarding the miracle of the Eucharist. The Council of Trent stated that after one finds *"nothing more that bread and wine,"* one should believe that three *"wondrous and admirable effects"* have occurred after the priest has uttered the words of the consecration of the Eucharist.

The first is that the true body of Christ the Lord, the same that was born of the Virgin Mary, and is now seated at the right hand of God the Father in heaven, is contained in the Sacrament of the Eucharist.

The second is that none of the substance of the elements of the bread and wine remains in the Sacrament.

And the third is that the accidents (bread and wine), which present themselves to the eyes or other senses, exist in a wonderful and ineffable manner without a subject. While the accidents of bread and wine can be seen, they have no innate substance and exist independently of any. This is because the substances of bread and wine are changed into the Body and Blood of Jesus Christ and they cease altogether to be bread and wine.

With the Church's official definition of the miracle of the Eucharist, we see the incredibly vast chasm that today separates the teachings of humanism from the Catholic Church's teachings on its greatest miracle, the mystery of the True Presence of Jesus Christ in the Eucharist. For the Church's teachings on the miracle of the Eucharist do not all fall under its own approved guidelines for discerning miracles. Not surprisingly then, this position, the concept of a formal teaching concerning miracles that is acquired strictly through terms of faith, leaves secular humanists aghast since they already are dismayed at the thought of miracles that exceed the order of nature.

Yet, according to the revelations of the Virgin Mary, the world is about to delve much deeper into this specific mystery of faith.

Although the Catholic Church's teaching of this mystery has been consistent over the ages, Mary repeatedly confirms that God wishes this mystery to come more alive in the world. Indeed, it is said that the Eucharistic Presence of Christ in the world will become the cornerstone of the new times. Likewise, numerous saints and mystics have long proclaimed the coming of these times.

Exactly how the world will evolve into a greater state of cooperation and living interaction with this reality is mystifying. Yet, we realize there is only one way it can occur: and that is through solid faith.

Faith! While a majority of Americans say that they believe in God, Catholics and all Christians often fail to find in Scripture a specific invitation to believe and accept "in faith" not only the reality of God, but also His divine plan. This plan is revealed in Scripture and discovered by each generation. And in its developement, God's plan has been generously enhanced with many reported miracles, signs and wonders to confirm its truth.

With each miracle, God hopes that at least one soul realizes that it needs less and less of such supernatural help, and can walk more and more on its own in just the light of faith. This is the path God prefers a soul to take. Indeed, Scripture calls us to believe in God with nothing but faith in the first place, for according to Scripture, everything we see and experience really is a miracle!

And so, according to divine revelation, all creation is a miracle or a sign to us of the existence of God. *"The heavens declare the glory of God..."* (Ps 19:1).

Likewise, the New Testament confirms this exhortation that understanding divine realities should be based upon faith. *"Ever since the creation of the world, the invisible existence of God and His everlasting power have been clearly seen by the mind's understanding of created things."* (Rm 1:20).

For those with strong faith, these two passages from Scripture are enough to uphold the belief in God, His plan, and for that matter, the doctrine of the Eucharist.

But Scripture goes on to explain and reveal to us God's divine plan. To make our faith secure and confident, we are given understanding of the creation of the world and man, God's establishment of various covenants with His people, and the consequence of sin on our eternal future.

Most of all, Scripture conveys the understanding that God's plan is centered around His Son, Jesus Christ, His Son's Cross and the profound mystery of the Redemption and the Resurrection.

Indeed, the life and death of Jesus Christ is the core of the meaning behind so many of Scripture's miraculous events. For the Passion, Crucifixion and Resurrection of Jesus Christ took shape in and through Christ's human body, a body that was totally human and yet completely and hypostatically united to His Divinity. And it is a body that through death was intended to bring eternal life to our souls and again someday to our bodies.

Thus, from the moment of Christ's conception, His human life is recognized as the core of the mystery of God's plan for His people. It was a divine plan to introduce Himself into the world forever, as both man and God; first, in the living, breathing body of Jesus Christ and then forevermore under the outward appearance of bread and wine. Scripture tells us that this Presence, though mystifying, is as physical and real as Christ's true human body.

For Catholics who believe and accept the Church's teachings, the greatest treasure in the Church is ,without dispute, the Holy Eucharist. In the Holy Eucharist Jesus Christ, under the appearances of bread and wine, remains united with His people. It is the source, unity and summit of Christian life and the summary of our faith.

While this doctrine remains rejected by the secular world as a whole, and by almost all other Christian churches at this time, Catholics are taught that they must receive Holy Communion (the body of Jesus Christ) at least once a year. By receiving Holy Communion, the Catholic Church teaches that a person is in obedience to the Lord's command to *"eat His body and drink His blood"*.

Although prefigured in numerous Old Testament verses of Scripture, it is in Christ's own words that we find the very beginning of this mystery, along with its profound implications for believers and its disconcerting realities for skeptics. But unlike contested mysteries embraced by the Catholic Church, such as the Virgin Mary's Immaculate Conception and Assumption, the essence of its teachings on Christ's True Presence in the Eucharist is clearly presented in the Gospels.

Starting with the sixth chapter of the Gospel of Saint John, in which Christ feeds five thousand men with five loaves and two fishes, Scripture begins to unfold and prepare the world for the coming mystery of the Eucharist.

According to John, the day after this miracle, the people were still impressed. They found Jesus, and He took the occasion to introduce the subject of "heavenly food" which He would give to the world. Jesus said:

> *Amen, I say to you, you seek Me, not because you have seen signs, but because you have eaten of the loaves and have been filled. Labor not for the food which perishes, but for that which endures to life everlasting which the Son of Man will give you"* (Jn 6:26-27).

Then, responding to their curiosity Jesus told them more:

> *Amen, amen I say to you, Moses gave you not the bread from Heaven, but My Father gives you the true bread from Heaven, for the bread of God is that which comes down from Heaven and gives life to the world"* (Jn 6:32-33).

In His words, Christ explains the superiority of this "bread" to the Old Testament "manna" which Moses gave the people. The Jews then confronted him: *"Lord, give us this bread always."* (Jn 6:34), whereupon Christ told them:

> *I am the bread of life, your fathers did eat manna in the desert and died. This is the bread which comes down from Heaven, that if any man eat of it, he may not die.*
>
> *I am the living bread which came down from Heaven; if any man eat of this bread, he shall live forever and the bread that I will give is My flesh for the life of the world* (Jn 6:48-51).
>
> *He that eats My flesh and drinks My blood has life everlasting, and I will raise him up on the last day. For My flesh is meat indeed, and My blood is drink indeed. He that eats My flesh and drinks My blood abides in Me and I in Him* (Jn 6:54-56).

Many of Christ's disciples, Scripture tells us, became dismayed. *"This saying is hard and who can hear it"* (Jn 6:60). Jesus, knowing what His disciples murmured, told them: ***"Does this scandalize you?"*** (Jn 6:61). Immediately, Christ told them again that this truth was incontestable, ***"Amen, Amen I say to you, unless you eat the flesh of the Son of Man, you shall not have life in you"*** (Jn 6:53). Scripture then relays that His words were too much for many, and these ones could *"follow him no more"* (Jn 6:66).

But the mystery continued to unfold. After many departed, Christ confronted the twelve, ***"Will you also go away?"*** (Jn 6:67). Peter, the rock of Christ's Church, testifies to the acceptance of the truth, *"Lord, to whom shall we go? Thou has the words of eternal life, and we believe and know thou art the Christ, the Son of God"* (Jn 6:68-69).

With this, Peter affirms the truth of the reality of Christ's True Presence in the Eucharist. Christ must be truly present in the Eucharist; indeed, the great apostle himself proclaims this belief.

A nineteenth century theologian, Father Michael Muller, C.S.S.R. defined in his book, *The Blessed Eucharist,* what all this meant to the apostles and consequently to millions of believers. Wrote Fr. Muller:

> *They believe the words of their Master without the least hesitation; they receive His words in that sense in which the others had refused to receive them; they receive them in their obvious meaning, as a promise that He would give them His real Flesh to eat and His real Blood to drink; they believe with a full faith, simply because His is "the Christ, the Son of God," too good to deceive, and too wise to be deceived; too faithful to make vain promises, and too powerful to find difficulty in fulfilling them. From this time forward the disciples were constantly expecting that Jesus Christ would fulfill His promise.*

And that day soon came. At the Last Supper Jesus took bread and blessed it. He then said, ***"Take ye and eat, for this is my body."*** Then holding the chalice, the Lord offered thanks and said, ***"Drink ye all of this, for this is my blood of the New Testament, which*** *shall be shed for many, for the remission of sins"* (Mt 26:28). At this moment, the Sacrament was instituted.

Father Muller again defines the significance:

> *When God speaks, what He commands is done in an instant. As He made the sun, the moon and the stars merely by saying:* ***"Let light be made"*** *so also at the Last Supper by His word alone, He instantly changed bread into His Body and wine into His Blood.****

Scripture supports this conclusion. Saint Paul admonished the Corinthians to remember, *"The chalice of blessing which we bless, is it not the communion of the Blood of Christ? And the bread which we break, is it not the communion of the Body of the Lord?"* (1 Cor. 10:16).

In the same Epistle to the Corinthians, Saint Paul exclaimed, *"Whosoever shall eat this bread or drink the chalice of the Lord unworthily, shall be guilty of the Body and Blood of the Lord. He that eateth and drinketh unworthily, eateth and drinketh damnation to himself, not discerning the Body of the Lord"* (1 Cor. 11:27-29). Thus, this statement confirms the Church's teaching that one must be in a state of grace (without mortal sin) to receive the Sacrament.

The early founding Fathers of the Church concurred with this teaching in their writings. Saint Ignatius, Bishop of Smyrna, who lived in the first century wrote:

> *Because the heretics refuse to acknowledge that the Holy Eucharist contains the same flesh which suffered for our sins and was raised again to life by God the Father, they die a miserable death and perish without hope.*

Saint Justin (d. 165) declared:

> *We call this food "Eucharist," of which no one should partake who does not believe in the truth of our doctrine, who has not been cleansed by the regeneration and remission of his sins and whose life is not in conformity with the precepts of Jesus Christ. Because we do not partake of this as ordi-*

nary food and drink, since in virtue of the word of God, Jesus Christ incarnate takes flesh and blood for our redemption. We know also that this food which in the natural order would become our flesh and blood, being consecrated in the prayer which contains His own divine words, is the flesh and blood of the same Jesus made man.

Through the centuries, the saints continued their admonitions to the faithful. Reports of Eucharistic miracles also began to be compiled, as Heaven supported the Church's greatest mystery with objective miracles to be perceived by the mind and senses of the faithful in order to solidify their trust.

Over and over, through arguments of reason and the testimony of the Church and Scripture, as well as numerous Eucharistic miracles, the mysterious but True Presence of Jesus Christ in the Holy Sacrifice of the Mass and the Eucharist has been presented and confirmed to the faithful for their belief and utilization. Furthermore, the Church has taught that not just individuals but also the whole world can profit from the infinite benefits of believing and participating in the Sacrament.

Indeed, the merits of receiving the Eucharist are more than logical. If by faith, people believe in the True Presence, then certainly the benefits would seem to be infinite in the their lives. For the more one partakes in the Body and Blood of Jesus Christ, the more one becomes like Christ in every way.

The Catechism of the Catholic Church is again explicit and clear on how the Sacrament enhances the lives of the faithful, both temporally in this world and spiritually as one strives for the next. According to the Catechism:

What material food produces in our bodily life, Holy Communion wonderfully achieves in our spiritual life. Communion with the flesh of the risen Christ, a flesh "given life and giving life through the Holy Spirit," preserves, increases, and renews the life of grace received at Baptism.

While the Church supports and teaches the richness of the sacramental life, it is another thing to say that the faithful have responded. Through the centuries, especially since the Age of Enlightenment, appreciation of the Sacrament has been increasingly eroded. Therefore, the crucial question becomes: "What do Catholics believe to be miraculous?" According to polls, the greatest miracle in the Church, a miracle that occurs hundreds of thousands of times a day, is said to be believed by less than 30% of all Catholics.

According to some Catholic theologians, this lack of belief has been a contributing factor, although a mystical one, to the great increase in violence, crime and moral disorder in the world today. For the Sacraments were meant to be supernatural protection from sin and temptation. Indeed, an increase in many worldwide problems directly followed a decline in the use of the Sacraments which were designed to protect souls.

Evil, it is said, can surmount even the greatest human will power. Only in Jesus Christ, His Word and His Eucharistic Presence, are people strong enough to resist. This is why the Church, in the Holy Mass, unites the Word of God with the celebration of the Eucharist. Together, the faithful are completely nourished in the mystery of Christ. Their souls are especially fortified to overcome the temptations and ravages of sin.

According to the Virgin Mary, it is particulary the faith in this Eucharistic nourishment which will effect the greatest changes in the new era. Mary says that much of the world will not only come to believe in this mystery, but also will partake in it. Indeed, it is said that the Triumph of the Immaculate Heart of Mary during our times will gloriously lead the world into a new era of true peace. At that time, the Holy Eucharist will be better known, appreciated and treasured. It will be a reign not just within the Church and individual lives, but in whole nations. Thus, the infinite power and grace available in the Eucharist will no longer be the world's greatest secret!

But the fact that this great mystery remains a secret to so many, is most fitting and appropriate, for the Eucharist began as such, - as a secret!

In fact, for centuries the liturgy of the Eucharist was known as the *"liturgy of the Secret"*. And the practice of gradually initiating the Catechumens into the more important mysteries of Christianity, through secrecy in both speaking and writing, was known as the *Disciplina Arcani,* the *"Discipline of the Secret".* Ironically, it was a secret unlike any other, for it was designed by God to eventually be universally proclaimed and accepted by all souls.

And it appears that the time to announce the new era is soon to come. Theologians tell us that at Fatima, the Virgin Mary not only revealed God's plan for the world to find true peace, but also his desire for the faithful to more deeply embrace the Church's greatest mystery in order to achieve that peace.

Most significantly, this is accentuated by the fact that Mary first appeared at Fatima on May 13, 1917. At that time. May 13 was the date on which the Church celebrated the recognition of Our Lady of the Blessed Sacrament. This title is the most theological of all Mary's titles after "Mother of God". At Fatima, Mary then called for the Communion of Reparation on the five first Saturdays, outlining and delivering a perfect plan to lead the faithful to her Son in the Eucharist.

Mary came to Fatima, theologians tell us, to help bring people back to her Son, especially in the Eucharist. Mary is also, theologians emphasize, the Mother of the Eucharist. And therefore, as John Haffert the co-founder of the Blue Army wrote in his superb book, *The Worlds Greatest Secret*, she is the *Mother of the Secret*, the world's most profound secret, the True Presence of Jesus Christ in every Mass and every consecrated Host over the last two thousand years.

Thus, it is apparent that through the "True Presence" will come "True Peace"! This is Fatima's most important message. And while there are those who choose to focus on the unknown contents of the third part of the Secret of Fatima, it is clear from what is already known of its contents, that it points the faithful to Christ's True Presence in the Eucharist.

The primary content of the Third Secret of Fatima has always been believed to involve an apostasy. The primary cause of this apostasy, Our Lady has repeatedly revealed, has been the loss of belief in the True Presence of Jesus Christ in the Mass, in the Eucharist and in the world. This is confirmed, once again by Mary's request at Fatima for the Communion of Reparation. Thus, we see that the Secret of Fatima, in essence, points to the Church's great secret, the True Presence of Jesus Christ. It is also then not surprising that the Secret of Fatima, like the Church's greatest secret, is no secret at all. Jesus Christ remains the answer to all that is known and unknown, in this life and the next.

May this book bring all souls who read it to the foot of Our Lord at every altar, as Our Lady calls them. Through the grace of God and with the Blessed Virgin Mary, may they then prepare mankind for the glorious new era of the Eucharistic reign of Jesus Christ which will rule throughout the world till the end of time!

CHAPTER ONE

"I WILL NOT REVEAL YOUR MYSTERIES"

His name was Tarcisius. Beyond that, his history is little-known. But the words etched on his tombstone demanded attention. For according to the inscription written by Pope Damasus I (366-384), Tarcisius *"chose rather to suffer death"* than to *"betray the secret."*

Indeed he did, for the secret he carried was believed to be divine.

According to tradition, Tarcisius was only a boy when he was confronted and killed by a pagan mob. This angry throng became interested in the boy after they had been informed that he carried a *"secret"* of the Christians.

It was fourth century Rome, and although Christianity was already several hundred years old, it did not as yet enjoy support from the Roman empire. Thus, many Christians risked the same fate as Tarcisius simply by admitting or practicing their faith.

The secret Tarcisius carried with him, and the one for which he chose to die, was something that most Christians of the time believed was worthy of such a fate. For it was the pinnacle of their faith, their pearl in the treasure chest, their shining star in the heavens.

At that time in history, most Christians possessed little. But the true gem which they shared in the mystery of their faith was so valuable that death was far preferable to betrayal. For they were well-aware of a certain betrayer who had gone before them, one who had willfully forsaken the living Christ, and none among them sought to imitate his poor example.

Almost two thousand years later, the Liturgical Communion Prayer of the Byzantine Catholic Rite invites the faithful as a body to verbally maintain and defend the secret Tarcisius died for: *"Accept me as a partaker of Your mystical supper, O Son of God,"* the congregation prays, *"for I will not reveal Your mysteries to Your enemies, nor will I give you a kiss, as did Judas ..."*

CHAPTER TWO

THE DISCIPLINE
OF THE SECRET

In 1900, the International Archaeologists Congress requested that Pope Leo XIII excavate beneath Saint Peter's Basilica. The Pope refused.

The archaeologists were hungry for new information concerning the lives of the early Christians. With the fall of Rome, the ancient mausoleums and catacombs were pillaged. Over the centuries, waves of hunters and looters left nothing to be discovered. But despite the futility of the wide-scale searches, the archaeologists knew that there was still one site which could bear great historical fruit: the catacombs of Vatican Hill.

This supposition proved correct. In 1939, as workmen sought to lower the body of Pope Pius XI into the floor of Saint Peter's Crypt, they accidentally channeled into a first century cemetery. The discovery was astonishing. With this, the Vatican relented in its original rejection of the archaeologists' request and the excavation began.

Decades of work yielded many rich discoveries. The most important among them was the tomb of Saint Peter himself. And with this descovery came information the Vatican hoped would shed light upon the faith: the very words the early christians left on the walls of the tombs of their deceased. These words lent much insight into the lives they led, and the deaths they suffered. Indeed, these words had the power to help the world understand the truth.

Throughout the catacombs, the name and symbols of Saint Peter were found everywhere. This included the simple inscription on his tomb which stated, "Peter Lies Within." "PE," "PET," and "PETRUS" were also deciphered as definite references to Saint Peter. But other symbols of the faith were found in even greater numbers.

These signs and symbols revealed more than just their meaning. They revealed, archaeologists insist, a community of secrecy. It was secrecy, they explain, that was based upon the various esoteric teachings of their new religion.

Indeed, according to cryptographic experts, the signs and symbols for Jesus, Mary, and Peter could not have been deciphered by the ancient pagans. They were too complex in meaning.

There were also symbolic fresco paintings found on the underground walls. Again, the images presented in these paintings, like the other signs and symbols, represented the core of Christianity. But to the pagans, they meant nothing.

However, an attempt to decipher these symbols and paintings in a Christian context reveals much, for most of the symbols did not represent baptism or the resurrection, nor good works or strong faith. Curiously, even Christ's many Scriptural teachings do not predominate in the mysterious art forms of the catacombs.

Instead, several symbols are repeatedly found. These same symbols recur time and time again on the walls and tombs, every place that the archaeologists discovered cryptographic writing.

And it is from these signs and symbols, as nothing else, that we discover what must have been the heart and soul of the early Christians' faith. For they shed light on what the martyrs were really willing to die for; they uncover the ultimate secret of their new faith.

Indeed, the catacombs show us that, like Tarcisius, the early Christians held in common one secret of supreme importance. This secret contained the meaning of their life on earth, as well as the secret of their Divine Life in Christ. In fact, it was the secret of life itself, all life.

It was even known for centuries as *the Discipline of the Secret ..."*

CHAPTER THREE

ONLY FOR THE WISE

The world at the time of Christ was truly an era of the esoteric. This pervading secrecy existed not just with Christianity, but with other religions and philosophies during the reign of the Greek and Roman empires.

For those born into the right class, the philosophies of the age could not be understood without being exposed to a certain amount of education. And those who became educated, were then exposed to the philosophies by the very process of education.

In and of themselves, the philosophies were not viewed as something to be shared with the masses. They were self-contained, rather secretive beliefs which were designed to insure self-perpetuating restraints on rule and class separation.

In response to the ways of the upper class, the esoteric nature of religions was often used by the disengaged as a similar path to exclusivity; a counter cultural system to introduce more meaning and definition to the purpose of one's life - especially since their lives often lacked upward economic and educational opportunity. Indeed, the "hereafter" was the greatest, and often the only, hope they had.

Together, both philosophical and religious activists feared contamination of their beliefs with magic. This was because the Mediterranean world during the early centuries before and after Christ contained many ritualistic beliefs and customs founded on superstition and alchemistical practices. Thus, numerous sects were esoteric for one reason or another.

But in studying ancient Judaism, we find another factor contributing to religious secrecy. Following the wisdom of their prophets, Old Testament Jews believed that secrecy was required of them by God.

In fact, Jewish writings of the time reveal a type of discipline in the preservation of their secrets. And the principal basis for this secrecy was founded in the apocalyptical.

According to scholars, apocalyptic writings were intensely secret writings. Secret, for the most part, for political reasons. However, it also seems likely that the Jews embraced this secrecy in their writings and traditions due to motivations and fears which stretched beyond the natural realm.

With the eyes of faith, one can deduce that God deliberately sought to protect His "chosen people." This protection extended beyond their mere human survival, and entered into the realm of their customs and beliefs. These were beliefs, according to God's original plan as outlined in the Old Testament, that were intended to be preserved for all the world to eventually embrace, such as the Ten Commandments.

From the earliest recorded times, the Israelites consistently adhered to their commitment to do God's will by keeping specific religious secrets. From the fate of Moses to the reason why only a part of the Torah was to be published, the need for secrecy was clearly understood. Indeed, a sacred book of Isaiah and numerous books of Ezra were said to be set aside only for the *"wise among the people."*

Repeatedly, the Old Testament and related works demonstrate this tendency toward confidentiality in their language and teachings. The prophet Daniel is told: *"Keep secret the message, and seal the book until the time of the end"* (Dn 12:4). And this "end" is reportedly revealed to him in visions.

Besides protecting the apocalyptic nature of the revelations, the laws and rules regarding the sacred readings also helped to protect the Jewish people from the Hellenistic culture that was spreading throughout Palestine before and after Christ. The early rabbis felt that this protection was essential to the faith. At the time of Jesus, a strong esoteric element was present in Judaism for this very reason. This also explains why the Scribes had such significant influence at that time.

Indeed, the Scribes were the bearers of *"secret knowledge."* It was said that they possessed the *"secrets of God,"* and *"understood"* His secret teachings. Specifically, these teachings fell into four primary categories: 1. incest laws; 2. the story of creation; 3. secrets of the Divine Nature; 4. the secrets of Heaven and the underworld. According to historians, these secrets also led to certain rules. And these rules, in turn, safeguarded the preservation and protection of religious tradition.

For example, only mature readers could read the account of creation. Likewise, teachers could mention the *"Most Holy Name"* only once a week, and certain passages of the Old Testament were not to be read at synagogue worship. In the Holy of Holies, it was forbidden that the worship of God be *"spoken."*

A secondary reason for these rules was to protect the sacred from profanation. Likewise, the rules protected the religion from corruption by heathenish superstitions. In fact, early writings taught that those who corrupted religion with superstition should *"close their ears or depart!"* Divine mysteries were preserved only for those who were *"worthy initiates, those who could be trusted with 'the holiest secret'."*

Thus, the role of the esoteric in early Christian teaching was in accordance with Jewish custom and the structure of religious teaching. But the teachings of Christ also contained many obvious tenets that openly called for the continuation of this approach.

The Gospels proclaim that Christ was the Messiah. But in the Gospel of Mark (8:30), we find that after Saint Peter's confession of this truth, Christ Himself urges secrecy: *"Then He gave them strict orders not to tell anyone about Him."*

From that moment, theologians tell us that Christ began to speak with apocalyptical significance, this is especially noted in the Gospel of Mark.

After Saint Peter's confession, Christ began to speak of His Passion. Again, this "secret" is confined to the disciples. According to Mark's Gospel, Christ's eschatological prophecies concerning signs of the end times are entrusted only to his most loyal disciples. Utilizing very mysterious speech, Christ reveals individual items of instruction regarding these mysteries. Again, He urges secrecy and discernment:

- *He who is able to receive this, let him receive it* (Mt 19:12).
- *I will destroy the temple made by human hands, and In three days I will construct another not made by human hands* (Mk 14:58).
- *All the prophets as well as the law spoke prophetically until John. If you are prepared to accept it, he is Elijah, the one who was certain to come. Hear carefully what you hear* (Mt 11:13-15).

In addition, Scripture reveals that some secret teachings of Christ were to be revealed in the future, according to His will.

Again, Christ's own words confirm their secrecy. And His instruction is to reveal them later, almost as the rabbis had done with their secretive teachings:

> *Do not let them intimidate you. Nothing is concealed that will not be revealed, and nothing hidden that will not be known. What I tell you in darkness, speak in the light. What you hear in private, proclaim from the housetops* (Mt 10:26-27).

> *You yourselves will not be the speakers. The Spirit of your Father will be speaking in you* (Mt 10:20).

In Mark's Gospel, Christ clearly emphasizes the deliberate need for secrecy regarding the full meaning of His words:

> *Things are hidden, only to be revealed at a later time; they are covered so as to be brought out into the open. Let him who has ears to hear me, hear* (Mk 4:22-23).

And later, in John's Gospel (13:30-31), Jesus partially reveals the meaning of the mysteries as they were unfolding:

> *No sooner had Judas eaten the morsel than he went out. It was night. Once Judas had left, Jesus said: "Now is the Son glorified and God is glorified in Him."*

After Christ's Ascension, the apostles continued with their effort to protect sacred mysteries from profanation. However, it must be emphasized that there were no secret "doctrines," as St. Irenaeus clarified in his *Adversus Haereses* (Against Heresies). Rather, this early Christian secrecy had to do with keeping knowledge of the Sacred mysteries from non-Christians. In the later writings, Sts. Augustine, Hilary, Leo and others, it is repeatedly stated that the Creed, elements of the Liturgy of the Eucharist and other traditions were not to be written, only to be learned.

Likewise, in Corinthians (I Cor 4:1), Saint Paul refers to himself and his trusted followers as *"servants of Christ and administers of the mysteries of God."* Saint Paul then states that to receive such a title, one must be *"trustworthy."*

Saint Paul also speaks of the need for divine wisdom in understanding the *"secrets of God"* (1 Cor 2:6-9). The great apostle then confesses that he has not disclosed everything, and that he has kept secret many facts which others were not ready to receive.

> *Brothers, the trouble was that I could not talk to you as spiritual men, but only as men of flesh, as infants in Christ. I fed you with milk and did not give you solid food, because you were not ready for it* (1 Cor 3:1-2).

> *For they were not ready for God's "hidden wisdom"* (1 Cor 2:7).

Thus, we see how careful St. Paul was in his teachings, as he even withheld some of them from Christians themselves. Other accounts found in the New Testament are likewise rich in the secrets of Christology. In the Epistle to the Hebrews, as well as different accounts in Saint Matthew and Saint Mark's Gospels, the deliberate and obvious absence of specific information continued to broaden the spectrum of the new religion's desire for secrecy. We know that Saint Paul even confesses that he kept a specific matter silent for *"fourteen years,"* and he admits there are still things he cannot speak of, *"I ... was snatched up to Paradise to hear words which cannot be uttered—words which no man may speak"* (2 Cor 12:4).

Likewise, the Book of Revelation, too, continues in the cryptic style and language of the apostles. Here we find not only the secrecy needed to preserve the purest integrity of the new religion, but also the continuation of the Jewish approach to apocalyptical secrets. Certainly, the most apocalyptical of all New Testament writings is the Book of Revelation, otherwise known as the Book of the Apocalypse. Indeed, the language and symbolism continuously utilized in this book are apparent, especially in the mysterious number of the Antichrist:

A certain wisdom is needed here, with a little ingenuity anyone can calculate the number of the beast, for it is the number that stands for a certain man. The man's number is six hundred sixty-six (Rv 13:18).

Most significantly, Revelation 13:9 invokes a *"special"* understanding of the faithful to interpret the secrets of the teaching: *"Let him who has ears heed these words."*

In Revelation 17:9, the faithful are also called to understand the secret meaning of the *"Great harlot of Babylon." "Here is the clue for one who possesses wisdom,"* the book states. From the mysterious meaning of *"the New Jerusalem"* to the *"beasts and their heads and diadems"* to the *"abomination of desolation,"* the language of the Book of Revelation seems to be completely shrouded in mystery.

Thus, in its early years, Christianity emerged from the womb with a plan for its survival. This plan embraced Jewish tradition and the teachings of Christ Himself, both of which called for secrecy.

Most of all, this secrecy was neither unreasonable nor random; rather, it was a deliberate route to the light - a light, its founders believed, would ultimately be received by the whole world, if only this new religion could safely emerge from its pagan surroundings.

But the dangerous world of the early Christians was filled with hate springing from many sources. From the pagan Romans to the orthodox Jews, Christ's message was perceived as a threat, one which the enemies of the new faith felt compelled to do away with.

Therefore, it is understandable how the early Christians must have felt about the dangers inherent in their "greatest" secret. For news that they were *"eating the body"* and *"drinking the blood"* of their God would not be well-received by their enemies. Nor would it enhance the chances of their survival, or the survival of their new religion.

CHAPTER FOUR

"GIVE NOT WHAT IS HOLY TO THE DOGS"

On Peter's tomb, and indeed, throughout the catacombs, the symbol for the Eucharist dominated. In fact, above and beyond all other imagery, the symbols used to depict this mystery regularly repeat themselves and, according to archaeologists, take many forms, including: a fish; loaves surmounted by fish; a bunch of grapes or a vine; and a cup often resembling a large vase.

These cryptographic inscriptions representing the Eucharist were found in abundance not only around Peter's tomb, but in the caves of Palestine, and along many miles of catacombs. In addition, numerous Eucharistic frescoes cover the catacomb walls. These frescoes depict the people eating bread and drinking wine. Some show the breaking of bread and banqueters gathered at table.

One very old fresco shows seven people at a table, all eating bread and drinking wine. A fresco from the Catacomb of Saint Calixtus shows seven more at a table with twelve baskets in the foreground. The baskets are standing higher than the table and are overflowing with bread, a clear reference to Scripture's Eucharistic account of the multiplication of the loaves. And in the Catacomb of Saint Priscilla, yet another "Lord's Supper" scene is found.

One picture found in a catacomb near the Via Appia Antica presents a threefold image which completely recounts the Eucharistic story. In the center is Christ, performing the miracle of multiplication. On the right hand side, Christ is again portrayed, this time in a gesture of blessing or thanksgiving, while five loaves of bread marked with the cross are visible in the folds of His cloak. The final image on the left shows the Samaritan woman drawing water from Jacob's well. It is the woman to whom Christ promised to give *"living water"* (Jn 4:13).

But most of all, besides the Eucharistic symbolism of the drawings and paintings, the cryptographic discoveries confirmed the great curtain of secrecy which existed in the lives of the early Christians, especially in their religious services.

The founders of Christianity lived a clandestine life permeated with fear. Thus, their religious rites were performed in the bowels of the earth, particularly in cemeteries where the superstitious Romans refused to go. Again, this was not without reason.

With the spread of Christianity came rampant and bloody persecution. Saint Peter himself was crucified, and Saint Paul was beheaded. In the Colosseum, Christians were repeatedly subjected to inhuman acts of torture, shame and martyrdom. Centuries later, the Church realized that like Christ, who died a bloody death on the cross, the blood of the early martyrs were the mystical seeds which allowed the Church to grow.

But why did the early Christians so willingly give up their lives? Certainly, the love and forgiveness offered by Christ endeared them to the truth of their faith. But if one can say the many cryptographic symbols of secrecy reveal anything about the early Christians, it must be their overwhelming convictions of Christ's True Presence among them. A presence they enacted in the Holy Sacrifice of the Mass and then received as food for their souls in the Eucharist.

This is what the numerous signs on the catacomb walls confirm. The early Christians were willing to die for a Living God. One who had died, and came back to life for them, a life He then shared with all in order to fulfill His Word. And His Word told them that He Himself would be their food!

Indeed, history tells us that the four Gospels were not assembled until the third century. In addition, the vast majority of early Christians were illiterate. Therefore, the lives and deaths of these individuals centered around what gave them the most meaning.

And the picture is clear. Just as Peter and Paul had done with them, they too, slowly and carefully initiated new believers into the faith. And this faith taught them that at its core was a most guarded mystery: the Holy Eucharist!

"Tarcisius," wrote Pope Damasus, "chose death rather than to betray the heavenly body to the raging dogs." Thus, the reality of the great secret of the Eucharist had to be true, for only concealed "bread" was found on the dead boy's body.

For early Christians, the protection of the Eucharist from any form of profanation became of the highest order. It was a secret that had to remain as such in order for the religion to survive. In fact, while the liturgy of the Eucharist comes directly from Scripture, the full account of the institution of the Eucharist is notably absent from St. John's Gospel. To some, this spoke loudly of the need for this mystery to remain, even in John's own words, highly secretive.

While some theologians have presented distinct reasons for the absence of this crucial Eucharistic event, others suspect that Saint John detailed his account of the Last Supper before it was possible to openly speak of the Eucharistic Mystery. Nothing in John's Gospel suggests that he regarded it as being of lesser significance. Rather, John's Gospel, as well as almost all of early Christianity's preserved writings, seems to point to a guarded and limited presentation of the great secret mystery in order to maintain the esoteric course prescribed by the words and deeds of the Church's founders, the apostles themselves. Thus, the sacred formula was not to be revealed to the general public. Saint John, some believe, knew this when he wrote his Gospel.

According to some scholars, there is also a detected tendency, even in Scriptural accounts of the Lord's Supper, to reveal the mystery in veiled terms. Some writers have wondered why Saint Luke quotes Christ's Eucharistic words in his Gospel, while in the Book of Acts, he uses ambiguous phrases such as *"the breaking of bread"* (Acts 2:42) and to *"break bread"* (Acts 2:46) to reference the same mystery. It is the supposition of many scholars that Luke's fluctuation was deliberate so as to confuse and bewilder non-Christians.

In the Letter to the Hebrews, any teaching of the Eucharist to beginners of the faith is absent (Heb 6:1-3). But at the same time, the author exhorts the faithful to become mature. Immediately afterward, he speaks of the enlightenment of men who have tasted *"the heavenly gift."*

While the authorship of the Letters to the Hebrews is contested, reviewers claim that it was written in a "high quality" style by someone who cites the Old Testament in a unique way. Some experts say that the author appears to have been educated and trained in a Hellenistic fashion, rather than Palestinian. Yet, the book reflects a deliberate knowledge of the necessity to preserve "the secret."

Likewise, in the First Epistle to the Thessalonians (1 Thes 5:27) and in the First Epistle to Timothy, (1 Tm 4:13), Saint Paul instructs the brethren *"to attend to readings and to doctrine"* in connection with the Eucharistic feast. While in the Letter to the Hebrews (Heb 13:10), the writer refers to the table of the Eucharist as an *"altar": "We have an altar from which those who serve the tabernacle have no right to eat."*

While some writings of the early Christians do speak openly of the Eucharist, it is believed that these accounts were necessary to defend the mystery against false understandings and enigmatic rumors. However, other writers and writings, apart from Scripture, confirm the quest for secrecy surrounding the Eucharist.

Saint Hippolytus (A.D. 215) writes, *"He shall not tell this to any but the faithful."* Likewise, the martyred Saint Justin confirms the fact that only *"the baptized may participate in the Eucharist."* Interestingly, however, he also fails to repeat Christ's exact words at the Last Supper.

Christian writings from the first and second century also show consistent and deliberate efforts to veil the true meaning and teachings regarding Christ's True Presence.

Most significantly, one early writing has been especially noted regarding this entire matter. According to experts, the words of Bishop Abercius of Hieropolis in Phrygia provide an accurate account of how the early Christians guarded their secret. Abercius traveled to Rome about ninety years after Saint Peter's death. The authenticity of his writings, according to scholars, has been confirmed by multiple sources.

Concerning the secret of Christ's True Presence in the bread and wine, Bishop Abercius wrote:

Faith everywhere led me forward and everywhere provided a fish of exceeding great size and perfection which a Holy Virgin drew with her hands from a fountain and ever gives this to its friends to eat, wine of great virtue, mingled with bread.

Scholars conclude that Abercius' writings were deliberate in their intense symbolism and mystery. But at the same time, they also perfectly expressed the doctrine of the Eucharist. It was a doctrine, Abercius also shows was already understood to include Mary, the mother of Christ.

Without a doubt, Bishop Abercius' guarded text concerning the mystery of the Eucharist would have pleased the Master. For indeed, the Lord Himself had warned his followers, *"Give not what is holy to the dogs"* (Mt 7:6).

Mother of the Secret

CHAPTER FIVE

THE LITURGY OF
THE SECRET

O utside the cold, damp catacombs, concealment became a way of life for the early Christians. Upon becoming a Christian, Tarcisius must have known this. But once underground, the faithful would gather and perform their religious rites. There, they were hidden from hostile gazes and Roman soldiers and were left alone to be with their God.

Because of new converts and strangers not familiar with the faith, the early Christian rites were divided into two parts. The first part of the liturgy, for those still learning the Catechism, involved prayers and ceremonies. This simpler rite of worship was deliberately designed for these Catechumens, to whom Saint Paul fed *"milk."*

But when the sacred meal began, only those who were full converts could partake. It was the beginning of the "Liturgy of the Secret."

It was also the continuation of the process in which the Mystical Body of Christ would be formed through the infusion of the Holy Spirit. This was the process by which Christians were, in Jesus' own words to the Father, *"made one as you Father are in Me, and I in You"* (Jn 17:21).

Thus, the "secret of secrets," the Holy Eucharist, was soon understood to reveal the truth in Christ's words and deeds, as recorded in the apostles' own words and in Scriptural accounts.

From Christ's institution of the Eucharist during the Jewish Passover, to the two disciples on the road to Emmaus who failed to recognize Christ until the *"breaking of the bread,"* the true relevance of the great secret is not clearly seen until the Liturgy of the Eucharist was instituted.

However, it is evident that the early Christians understood that Christ's words at the Passover Meal were not symbolic. They were meant to be taken literally. Various Scriptural accounts reveal this, especially those regarding Christ's Last Supper.

Most significantly, while Christ knew these were His last hours on earth, He made no effort to summarize any of His teachings, no effort to repeat His message of love, repentance and forgiveness. Neither did the Last Supper involve stories, parables or miracles of healing. Instead Christ specifically instituted a new process that He instructed His apostles to repeat in His memory.[1] And His words were precise: *"I have greatly desired to eat this Passover with you before I suffer."*

During the meal, Jesus took bread, blessed it, broke it and gave it to His disciples. *"Take this and eat it,"* He said, *"This is My Body."*

Then He took a cup, gave thanks, and gave it to them, saying, *"All of you must drink from it. This is My Blood, the blood of the covenant to be poured out on behalf of many for the forgiveness of sins."*

With this, many of Christ's words and actions were fulfilled in their true meaning, and they began to be understood. Indeed the cryptographic symbols adopted by the early Christians reveal their enlightened understanding of Christ and His words.

Most of all, this new understanding allowed them to do what the Lord asked of His apostles at the Passover Meal, to *"eat His Body and drink His Blood."* Thus, then, just as with Tarcisius, it gave them the courage to die rather than to betray this vow.

But for many years, fear continued to keep this secret of the True Presence from being recorded in its proper text and manner. The early Christian scribes and scholars wrote little about the Eucharist or any matter of the faith. But tradition carefully handed down these crucial truths.

John Haffert, the author of numerous books and the co-founder of the Blue Army, notes the incredible reality of how the Liturgy of the Eucharist was founded in secret, out of necessity and practicality. Writes Haffert:

> *No ordinary mortal would come equipped with the inventiveness necessary to make up a story like the Eucharistic one. Or, if some strange being did invent it, no ordinary meal would perpetuate it. For such an idea to have originated and to have endured, it would have to be more certain than surmised in the minds of Christians. They were willing to **die** for it. Moreover, it was not a tenet calculated to recruit new members to the struggling, infant Church. On the contrary! It was a tenet which would repel most people; they would consider it too fantastic for belief and an insult to their common sense. Nevertheless, the little band of Christians stuck to it and passed it on to their children, and their children to their children, through the years. And they **did** die for it.*[1]

It was tradition alone which held together the chain of teaching in unbroken sequence through the years of persecution and secrecy. As a matter of fact, comparatively few people in pagan Rome could read. The Gospels and the whole collection of sacred writings that we now call the Bible were not assembled and compiled into one book until after the periods of the persecution. The deposit of Faith then was handed down orally from one Christian to another for almost four centuries until the Bible was compiled and until other manuscripts and books of all sorts could publicly record it.

> *Today, thanks to the ever-advancing science of archeology, we are beginning to find evidence which corroborates the writings as well as the tradition. But we may never find corroboration of all details, nor have the writings themselves recorded every detail. We still must look to tradition to flesh out the skeleton of the written word which wasn't filled out until the time of secrecy.*[2]

Other Scriptural words about Christ's teachings and actions also take on their true meaning with the institution of the Liturgy of the Eucharist.

The Jews foretold for years that the Messiah would be born in *"the house of bread,"* a translation which in Hebrew literally means *"Bethlehem."* At His birth, Christ was laid in a manger, which was really a trough for animals to eat grain. Likewise, Christ's very first miracle changes water into wine. Again, the symbolism is evident for those "who have faith."

On two occasions, Christ feeds the thousands through the "invisible" duplication of loaves of bread and fish. In the same way His True Presence in the Eucharist is endless and infinitely divisible. It was no accident that, after His Ascension Christ, left behind twelve apostles to carry on and dispense His teachings on the bread of life. But were these twelve a symbolic fulfillment of the fact that Scripture tells us *"twelve baskets"* remained after Christ fed over five thousand? And was the fact that *"seven baskets"* remained after Christ fed more than four thousand indicative of God remaining with His people, now as their very food, until the end of the world? For the number seven has always been said to be God's number.

Consistent with the later teachings of the Church on the sacredness of the Eucharist, we find that every little scrap of bread was collected and placed in baskets at the end of the miracle. Again, was this not a definitive sign of the call for recognition of the holiness of the Sacrament?

Even the Transfiguration of Christ compels us to wonder at its Eucharistic overtones. Moses fed his people manna from the heavens and Elijah called down upon his sacrifice a heavenly fire. In these acts the power of God was brought forth, much in the same sense as it is at the moment of consecration - the power of the Holy Spirit consuming the bread and wine into food from heaven by command of the priest.

Indeed, the roles of the Old Testament prophets bring to light the reality of how much their lives and writings are connected with the life and mission of Christ.

Jeremiah spoke of a savior who would be linked to the Passover, the mystery of God's delivery of the Jews out of Egypt. Once again, this is seen as no coincidence. For when Christ promised bread which would enable His listeners to live forever, they responded, *"We want the bread!"*

It has been often pointed out how Christ Himself was the lamb who was to be sacrificed, and whose blood was to be shed for the sins of mankind and for their salvation. Likewise the blood of the Passover lambs marked the doors of the Jews on Passover night so that they would be saved from the Angel of Death.

Throughout the Old Testament, the writings of Isaiah, David, Ezekiel and Hosea allude to the mystery of the Savior and to the mystery of His yet-to-be revealed True Presence in the Holy Sacrifice of the Mass. It was a Holy Sacrifice that would be repeatedly offered throughout the world over generations and generations, just as the prophet proclaimed:

> *...from the rising of the sun, even to its setting, my name is great among the nations; and everywhere they bring sacrifice to my name, and a pure offering* (Mal 1:11).

The Eucharistic Liturgy today holds the truth of many Scriptural references to this great mystery, which the Church faithful proclaim by worshiping *"Through Him, with Him and in Him."*

Indeed, the very word "Host" means sacrifice. Christ Himself is this sacrifice, and His invisible Presence is to be acknowledged by the priest and the faithful. Just as Christ was present to the disciples who broke bread with Him on the road to Emmaus, the invisible Savior is truly present to us. All we have to do is recognize Him in the "breaking of the bread."

At Emmaus, once the disciples recognized Him, Christ vanished. This is a sign to us that He need not be visible to be truly present. Indeed, Christ's sacrifice on the cross is forever revisited in a bloodless manner, a reminder to all that He died on the cross for the sins of all. Again, the words of the prophet ring out, *"everywhere...a pure offering, for great is my name among the nations, says the Lord of Hosts"* (Mal 1:11).

Like her Son, Mary's own unique role in the mystery of the Eucharist was also reportedly prefigured in a vision of the virgin on a cloud over Mount Carmel received by the prophet Elijah. After seeing Our Lady, Elijah then went down into the desert and there participated in another mystery, what some say was a prefigurement of the Holy Eucharist.

John Haffert, in his book, *Sign of Her Heart*, explains:

In the days of prophecy, Saint Elijah saw a cloud appear over Mount Carmel, foot-shaped. It was a vision of Her who was to arise immaculate from the sea of humankind and to crush Satan beneath Her heel, as She brought forth the Salvation of the world. It is traditional that Elias founded the family of Carmel for her. But after he had beheld this prophetical vision of Our Lady of Mount Carmel, he went down into the desert and there partook of another mystery, a prefigurement of the Holy Eucharist.

He had fled to the desert because he feared the wrath of the wicked Queen Jezebel, whose false prophets he had slain on Mount Carmel. He sat heavily beneath a juniper tree and begged God to take away his soul. Instead, an angel came and fed him a piece of bread. In the strength of that bread, the prophet walked for forty days. The Fathers of the Church interpret it as a prophetical symbol of the Eucharist.

"Now, if the bread given under the juniper tree and ministered by an angel is a type of the Holy Eucharist," asks the Scriptural commentator, Sylveria, *"why indeed, was not that bread which angels ministered to Elias at Carith a foreshadow of the Eucharist? Or why should not the bread given by Divine Power in the house of the widow of Sareptha obtain this great honor? I answer that this bread given under the juniper has been so greatly sublimated because Elias came to the juniper from Mount Carmel where he had seen, in a small cloud, the Immaculate Queen of Heaven whom he had thereupon loved and wholeheartedly venerated. From this apparition and veneration he had disposed himself to partake, in type and figure, of such an ineffable mystery as the Eucharist."[2]*

Although it may sound simply like a play on words, it is true that when we go to Mary in the Scapular we go to Jesus in the Eucharist. Father Faber says: "In the devout life, it is almost the same thing to say of a man that he has a great devotion to Our Blessed Lady or that he has a great devotion to the Blessed Sacrament."[3]

While over the centuries, the offering of the Holy Sacrifice of the Mass would spread to every nation, it is said that the very first Mass, after the Last Supper, was offered on the seventh day after Pentecost.

Private revelations of various mystics give us accounts of this historic event. But, perhaps the account of the Venerable Mary of Agreda reveals something special. For in her account, as detailed in the book, *The Mystical City of God*, we find how God arranged every critical detail of the important gathering.

Most of all, we again find at the center of this story, the special and singular role God reserved for the Blessed Virgin Mary, the Mother of Jesus Christ, the Mother of the Eucharist. For Mary of Agreda's words reveal the Virgin's important yet humble and obedient role at the very first Mass in history:

The Apostle (St. Peter) partook himself of the Sacrament and communicated it to the eleven Apostles as most holy Mary had instructed him. Thereupon, at the hands of Saint Peter, the heavenly Mother partook of it, while the celestial spirits there present attended with ineffable reverence. In approaching the altar the great Lady made three profound prostrations, touching the ground with her face.

> *She returned to her place, and it is impossible to describe in words the effects of this participation of the Holy Eucharist in this most exalted of creatures. She was entirely transformed and elevated, completely absorbed in this divine conflagration of the love of her most holy Son, whom She had now received bodily. She remained in a trance, elevated from the floor; but the holy angels shielded Her somewhat from view according to her own wish, in order that the attention of those present might not be unduly attracted by the divine effects apparent in Her. The disciples distributed Holy Communion, first to the disciples and then to the others who had been believers before the Ascension. But of the five thousand newly baptized only one thousand received Communion on that day; because not all were entirely prepared or furnished with the insight and attention required for receiving the Lord in this great sacrament and mystery of the Altar."[4]*

Thus, we find in faith through the words of Mary of Agreda how the sublime mystery of the Eucharistic sacrifice was already understood and accepted by the Virgin Mary and the apostles right from the beginning. It is a complex mystery, yet a simple one if truly believed. Nonetheless, a simple story might best bring to life this mystery of mysteries.

Upon giving his little girl a crucifix, a father once asked his daughter, *"What is the difference between the figure on the cross and the Host held up at the Consecration of the Mass by the priest?"*

The child replied, *"When I look at the figure on the cross, I see Jesus, but He's not there. When I look at the Host, I don't see Jesus, but He is there!"[5]*

CHAPTER SIX

THE MYSTICAL BODY OF JESUS CHRIST

From the earliest days of the Church, Christian theologians understood that Christ Himself was the high priest who offered His sacrifice on Calvary. The offering was Christ Himself, His Body and His Blood. In the Liturgy of the Eucharist, Christ Himself is again offered, His Body and His Blood. The only difference is that Christ does not die again, but offers Himself in a mystical manner under the appearance of bread and wine.

Over the centuries, Christian beliefs about the Eucharistic Sacrifice have remained consistent. In the mid-sixteenth century, the Council of Trent provided the summation of the Eucharistic Liturgy:

> *Jesus Christ, our God and Savior, although He was to offer Himself once and for all to God the Father on the altar of the cross by His death, there to work out our eternal redemption, yet since His priesthood was not to be extinguished by His death, He at the Last Supper, on the night that He was betrayed, wanted to leave to ... the Church a visible sacrifice. The exigencies of our nature demand it. The sacrifice of God once and for all wrought upon the cross, should be reenacted and its memory abide to the end of the world, and its saving power applied (anew to each generation) for the remission of those sins into which we fall day by day ... He offered His Body and Blood to God the Father*

*under the appearances of bread and wine, and gave them under the same appearance to His apostles. These men He then appointed priests of the New Testament—they and their successors—by His words, **"Do this in remembrance of me."** So He gave the command to offer the sacrifice as the Church has understood and taught.[1]*

Four hundred years later, Vatican II stated:

At the Last Supper, on the night He was handed over, Our Lord instituted the Eucharistic Sacrifice of His Body and Blood to perpetuate the sacrifice on the Cross throughout the ages until He should come, and thus entrust to the Church, His beloved Spouse, the memorial of His death and resurrection: A sacrament of devotion, a sign of unity, a bond of charity, a paschal banquet in which Christ is received, the soul is filled with Grace and there is given to us the pledge of future glory. (Vatican Council II)[2]

This understanding of the Eucharistic Sacrifice, firmly rooted in Scripture, gives just as much credence to tradition. For the declarations of the Council of Trent and Vatican II do not stray from what the early Fathers of the Church laid down in writing concerning the Eucharist.

As with Bishop Abericius, a consistent theology of the Eucharist is visible in the Church's oldest writings. Most noteworthy are the writings of Saint Justin (d. A.D. 165) and Saint Hippolytus (d. A.D. 235). Both saints defended the secret of the Holy Sacrifice in their writings without disclosing its full mystery.

Highly characteristic of the older writings is the wisdom found in the words of Saint Ignatius of Antioch who died around the year A.D 107. In Saint Ignatius' writings we find how profoundly the early Church understood the power of the Eucharist. In his warning to the faithful of Philadelphia, Saint Ignatius wrote against the evils of schism and division. The saint challenged, *"Strive then to make use of one form of thanksgiving, for the flesh of Our Lord Jesus Christ is one and one is the chalice in the union of His Blood, one altar, one bishop."*

Saint Cyprian, who was beheaded for his refusal to sacrifice to pagan gods, wrote about the Eucharist:

Finally, the sacrifices of the Lord proclaim the unity of Christians, bound together by the bond of a firm and inviolable charity. For when the Lord, in speaking of bread which is produced by the compacting of many grains of wheat, refers to it as His Body, He is describing our people whose unity He has sustained, and when He refers to wine pressed from many grapes and berries, as His Blood, He is speaking of our flock, formed by the fusing of many united together.

In spite of persistent persecutions by the Roman emperors Decius and Diocletian, the number of Christians by A.D. 300 was an estimated five million, out of a total population of fifty million in the Roman empire. In A.D. 311, Emperor Galerius ended the persecutions of Diocletian.

Two years later, Emperor Constantine granted religious tolerance throughout the Roman empire after a vision guided him to lead his army into a victorious battle under the sign of the cross.

By A.D. 324, Constantine actively supported the religion. He built churches and instituted laws, one of which honored Sunday, the day of the Holy Sacrifice of the Mass. In the year A.D. 337 Constantine was baptized on his deathbed.

Together with the actions of Constantine, the fourth century ushered in some of the greatest highlights in Church history. The first Council was held in Nicea (Turkey) in A.D. 325. This was also the century that saw the end of martyrdom as a witness to the faith in the Roman Empire.

But new problems arose, most noteworthy the Arian Heresy. These divisions and the declaration of Theodosius in A.D. 381 that Christianity be the only official religion of the Roman Empire, now challenged the Church to defend its teachings in a more defined fashion. This challenge included the need for the Church to more openly explain its teachings on the "Discipline of the Secret," the Sacrifice of the Mass and the Holy Eucharist.

But God did not leave the Church helpless in its need. Great defenders of the faith, and especially of its greatest mystery, arose during this period.

Concerning the mystery of transubstantiation, Saint Ambrose (340-397), the Bishop of Milan, wrote:

> Let us be assured that this is not what nature formed, but what the blessing consecrated, and the greater efficacy resides in the blessing than in nature, for by the blessing nature is changed.

In support of the truth of this mystery, Saint Ambrose also invoked many of the miracles described in Scripture, including Christ's birth of the Virgin Mary. Then, turning to the work of creation, he stated:

> Surely the word of Christ, which could make out of nothing that which did not exist, can change things already in existence into what they were not. For it is no less extraordinary to give things new natures than to change their natures.

Saint Cyril of Jerusalem (315-386) wrote about the Holy Sacrifice of the Mass, and the omnipotent power of Christ in His True Presence:

> After the spiritual Sacrifice, the unbloody act of worship has been completed. Bending over this propitiatory offering we beg God to grant peace to all the Churches, to give harmony to the whole world, to bless our rulers, our soldiers, and our companions, to aid the sick and afflicted, and in general to assist all who stand in need; and then we offer the Victim also for our deceased holy ancestors and bishops and for all our dead. As we do this, we are filled with the conviction that this Sacrifice will be of the greatest help to those souls for whom prayers are being offered in the very presence of our holy and awesome Victim.

Most noteworthy are the writings of the great fourth century convert, Saint Augustine (354-430). Saint Augustine lived a monastic life with friends after his conversion to Christianity. He was converted through the prayers of his mother, Saint Monica, and the preaching of Saint Ambrose. He came to be recognized as one of the most productive and influential writers in the history of Christianity.

Concerning the True Presence, Saint Augustine wrote:

> *It was in His flesh that Christ walked among us and it is His flesh that He has given us to eat for our salvation. No one, however, eats of this flesh without having first adored it ... and not only do we not sin in thus adoring it, but we would sin if we did not do so.*

In A.D. 343 the Council of Sardica declared that the Pope, the Bishop of Rome, maintained full authority over all the Churches of the West. In 378 the Emperor Gratian confirmed this ruling. Pope Damasus (A.D. 366-384) then declared that the Pope's authority came not from the Council but from the Lord Himself. He cited Matthew 16:18: ***"And I say to thee, thou art Peter and upon this rock I will build my Church, and the gates of hell shall not prevail against it."***

With this, the Church firmly solidified its authority. It was the one holy, catholic and apostolic Church of Jesus Christ. The Church also openly declared that it was the living Mystical Body of Jesus Christ; and the secret it sought to protect was clearly the foundation of its very existence.

But this mystery of mysteries has, in many ways, remained a secret. And until the late twentieth century the Church even approved in language this secret. For in reality, it wasn't until 1964 that Vatican Council II openly substituted *"Liturgy of the Eucharist"* for *"Liturgy of the Secret."* [3]

Mother of the Secret

CHAPTER SEVEN

OUT OF MECCA

In God's eternal wisdom, His Church was carefully nourished and protected for centuries in the catacombs of Rome and the caves of Palestine. Through unwavering faith it grew. Yet, the Church's early history is still filled with numerous mystical stories of visions and voices.

These stories of heavenly intervention run the gamut from Christ's reported confrontation with Saint Peter to the confrontation of Pope Leo with Attila. Peter sought to exit Rome. But after hearing the words of Jesus, he returned to submit to his death. Likewise, Pope Leo's dramatic standoff with Attila the Hun outside of Rome in 452 ended with Rome spared and the return of the Huns to beyond the Danube. Attila would later say that the menacing presence of "two vested individuals" who threatened him with death as they stood with swords drawn next to Pope Leo resulted in his retreat.

While these are fascinating tales, the entire history of the early Church is no less captivating. Indeed, as the faith of the early Christians was buoyed by their strong convictions in Christ's words and in His True Presence, these courageous souls brought the Church from underground to the center of the civilized world.

Most significantly, the fact that all of this was accomplished without a violent revolution is the true sign of God's hand. Indeed, the Church emerged through suffering and sacrifice, just as Christ's words call all people to confront their own struggles and challenges.

After the retreat of the Huns, the Church quickly began to spread its wings. New orders emerged, as the Church grew in number, influence and wealth. Most of all, history shows that it was faith that made the Church grow just as it was faith that allowed it to survive.

While the history of the early Church reveals stories of supernatural interventions, more than anything else, the significant growth of the Church shows that the mysteries of this new religion were seized and accepted by millions on "faith." Indeed, and at the center of these mysteries remained the Holy Sacrifice of the Mass, the True Presence of Jesus Christ in the Church and in the Eucharist.

By the fourth century the Mass showed a decisive shift in liturgical sensibility. As the celebration of the Eucharist emerged into the public realm, important changes were found in both ritual action and ritual interpretation.

At the point when Holy Communion was distributed during the Mass, gestures of reverence and adoration appeared, as the Eucharist was seen as a ritual drama that rehearsed the events in Jesus Christ's life, death and resurrection. Some leaders taught that the altar was not so much a table, but the tomb where Christ was laid and then resurrected through the liturgical celebration. Altogether, this was the process through which emerged the complete celebration of the Sacrament.

Likewise, the celebration of the Eucharist from the fifth through ninth centuries was surrounded by many intellectual struggles.

These differences centered around attempts to properly interpret in language a realistic perception of the Lord's Presence in the Sacrament. A complete piety surrounding the Eucharist also emerged, as the practice of extra-liturgical veneration of the Eucharist's species began. However, customs like Eucharistic veneration, benediction, processions, and visits to the Blessed Sacrament had not yet developed.

For the most part, during this period the Church continued to grow within and in numbers. Various councils established and clarified the Church's teachings and defined its Sacraments. And it should be noted that the Church's teachings concerning the True Presence were, for the most part, unchallenged during these centuries.

But while the Church grew and spread out over many lands, the seventh century brought with it the rise of a great danger. Out of Mecca, a man named Mohammed arose among the people. He proclaimed revelations and visions of God, declaring there was no God but Allah, and that he was his messenger. Hence, the Mohammedan faith of Islam was born.

Mohammed's teachings were captured in a book called the Koran, which contains 114 chapters. Among the teachings were several ominous ones for Christians, including the denial of the divinity of Jesus Christ and the Most Holy Trinity.

By the year 660, Mohammed's successors completed and assembled all of his writings. They then began the violent spread of the Islamic faith. This was the first "major" assault on the Church, especially Islam's attack on Christ's divinity.

According to the revelations of the Virgin Mary, the second major assault was to be the Protestant Reformation. In this assault Christ's True Presence in His Church was also directly denied, only in a different manner.

Today, Our Lady's words from her numerous apparitions reveal how a third major confrontation awaits the Church. It will be a decisive confrontation, the Virgin told Sister Lucia Santos of Fatima. And this confrontation will again attempt to accomplish what the first two assaults failed to do through military force and doctrinal revolution. Moreover, Mary says, it will be mystically linked to what began with the Church's first major challenge out of Mecca in the seventh century, since all assaults on the Church are inspired and motivated by the world of darkness and its evil inhabitants.

Indeed, Satan has been determined to destroy belief in Christ's True Presence in the Church since its founding. But as Scripture guarantees and Mary assures us, God will defend and preserve this mystery.

Curiously, not very long after Mohammed's writings began to spread, it appears that Heaven moved in a mighty way to uphold the faith in Christ's True Presence in His Church. For around the year A.D. 700, a miracle occurred in Lanciano, Italy that even today scientists cannot explain or deny.

Mother of the Secret

CHAPTER EIGHT

THE KINGDOM OF GOD

With the beginning of the second millennium, documented reports of Eucharistic miracles are consistently found. But the most famous Eucharistic miracle in Church history remains the great miracle of Lanciano, Italy, which reportedly occurred around the beginning of the eighth century.

Tradition has it that Lanciano is named after the "lance" that pierced Christ's heart. Reportedly, the Roman centurion Longinus, who thrust the lance into the side of Christ, striking his heart, was from Lanciano (originally "Anxanum").

After seeing the dramatic events that occurred upon Christ's death, Longinus believed Christ was the Savior. His belief was aided by a personal experience. The centurion had poor eyesight, but after his eyes were touched with the water and blood from Christ's body, his vision was completely restored. From this experience, Longinus then quit the army and became a convert. He died a martyr and is now known as Saint Longinus whose feast day is March 15.

The Miracle of Lanciano reportedly occurred around the year A.D. 700 when a priest-monk of the order of Saint Basil was celebrating Mass.

Because of his weak faith, the priest doubted the transubstantiation (the changing of bread and wine into the real and True Presence of the Body and Blood of Jesus Christ). But when he uttered the words of the consecration, the Host suddenly changed into a circle of flesh and the wine into visible blood. News of this miracle quickly spread.

Since then, the miraculous Host and five pellets of blood have survived for over 1200 years. Numerous scientific tests have challenged this event, the latest being in 1970. The results from that investigation were:

1. The blood is real blood and the flesh is real flesh. It is human blood (type AB) and the flesh is striated muscular tissue of the myocardium. (The blood is the same type as found on the Shroud of Turin.)
2. While spoilage and contamination should have occurred, all the chemical properties (minerals, proteins etc.) of the blood have remained, although this is scientifically impossible because of the components of the blood and its age.
3. The flesh and blood should have deteriorated and vanished hundreds of years ago for it contains no preservatives.[1] (Physical, biological, and atmospheric agents were exposed to it for centuries)

On March 4, 1971 Professor Odoaido Linoli and his team of scientists announced their conclusions in a detailed medical and scientific report to a prestigious assembly from all walks of life and all disciplines. Again, after 1200 years, the miracle of Lanciano was still that - - a miracle!

It will never be known whether or not Heaven's timing for this incredible miracle was meant to connect with the seventh centrury events involving Islam's denial of Christ's divinity. However, not long after Lanciano, more reports of mystical phenomena surrounding the Eucharist were found.

During the ninth century, debates over language explaining and defining the True Presence continued. Some writers cited reports of "bleeding hosts" and "miraculous apparitions of the Lord in the bread" to support their positions.

However, Church authorities dismissed these stories and insisted that attributing any significant meaning to their reality detracted from the mystery of the True Presence.

In fact, it would no longer have been proper to call the Eucharist a mystery if credence were given to these claims. It was argued that God had chosen to veil Himself in the Eucharist, and to do otherwise would damage the Sacrament. If God occasionally chose to manifest Himself externally that is one thing; but the Eucharist was meant to demand recognition from the faithful's minds, not their senses. Thus, the writers of the Church sought to keep their views in the proper perspective of faith in order to truly preserve the integrity and meaning of the mystery. However, around the year 1000, a second Eucharistic miracle of significant stature occurred, and its story is well-documented.

In Trani, Italy a Jewish woman who hated the Catholic Church and practiced witchcraft reportedly conspired to steal a consecrated Host. Upon receiving the Host, she took it to her store to burn it in a pot of boiling oil. But as soon as the Host touched the oil, it turned into real flesh. Afterward, the flesh began to bleed. This bleeding became profuse, to the point where blood flowed everywhere. In terror, the woman tried to hide what she had done. But soon neighbors came. The bishop arrived, and the whole town came to revere the miracle. To this day, the blood-soaked Host is still incorrupt (free of decay) and preserved in the local cathedral. This miracle has been repeatedly authenticated over the centuries by bishops and even by Pope Urban VI.

Once again, the timing of this documented miracle is very curious. For not long afterward, the Church experienced its very first major heresy involving Christ's True Presence in the Eucharist.

Only four years after the Great Eastern Schism in 1054, an attack on the Church's teachings of the Lord's True Presence in the Eucharist was waged. Scholars would later recognize this as a major heresy in the Church.

The Berengarian Controversy surrounded the doctrines of a teacher and philosopher named Berengarius of Tours. Berengarius' philosophical language was the source of this debate. He sought to define "the change" that occurs in the bread and wine and the nature and structure of the Sacrament.

These were prickly theological questions. At the time, medieval political realities profoundly affected the debate. At a synod held in Rome in 1059, during the Pontificate of Nicholas II, Berengarius was forced to make a confession of faith:

> *I, Berengarius, ... acknowledging the true and apostolic faith, anathematize every, especially that one for which heretofore I have been infamous, [heresy] which attempted to prove that the bread and wine which are placed on the altar remain merely a sacrament after consecration—and not the true body and blood of our Lord Jesus Christ; and further, that [the body and blood] are touched and broken by the hands of the priests and crushed by the teeth of the faithful in a sacramental manner only—and not physically. I assent to the Holy Roman Church and the Apostolic See, and I confess with mouth and heart that ... the bread and wine which are placed on the altar are not merely a sacrament after consecration, but are rather the true body and blood of our Lord Jesus Christ—and that these are truly, physically and not merely sacramentally, touched and broken by the hands of the priests and crushed by the teeth of the faithful."*

As noted, Berengarius was labeled a heretic. He died in the year 1088. However, between 1160 and 1208, three different schools of thought concerning the moment of consecration developed from this controversy. While all three schools acknowledged Christ's True Presence, a new age was upon the world and the Church.

It was not until the Age of Enlightenment that the True Presence of Jesus Christ in the Church and in the Eucharist was denied and rejected. However, in retrospect, the eleventh century Eastern Orthodox schism and Eucharistic controversy reveal the intellectual seeds of the later schism. Although Christ's True Presence was upheld throughout both events and the Orthodox Church continued to validate the divine reality of the Sacrament, new ideas began to challenge the Church's teachings.

Like sin, which becomes stronger and more inviting with each visitation, the schism of 1054 is now seen as a crucial phase in a growing impetus that would later seek to disassemble all Christian thought. Even though the Church has been rocked by heresies and confrontations since its beginning, the events of 1054 proved to the world that the Catholic Church could be wounded.

Although Church leaders and theologians valiantly defended its theology, by the twelfth and thirteenth centuries, the writings of philosophers indicated that the world was about to change.

It would be a change directed away from such things as faith and religion, which surrender to a higher order ensconced in the invisible and supernatural, to a new world order based upon the mind and the senses.

But Heaven wasn't missing anything. By the twelfth century, the True Presence of Jesus Christ in the Eucharist as an invisible truth was repeatedly confirmed by visible manifestations of bread and wine. Like the miracle at Lanciano, the Body and Blood of Jesus Christ repeatedly manifested itself in incredible miracles that both stunned and excited the faithful.

Whether or not these events were coordinated by God to counter the prevailing heretical times is unknown. But with faith in the Church's teaching and knowledge of its history of survival, it is quite apparent that the living God of all mankind, Jesus Christ, deliberately and repeatedly chose this period to divinely intervene in a dynamic way.

While secular humanism in the twelfth century was only a budding school of thought, it obviously led the world into another era of paganism. This paganism was falsely supported by a mis-guided intellectualism. Thus, with each Eucharistic miracle, per-haps God sought to overcome the minds of men by appealing di-rectly to their senses. As we find in the Scriptural stories of Christ's many miracles, people's faith cannot deny what they see and hear, no matter what they are told and no matter who is telling them.

Indeed, the intellectuals of the early middle ages, like the spiri-tually blind Pharisees and Scribes of Christ's time, faced the diffi-cult task of convincing people to deny what they believed through personal experience.

Likewise, the Church taught that Jesus Christ proclaimed that the *"Kingdom of God was at hand."* And with each Eucharistic miracle came continuing evidence that it was not going to go away...

Mother of the Secret

CHAPTER NINE

"ALL FOR JESUS, THROUGH MARY"

The popes of the twelfth and thirteenth centuries constantly re-aligned the Church with different kings and nations to preserve the freedom of the papal states. Hence, a balance of power within Europe was maintained. Likewise, any single ruler was prevented from controlling the Church.

During this same period, the Church embarked upon military expeditions, or Crusades, to liberate the Holy Land from Moslem control. It was a turbulent time.

But as history has shown, the Church responded to the troubles of one century with a dynamic spiritual renewal in the next. New orders, monasteries, and political movements evolved. Likewise, new schools emerged and brought with them a shift in the focus of the faith. For example, images of a crucified and suffering Christ reflected the peoples' struggles and life's uncertainties. People's piety also became more personal and individualistic as devotion to Mary and the saints flourished.

Most significantly, numerous Church councils reaffirmed Christ's True Presence in the Eucharist as the term *"transubstantiation"* began to be implemented.

The twelfth century also brought the beginning of Scholastic Theology, the theology of the schools. Preparing to deal with the problems of the coming Age of Enlightenment, church leaders began to emphasize reason in the understanding of the mysteries of faith and theology.

Indeed, the theologians of the era wanted to form a synthesis using the teachings of the Bible, the writings of the early Church fathers, and philosophy to explain the faith. They believed faith and reason complemented each other.

But this renewal also led to a new crisis, as dissident groups emerged and another major heresy confronted the Catholic Church.

The Albigensian Heresy spread quickly and attracted many. The Church and its political allies of the day fought long and hard to oppose it. Also characteristic of this period was a great outbreak of reports of mystical interventions and signs, signs that appeared to show Heaven coming to the aid of the Church Militant.

The most prominent mystical interventions were the apparitions of the Blessed Virgin Mary to Saint Dominic. In the year 1214, the Virgin Mary reportedly appeared to Saint Dominic and gave him the Rosary as a powerful means of converting the Albigensians and other sinners.

According to Blessed Alan de Roche's book, *De Dignitate Psalterii*, Saint Dominic withdrew into a forest near Toulouse to pray and fast for the gravity of the situation. For three days and three nights, he prayed unceasingly for the conversion of the Albigensians.

Finally, the Virgin Mary appeared to him accompanied by three angels and said, *"Dear Dominic, do you know which weapon the Blessed Trinity wants to use to reform the world?*

"Oh, my Lady," answered Saint Dominic, *"you know far better than I do because next to your Son Jesus Christ you have always been the chief instrument of our salvation."*

Then Our Lady replied:

> *I want you to know that, in this kind of warfare, the battering ram has always been the Angelic Psalter which is the foundation stone of the New Testament. Therefore if you want to reach these hardened souls and win them over to God, preach my Psalter.*[1]

Saint Dominic arose and went to the cathedral and began to preach about the Rosary. At the beginning of his sermon, a storm broke out and the earth reportedly shook. Then, an image of Mary raising her arms to Heaven three times was seen. This was interpreted by the people as a sign that the Virgin was calling down the vengeance of God if they failed to convert. Through all of this, Saint Dominic continued to preach about the Rosary.

The people of Toulouse reportedly embraced the saint's teachings, as conversions and renunciation of the Albigensian faith occurred. The Rosary then quickly spread as Saint Dominic's example and fervor ignited the Christian world.

This era also witnessed the rise of many great leaders of the faith. Saint Dominic (1170-1221), Saint Bernard of Clairvaux (1090-1153), Saint Elizabeth of Schoenau (1127-1164), Saint Francis of Assisi (1181-1226), Saint Simon Stock (1165-1265), Saint Mechtilde (1240-1298) and Saint Gertrude (1256-1302) were all heroic figures of the times and were all devoted to the Eucharist.

Saint Francis of Assisi was especially devoted to the Eucharist. Five out of the eight letters he wrote that are still in existence deal with the Holy Eucharist. Wrote St. Francis:

> *...in this world I cannot see the most high Son of God with my own eyes except for His most holy body and blood. Everyday He humbles Himself just as He did when He came from His heavenly throne into the Virgin's womb ... when He descends from the bosom of the Father into the hand of the priest at the altar.*

Another great defender of the faith and the True Presence at the time was St. Thomas Aquinas. Upon the request of the King of France, Saint Thomas Aquinas traveled to France in 1269 to speak to students about the True Presence of Christ in the Eucharist. After fasting for three days and praying, the great saint wrote a treatise that was presented and accepted unanimously at the university.

After this Saint Thomas reportedly received a vision of Christ, who told him, *"Thou has written well of the Sacrament of My Body."* The saint reportedly then went into ecstasy and levitated above the ground before many witnesses.

Likewise, Saint Anthony of Padua was also a defender of the Eucharist. Saint Anthony was born in the twelfth century, and the Eucharistic Miracle of Saint Anthony and the Donkey reveals to us his great confidence in the True Presence.

One day, Saint Anthony was confronted by a man named Bovillo who heard of Saint Anthony's great gifts, and who did not believe in the True Presence. The man told Saint Anthony that he would starve his mule for three days. At the end of the three days, Saint Anthony was to stand on one end of the square holding the Eucharist and the man would stand on the other end, holding a pail of the animal's favorite food. It was agreed that if the mule went to Saint Anthony, the man, a hater of Catholics, would stop persecuting the Church.

The mule was starved for three days. At the same time Saint Anthony fasted and prayed for three days.

At the agreed upon time, the two men took their places in the town square. The man showed the mule the food, while Saint Anthony softly spoke to the animal. The great saint then reportedly said, "Creature of God, in His name, I command you to come here and adore Him, so that it will give truth to all of the Real Presence of Jesus in the Blessed Sacrament of the Eucharist."

Almost instantly, the mule ignored the food and went over to where Saint Anthony held the Host. The animal knelt down on both legs and lowered his head in adoration. With this, the heretic proceeded to believe. There is a shrine to this day in Rimini, Italy, in honor of this Eucharistic miracle.

All of these saints are remembered for their great defense of the faith. But most curiously, they share something else. They all reported visions of Mary and Jesus. These visions directly or indirectly would come to affect their actions, and eventually, the entire Church.

Indeed, the thirteen century reveals many stories of heavenly visions. One such story deals with the Seven Servite Saints. In the year 1233, there lived in Florence seven rich, distinguished young businessmen. Their ages ranged from 27 to 35 and all proclaimed public devotion to Mary. Five years before, they had joined the Confraternity of the Laudesi Laudes (Praises) of Mary. Thus, they attended meetings on a regular basis to honor and sing to the Queen of Heaven.

On the feast of Mary's Assumption, in the year 1233, all seven men experienced a mystical encounter with the Virgin Mary. After receiving Holy Communion, each man saw an apparition of Our Lady, accompanied by many angels. Mary then gave them a message requesting that they depart and follow a new path. Six years later, Mary again appeared to the now hermits and requested the founding of the Order of Servants of Mary. They complied with the Virgin's request. Pope Leo XIII canonized the seven in 1888.

With this story and the many others involving the great saints of the times, we see the unfolding of a series of numerous heavenly interventions surrounding the Virgin Mary and the Church. Indeed, Mary herself said that she was sent to earth to defend the sacred and holy mysteries of the Church.

The twelfth and thirteenth centuries also witnessed an outbreak of Eucharistic miracles. Such miraculous events were reported in France, Italy, Spain, Portugal, Czechoslovakia, and Germany during an unprecedented period of heavenly signs which confirmed the True Presence. Never before had one century documented so many confirmed reports.

Thus, the Eucharistic miracles were incredible events with undeniable significance. Indeed, in them, God perhaps sought to combat the errors of the day and possibly the approaching crisis of the sixteenth century. Most of all, many of the stories of these Eucharistic miracles must be individually examined in order to understand their overall significance to this era and to the Church.

In the year 1153, in Blaine, France a different kind of Eucharistic miracle occurred. On a feast day of the Holy Spirit, while the archbishop of Soissons elevated the Host in consecration, the people in the Church saw a vision of a small child instead of the Host.

The vision was so powerful that many non-Catholics reportedly requested to be baptized. Following the miracle, the Host was venerated for centuries. Today the miracle is still affirmed by the Church although no special observances are held anymore.

In Ferraro, Italy, on March 28, 1171 at a Mass on Easter Sunday, a consecrated Host began to spurt blood at the moment it was broken into two parts. Witnesses also reported that the Host turned into flesh. Pope Pius IX visited the Church in 1857. The miracle is still venerated to this day.

In 1194, a woman in Augsburg, Germany received Holy Communion and took it home where she kept it for five years. She sealed it between two pieces of wax creating a homemade reliquary. After five years, she confessed this secret to her priest. Upon opening the reliquary, it was found that the Host had turned to flesh and had red streaks.

After the miraculous Host was moved to the cathedral, a second miracle occurred. This time the Host swelled in size and broke out of the wax container. The local bishop recognized the miracle on May 15, 1199. Likewise, many miraculous healings have been reported in association with the traditional services that celebrate the two miracles.

In the year 1228, two women in Alatri, Italy, conspired to remove a consecrated Host. After communion, the one woman hid the Host in her home in a small pouch. Two days later, burdened by her conscience, she decided to take the Host back to the Church. But upon opening the pouch, the woman discovered the Host had turned to flesh. The Host was then transferred to the cathedral for veneration. In 1978, the seven hundred fiftieth anniversary of the miracle, a special celebration was observed.

At Saint Ambrose Church of Florence, Italy on December 30, 1230, a priest left some drops of consecrated wine in the chalice. The next day it was observed that the wine had turned to blood. Other miracles followed and in 1266, Pope Clement IV declared the authenticity of the Miracle of the Eucharist of Florence.

In 1595, a second Eucharistic miracle occurred. This time six consecrated Hosts that had fallen near fire were united into one large Host. In 1628, the Hosts were declared incorrupt by the Bishop of Florence.

In 1280, a woman in Lanciano, Italy, with a troubled marriage was advised to take a consecrated Host to her home and to place it in a pot and cook it. She was advised to place the ashes of the Host in her husband's wine and soup. This would supposedly invigorate his passion for her. But upon placing the Host in the pot, it suddenly began to smoke. It then turned into flesh and bled profusely. Out of fear, the woman then buried the host, along with the pot in her stable. Seven years later she confessed, and the bleeding Host was discovered incorrupt. While the Eucharistic miracle actually occurred in Lanciano, it was then moved to Offida and it is still there to this day.

In 1263, a priest named Peter of Prague was traveling to Rome to find help for his struggling faith. On the way, he stopped in Bolsena, Italy, seventy miles north of Rome, where he celebrated Mass at the Church of Saint Christina. At the time of the consecration, the priest elevated the Host and said, "This is My Body." The Host then turned into flesh and began to bleed. Immediately, Father Peter traveled to nearby Orvieto to personally tell Pope Urban IV of the miracle. It is said that from these events the Holy Father was led to declare the Feast of Corpus Christi on August 11, 1264, in honor of the Blessed Sacrament. At that time, the Church had been still struggling against a heresy known as Berengarianism, that opposed the True Presence.

Near Venice in 1294, a woman who regularly washed the altar cloths began her normal undertaking. However, this time as she washed the altar cloth, a red stain slowly began to grow and grow. The harder she rubbed, the larger the stain became. Finally, blood began to rush out from the cloth. Upon inspection, the woman found a Host which was the source of the bleeding. Quickly, the entire village, including the priest, discovered what was happening. In 1972, the Eucharistic Congress held in Udine, declared that the Miracle of Valvasone was one of the miracles of the Eucharist that still had visible traces which the faithful could venerate.

South of Fatima lies the village of Santarem, Portugal. In the early thirteenth century an unhappily married woman sought to remove a consecrated Host from a church and to take it home on the advice of a sorceress. But within a few moments, the Host began to bleed. The blood covered the woman's hands and dripped a trail behind her. After she ran home, she placed the Host in a chest. During the night, a mysterious light came forth from the trunk and illuminated the entire home. An investigation followed, and the miracle was recognized. The Host still exists today, over 700 years later.

In northeastern Spain, in the year 1239, a Catholic king named Don Jaime prepared for an invasion from the northern African states.

As part of the preparation, the King ordered a Mass for his soldiers. But a surprise attack forced the priest to quickly hide six consecrated Hosts. After the battle, the Hosts were found to be missing from the cloth they were buried in, only to be replaced by six blood stains. A church was built in Daroca to commemorate the miracle which still is celebrated.

In the thirteenth century, the city of Olmutz in Czechoslovakia, braced for an invasion by the Tartars. The leader of Moravia at that time, Jaroslas of Sternberg, ordered his army to receive the Holy Sacrament before battle. In battle, five consecrated Hosts were carried by a priest on horseback. After winning the battle, the Christians found that the five consecrated Hosts each exhibited a clear, shiny circle of a rosy color. The Hosts had miraculously changed, and the victorious Christians celebrated the miracle.

In 1257, two years after a chapel in Regensburg, Germany, had been built on the site where some Hosts had accidentally fallen, a priest incurred doubts about the True Presence of Christ in the Eucharist. Suddenly, the corpus on the large altar cross sprung to life. The hands of the crucified Lord removed the chalice from the priest's hands. When the shocked priest repented sincerely, the chalice was handed back to him. For centuries the miracle was remembered and celebrated.

In 1274, a thief removed a pyx from Saint Gervais Church in Paris. Later, as he opened the case to throw away the Host, the Host rose upward and began to flutter above his head. A throng of people gathered, including the priest who had consecrated the Host. The Host then fell into this priest's hands. Following the miracle, the bishop ordered special services to be held, which were observed for years.

In Paris in the year 1290, a poor woman who had pawned her dress for some living expense money, returned to the pawnbroker to borrow her dress back for Easter Sunday. The pawnbroker, a non-Christian, asked for a consecrated Host in return. Upon receiving it, he drew a knife and proceeded to stab the Host. Instantly blood squirted everywhere splashing everyone present. He then threw the Host into a fire. When this failed to hurt the Host, he threw it in a kettle of boiling water.

The water turned red with blood and then ran out of the kettle into the street. A woman passerby entered the house and saw a vision of Christ standing before the kettle. Suddenly Christ vanished and she witnessed the Host floating in midair. The Host descended into a vase which the woman had grabbed. It was then taken to a nearby church. Afterward, the king along with the local bishop authorized the home to be converted into a chapel.

In 1280 outside the village of Slavonice in Czechoslovakia, a stolen Host was discovered miraculously floating above a mysterious fire. The Host was deposited in a vessel by a priest. He then proceeded to the city where the church was located. But suddenly, the Host again disappeared. It was found once more floating in the fire above a heap of stones. After retrieving it and returning it to the Church, it was found to have returned again to the fire. This time, a promise was made to construct a sanctuary on the place of the discovery of the missing Host. The local bishop consecrated the chapel and for centuries, pilgrims journeyed to Slavonice. The anniversary of the miracle is still observed.

In Aninon, Spain around the year 1300, a fire totally destroyed the Church of Our Lady of Catillo. Everything was destroyed in the church, even the tabernacle that held consecrated Hosts. However, in searching through the ruins, five bleeding Hosts were found and a sixth Host was stuck to the pall. The miracle was later approved in 1613 by the Vicar General and the anniversary of the miracle is still celebrated.

During the early 1300's a priest from the town of Cascia, Italy, near Siena, was suffering with doubt over the True Presence. His priesthood was lackluster in faith, and he had become apathetic. One day while on a house call to a sick person, he casually tossed a consecrated Host between two pages of his breviary. Upon arrival at the sick person's home, the priest opened his book only to find two bloodstained pages where the Host had been placed. Over the years, this miracle has been venerated. It was verified by the bishop, and in 1930 on the sixth centennial, a new chapel was built in honor of the Eucharistic miracle.

In a small Spanish village named Cebero, around the year 1300, a pious peasant named Juan Santin plodded through a severe snowstorm to attend daily Mass. A disgruntled priest, however, had begun the Mass prior to anyone's arrival. Indeed, he bemoaned the very necessity of offering the Holy Sacrifice. At the exact moment of the consecration, the doors of the Church burst open with wind and snow, as Juan had finally arrived. Simultaneously, the priest's hands were now raised above his head holding the paten with the bread and the chalice with the wine in consecration. The peasant, seeing this, fell to his knees in adoration. Suddenly, the Host turned to flesh and the wine into blood. The remorseful priest broke into tears as both he and Juan were awestruck over the miracle. Pope Innocent III authenticated the miracle, and it is celebrated to this day.

Thus, we find the twelfth and thirteenth centuries were filled with reports of mystical events. From the Virgin Mary presenting the Rosary to Saint Dominic, to the numerous Eucharistic miracles, it is apparent that Heaven was supplying the Church with new weapons from above to defend its sacred mysteries. Undoubtedly, Heaven knew that the Church would need these weapons in the urgent and dangerous times that lay ahead.

Likewise, it must be noted that the full and detailed accounts of the many Eucharistic miracles also continued to reveal links to the Virgin Mary. For it appears that Heaven was laying the foundation for the coming of her times - times that would reveal her mighty role in helping the Church to protect her Son's True Presence and eventually lead to Fatima's promise of the triumph of Mary's Immaculate Heart throughout the entire world.

Perhaps the rule of St. Bernard of Clairvaux, who was said to have *"carried the twelfth century on his shoulders,"* reveals how God was establishing the importance of Mary in His divine plan.

"All for Jesus," St. Bernard declared, *"through Mary!"*

CHAPTER TEN

THE REALITY OF CHRIST'S TRUE PRESENCE

Throughout the fourteenth century, Eucharistic miracles, saintly visions, and apparitions abounded, as Heaven continued to pour out its signs and wonders in order to strengthen the faithful. All the while, the Church marched forward toward heresy, confrontation and division, and a storm of unparalleled proportion.

Indeed, a new era was dawning, not just in the Church, but in the world. New philosophies based on Rationalism were gaining in popularity, as faith and religion were repeatedly assaulted by secularists.

Within the Church, a Great Western Schism arose in the fourteenth century. Three men simultaneously claimed to be pope during one of the most difficult times in Church history.

Finally, the Council of Constantine (1411-1418) deposed two popes, persuaded a third to retire and elected a new pope, Martin V (1417). But this entire affair greatly weakened the papacy and led to new problems. The authority of the Church and its teachings were now directly challenged, especially its teaching of the Eucharistic doctrine of "transubstantiation."

An Oxford scholar named John Wycliffe (1330-1384), who had little serious study of Scripture, published his translation of the Bible. Wycliffe taught that the Bible, not tradition, was the sole rule of faith. It quickly became one of the most well-circulated works of the times. Most significantly, Wycliffe's ideas about transubstantiation then affected others, such as John Huss (1369-1415). These critics then led an increasing number of people to rebel against Church teachings. According to scholars, all these circumstances were the early sparks of the Protestant uprising. But again, it must be emphasized that during this period, a plethora of miracles, accompanied by reports of numerous mystical interventions, occurred.

In fact, an acknowledged era of mysticism arose. This was exemplified by such great saints as St. Catherine of Siena who boldly defended the Church and its sacred mysteries.

Blessed Raymond of Capua, who wrote about the life of Saint Catherine of Siena and who was her confessor, reports that she received a special apparition of the Lord in 1372. During this apparition, St. Catherine was allowed to drink the blood of Christ from His side. After this, for the remaining years of her life until her death, she ate no food other than the Eucharist.

With so many new problems arising within the Church and the world, it appears that Heaven wanted, through the great saints and numerous miracles, to keep the faithful's eyes on the truth: Jesus Christ was truly present and alive in His Church. Indeed, priests also began to hold the consecrated Host high before the faithful in a demonstrative sign of Christ's True Presence among them.

There were many reports of Eucharistic miracles just as there had been in the previous two centuries. Once again, let us take a look at some of them in order to see how actively God revealed Himself to His people in so many special ways.

In 1317, a priest from Viversel, Belgium, took Holy Communion to a man in the village who was ill. Upon arriving, the priest placed a Host in a ciborium. When the priest left the room for several minutes, a man in the state of mortal sin picked up the Host. Suddenly, the Host began to bleed and the scared man fled. When the priest returned and saw the bleeding Host, he took it to another pastor. This priest advised that the Host be taken to a convent in Liège. When the Host was placed on the altar in the convent church, those present witnessed a vision of Christ crowned with thorns. This second miracle was seen as confirmation of Heaven's desire for the Host to be there. The miraculous Host still exists to this day.

In Blanot, France on March 31, 1331, a Host fell out of the mouth of a woman named Jacquette. It landed on a special communion cloth, designed for such accidents. Upon searching for the Host, it could not be found, only a red spot was seen. After Mass, the priest attempted to wash out the red stain, only to find that the red spot began to grow and grow. The basin also became filled with bloody water. An investigation followed and was completed with Pope John XXII's favorable verdict. The miracle is still solemnly celebrated in Blanot to this day.

On March 15, 1345, a very sick man named Ysbrant Dommer received Holy Communion at his home in Amsterdam, Holland. After the priest departed, Ysbrant expelled the contents of his stomach into a basin. A woman who was there then threw it all into a large open fire in the hearth. The following day the same woman discovered the Host, shining and whole, in the coals. She placed it in a cloth and then into a chest A priest came and took it to the parish church of Saint Nicholas, where he placed it in a pyx. The next morning the priest found the pyx empty. Somehow, the Host reappeared in the woman's chest. After a third incident, the priest became convinced of the entire miracle. An inquiry was held, and the bishop's verdict was favorable for the events. Over the centuries, celebration of this miracle has continued.

While celebrating Mass on April 25, 1356, a priest in Macereta, Italy, experienced a moment of doubt about the reality of Christ's True Presence. Upon breaking the Host at the consecration, fresh blood began to drip from the pieces of the Host. Some of the blood fell beside the chalice, staining the corporal. A canonical commission authenticated the miracle, and it is honored to this day in Macereta on the feast of Corpus Christi.

On October 4, 1369 a man named Jean of Louvain stole fifteen small Hosts and one large Host from the Church of Saint Catherine in Brussels, Belgium. Jean had been paid sixty gold coins by a Jewish man named Jonathan for this criminal act. Two weeks after the theft, Jonathan was murdered in his own garden. His wife gave the Hosts to a group of men who assembled in a synagogue in Brussels on Good Friday April 4, 1370. The men commenced to stab the Hosts with knives. Immediately, blood flowed from the Hosts. Seized with terror, they fell to the ground in fear. In an effort to get rid of the bloody Hosts, they hired a woman named Catherine to transport them to Cologne. Instead the woman took them to Pierre Van Eede, the Curé of the Church of Notre Dame de la Chapelle.

In 1968, a disclaimer was published by the diocesan authorities to lift any blame on the Jewish community for the events. The miracle, however, is still venerated.

In the year 1345, outside of Krakow, Poland, near a village named Bawo, one night mysterious lights were seen emanating through a swamp-like area of marshes. Simultaneously, flashes of lightning filled the skies above the swamp. On the same day, word came that someone had broken into All Saints Catholic Church and removed a pyx containing a consecrated Host. The local bishop called for prayer and penance. After three days, he led a party into the swamp and retrieved the pyx with the Host undefiled. The miracle occurred during the octave of Corpus Christi, and documents from 1392 still exist in testimony of its actual occurrence.

In the year 1379, a Eucharistic miracle occurred in the village of Boxtel in Holland. At the Church of Saint Peter, a priest named Father Van der Aker, celebrated Mass and had an accident. Just as he was about to consecrate the bread and wine, he accidentally spilled the wine on the corporal and the altar cloth. Although he had used white wine, the cloth was stained a deep red color. Repeated efforts to wash out the stains failed, and due to embarrassment and fear, he hid the cloths. Father Van der Aker died that year, but before dying he told his pastor, Father Henry, what had happened. The following year it was decreed that the cloths were to be venerated annually as relics of the Precious Blood. The village became a pilgrimage shrine, and the miracle is celebrated to this day.

A wealthy noblewoman of the town of Middleburg, Netherlands, required her servants to go to confession and communion each year during the holy season of Lent. Her servants obliged. But in 1374 one of them, a man named Jean, failed to go to confession prior to receiving Holy Communion. At the moment the Host touched his tongue, it turned to flesh. Jean panicked and was unable to swallow. He then bit into the flesh causing three drops of blood to come out of his mouth and onto the cloth draping the communion rail. The priest removed the Host and placed it on a vessel. It was later transferred to Belgium. The Host, relics and original papers exist to this day.

At Saint Oswald Church in the town of Seefield, Austria, a Eucharistic miracle occurred on Holy Thursday in the year 1384. At that time, a man named Oswald Miller, who was a knight and guardian of Schlossberg Castle, came along with his men to the church. He proceeded to the altar after Mass and demanded a large Host instead of the smaller ones usually given. Since his sword was drawn, the priest acceded to his wishes. But at the moment the Host touched the knight's tongue, he sank to his knees into the ground. Seizing the altar in desperation, the knight implored the priest to remove the Host. The Host was observed to have turned red as if saturated with blood and it then was safeguarded. A new church stands today over the old one. Inside, the knight's sunken footprints are still preserved. In 1984, the miracle's six hundredth anniversary was observed.

In 1330, a young girl of nine named Imelda Lambertini entered the Dominican Convent of Santa Maria Maddalena in Valdipietra, near Bologna, Italy. On the feast of the Ascension in 1333, the twelve-year old Imelda longed for Holy Communion. After Mass, the sisters of the convent noticed that a bright white Host was suspended in the air above Imelda's head. A priest came and held out a paten onto which the Host descended. He took this as a sign that he was to give Imelda First Holy Communion. Upon receiving the sacrament, the child went into ecstasy and died. The date was May 12, 1333.

In 1922, a community called the Dominican Sisters of the Blessed Imelda was established in her name. Blessed Imelda was named the Protectress of First Holy Communion by Pope St. Pius X. Her body remains incorrupt.

Between Frankfurt and Wurzburg lies the town of Walldurn, Germany. In the year 1330, a priest named Father Otto was celebrating Mass at Saint George Church when he knocked over the chalice. The contents spilled, forming in actual blood what appeared to be a miraculous image on the corporal. The image depicted a crucified Christ, surrounded by eleven heads of Christ crowned with thorns. The priest hid the cloth, but prior to his death, he notified his confessor. The miracle was sent to Rome where it was authenticated by Pope Eugene IV. It is still celebrated on its anniversary date to this day.

At the church of Santa Maria Assunta in Bagno Di Romagna, Italy in the year 1412, a priest was struggling with his faith. As he was offering Mass one day, he continued to have his doubts about the True Presence of Jesus in the Eucharist. Suddenly, after the consecration, the priest looked into the chalice and saw that the wine had turned into blood. The red blood then began to boil! This caused some of it to spurt out of the chalice and onto the corporal. The blood seemed to be alive. The priest alerted the congregation who experienced a powerful conversion. Almost 400 years later, after Pope Pius VI convened a commission to investigate, the relics were put on display for the faithful to venerate. In 1912, a large celebration was held to commemorate the miracle. In 1958, a scientific study confirmed that the stain on the corporal cloth was blood.

Around the year 1433, a non-Christian reportedly abused a Host causing a stream of blood to issue forth from it. While the specifics of the miracle are not recorded, the Host was sent to Rome on the request of Pope Eugene IV. It was later transferred to Dijon, France, where it was credited with healing King Louis XII. The Host was later destroyed during the French Revolution in 1794.

In 1453, two ex-soldiers pillaged a church, removing together with other things, an ostensorium containing a large consecrated Host. Upon entering Turin, Italy, their mule stumbled causing all of their possessions to tumble to the ground. The Host, however, rose into the air. It then remained suspended in the air, giving off splendid rays of light. The miracle occurred in a crowded marketplace. The names of ten witnesses are still chronicled to this day. A priest named Bartolomeo Coccono notified the Bishop of Turin, Ludovico of Ramagnano. The bishop traveled to the site, venerated the Blessed Sacrament, and then opened a ciborium into which the Host descended. By the order of the Holy See, the Host was consumed in the year 1584, after being perfectly preserved for 131 years.

This miracle, because of brilliance of the Host, is known as the Sun of Justice. Various popes including Popes Pius XII, Gregory XVI, Clement XIII, Benedict XIV, St. Pius X and Pius XI have all recognized the miracle. In 1953, on the fifth centennial of the miracle, special services were held in Turin.

In the year 1405, a wealthy young man named Jean du Bois from, a village in Belgium, received visions of a suffering Christ on three consecutive nights. On the third day, a priest celebrating Mass at a small chapel on Jean du Bois's property noticed that a large portion of a Host which he had consecrated by himself three days ago was still stuck to the corporal cloth. As the priest tried to pry it loose, it began to bleed. The priest panicked, but Jean du Bois, who decided to attend Mass that day, rushed to the altar to comfort the priest by assuring him that the "miracle was of God." Apparently, the three nights of visions of a suffering Christ were connected to the displaced Host in the chapel. Blood then flowed from the Host for five days. Local church authorities, including the Bishop of Cambrai, Pierre d'Ailly put the corporal through tests. Years later, an official investigation was commissioned by the then Cardinal d'Ailly. On October 10, 1413, a Papal Bull confirmed the authenticity of the miracle. The miracle of Bois Seigneur Isaac is still open for veneration in the little town of Ittre, Belgium.

During the mid 1400's a Eucharistic miracle took place in Langenwiese, an area between Poland and Czechoslovakia. A group of thieves entered a church specifically to steal and desecrate consecrated Hosts. They placed them in a white linen cloth only to find them bleeding a short time later. Stricken with fear, they hid them in a forest.

A second miracle then occurred. A Polish man in a carriage was forced to stop by the actions of his horse. The horse at a certain point along the road through the forest completely halted and proceeded to lay down on the road. The frustrated man then discovered the Hosts during his efforts to revitalize his dormant animal.

After contacting a priest, the Hosts were returned to Langenwiese. As many as 50,000 pilgrims at a time would later travel to the city as it became a center for pilgrimages during the middle ages. The Hosts had been originally consecrated by Saint John of Capistran.

In Ettiswil, Switzerland in the year 1447, a woman, under the commission of cultists, traveled from Germany to Switzerland in order to steal some consecrated Hosts from a Catholic Church. She succeeded in removing one large and five small Hosts. However, during her escape she found her pocket to be unusually heavy. Somewhat spooked by it all, she decided to abandon her satchel with the Hosts in a cemetery lot of nettle bushes. A young girl named Margaret Schulmeister, who was grazing her pigs, noticed that her animals were acting strangely near this nettle patch. Upon inspection, she saw brilliant white light radiate from the bushes. After spreading the weeds apart, she discovered the six small Hosts in the shape of a flower with the large Host in the middle. The six small Hosts were removed and returned to the church. However, the large Host could not be recovered and it was determined that it was to remain on this site as the Lord seemed to be indicating. A large stone covered the Host and a chapel was erected. The chapel still stands to this day.

As in previous centuries, the fine details of many of the Eucharistic miracles reveal the Virgin Mary's involvement as reported apparitions of Mary continued to multiply. Some of the heavenly encounters brought revelations that were most often associated with local needs and concerns.

Most significantly, it is recorded that during this period the Virgin Mary came once again to insist that the Rosary be prayed by the faithful. After the era of Saint Dominic, a century and a half of time had brought with it a loss of fervor for the prayer.

So, once again the Virgin Mary appeared. This time she came to Blessed Alan De La Roche in the year 1460. Prefiguring her later interventions and requests, Mary told Blessed Alan how the Rosary could help perfect his imitation of her Son.

The Rosary was, the Virgin confirmed once again, *"the Weapon"* that the most Holy Trinity wanted to use *"to reform the world,"* for the Queen of Heaven knew that a flood of sin would soon submerge mankind.

CHAPTER ELEVEN

FROM CANA TO CALVARY

Holy things must be treated in a holy way and this sacrifice is the most holy of all things. And so, that this sacrifice might be worthily and reverently offered and received, the Catholic Church many centuries ago instituted the sacred Canon. It is free from all error and contains nothing that does not savour of holiness and piety and contains nothing that does not raise to God the minds of those who offer the Sacrifice. For it is made up from the words of Our Lord, from apostolic traditions, and from devout instructions of the holy pontiffs.

Council of Trent,
On the Sacrifice of the Mass

Over the centuries the Holy Spirit has inspired many popes, saints and Church leaders to take action in defense of the Church's sacred mysteries; yet it is through Mary's apparitions and revelations that we find one of Heaven's unique calls to come back to the sacred.

Indeed, Mary's call urges us to return to a faith that has its cornerstone in the sacred mysteries of the liturgy, especially in the mystery of the Eucharist. Likewise, the Virgin comes to earth to defend this mystery. Father Edward Carter, S.J., writes in his book, *Mother At Our Side:*

The Eucharistic sacrifice unites all these aspects of our lives with the love, the beauty, and the strength of Jesus' offering and presents them to the Father in the Holy Spirit with Mary our Mother at our side. As Mary was present at Calvary's offering, so is she present as that sacrifice really becomes present in an unbloody manner in the Mass.[1]

In fact, the Blessed Virgin's apparitions clearly reveal her role in guarding and upholding the Church's most sacred mystery. Many occasions of Mary's intercession through statues, icons and miraculous objects have been reported over more than the last 1500 years. And these signs prefigure her modern-day apparitions.

Likewise, hundreds of sacred images, also associated with stories of Mary's intercessions, draw our attention to the True Presence of Our Lord in the Church. More often than not, these famous statues and images show Our Lady holding the Christ Child or the crucified body of her Son. Without question, the miracles almost always are meant to depict how the living Christ responds to the intercessions of His mother, just as He first did at Cana.

But it is especially with Our Lady's apparitions to Juan Diego and his uncle Juan Bernardino at Guadalupe, Mexico in 1531, where we find Mary's actions clearly and deliberately point specifically to her Son's True Presence in His Church.

Indeed, theologians point out that the apparitions at Guadalupe coincided very closely with Martin Luther's revolt against the Church in the sixteenth century. The Protestant revolution instigated the rejection of many Catholic beliefs, traditions and practices. Yet, probably the abandonment of the Holy Sacrifice of the Mass was the most serious of its effects. With no Mass, the Eucharist, the Living Presence of Jesus Christ that is meant to be a source of strength for all souls, was also abandoned.

According to some writers, this was a primary goal of Martin Luther's efforts. It was an insidious goal, for it sought to deliberately remove belief in the supernatural graces available in the Sacraments, thus removing the belief in Christ's True Presence in the Catholic Church and the world.

Monsignor Patrick F. O'Hare, L.L.D. in his 1916 publication, *The Facts About Luther,* writes how Luther's efforts were unparalleled in history. For never before, writes Fr. O'Hare, had anyone so dramatically sought to remove "specific doctrines" concerning God from an existing religion:

Possessed now by the spirit of disorder and opposition to law, and jealous of the authority of the Church and the God-given supremacy of her visible head, he conceived the idea of a new religion, which he thought in his vanity he was capable of formulating. Forthwith, without the shadow of a pretense of direct and divine commission, he began to construct what he foolishly considered a church, and then assumed the right to inflict and impose his self-made work upon his fellow men.

In his wild scheme he aimed at getting rid of the Church's sacramental system and banishing altogether from men's minds the very idea of an outward and visible sign of an inward and invisible grace. He intended to take from men the only certain voice which, speaking in the name of God and representing Him, delivered infallible truth to the world and announced authoritatively the means whereby sanctification and salvation were to be secured.

He purposed, in a word, to overthrow, annihilate and displace the Mother Church, and thus deprive men of her divine guidance unto truth, morality and life eternal. In his conceit he imagined that men should be left wholly to their own unaided and fallible reason, and hence he proclaimed the right of all, without any Church interference, to follow in matters of belief their own intellect as sole and final judge. In advancing this claim, so destructive to the authority of the Church, he asserted a right never before recognized; a right, let it be understood, never known under any other form of revealed religion; a right never allowed even under the Jewish theocracy; and a right hardly ever exercised among the more enlightened pagans. His program was one of the most daring in all human history.[2]

Not long after Luther's initial efforts to dismantle the teachings of the Catholic Church, a multitude of other heretical teachings began to circulate. Between 1522 and 1529, about forty different protestant catechisms were produced by the disciples of Luther. This included Luther's own larger catechism, the Devosch Catechisms, in 1530.

Other protestant leaders followed soon thereafter, Bucer in 1534, Calvin in 1536 and Berne in 1552. Many protestant publications rapidly spread abroad, for example the Heidelberg Catechism of the Dutch Reformed Church in 1563. This catechism spread into Switzerland, Austria and Holland. All of these efforts shared one common goal: elimination of the Catholic Church's sacramental system!

While many suspect that the Church's teachings at the time were weak, inconsistent and unorganized, thus contributing to the rapid spread of the Reformation, a close examination of the times reveals the opposite.

In fact, the work of teaching religion and of preaching was anything but neglected during the centuries which led up to the Reformation. Some writers even contend that the faith was yielding its highest fruits of piety and holiness in every rank of society.

But the damage was done. When the Council of Trent convened on December 13, 1545, the Church began to construct a uniform and comprehensive manual which would supply parish priests with an official book of instruction for the faithful. This work became known as the Catechism of the Council of Trent.

Although not originally mentioned at the Council's convocation, during the fourth session on April 15, 1546, the draft of a decree calling for a catechism was read. The idea met with general approval but was not published until 1566 under the reign of Pope Pius V. The contents of the Catechism were designed to provide for the faithful an official book of instruction of all Church teachings and Christian doctrines.

Especially in its detailed explanation of the Sacraments, the Catechism reflects the Church's most profound mysteries in a fervent and inspiring manner. With great authority and certitude, the Catechism defined the Lord's True Presence in the Eucharist and the consequences of rejecting this truth. The Catechism states:

As of all the sacred mysteries bequeathed to us by our Lord and Saviour as most infallible instruments of divine grace, there is none comparable to the most holy Sacrament of the Eucharist; so, for no crime is there a heavier punishment to be feared from God than for the unholy or irreligious use by the faithful of that which is full of holi-

ness, or rather which contains the very author and source of holiness. This the Apostle wisely saw, and has openly admonished us of it. For when he had declared the enormity of their guilt who discerned not the body of the Lord, he immediately subjoined: "Therefore are there many infirm and weak among you, and many sleep."

In order that the faithful, therefore, aware of the divine honors due to this heavenly Sacrament, may derive therefrom abundant fruit of grace and escape the most just anger of God, pastors should explain with the greatest diligence all those things which may seem calculated more fully to display its majesty. (Catechism of the Council of Trent)

While the Mystical Body of Christ on earth was responding to the events of the times, so was Heaven in a most profound manner. For the errors of the times were not confined to the sixteenth century. Indeed, God clearly began to lay the groundwork for future events. These were events that would span the coming centuries. Most significantly, the effects of the errors of the Reformation would lead to more errors and a prophesied climax hundreds of years later. And according to many, the world is now approaching this climax.

At Guadalupe, Mexico, in 1531, the Virgin Mary appeared to a peasant Aztec Indian and began the conversion of the Americas. While the apparitions of Our Lady of Guadalupe are well-known today mostly because of the supernaturally imposed image of the Virgin Mary upon Juan Diego's tilma, Mary's intervention at Guadalupe also began a new round of heavenly efforts to draw attention to the True Presence of Jesus Christ in the Blessed Sacrament.

Indeed, Mary's role at Guadalupe and through the later centuries even earned her the title of "Our Lady of the Blessed Sacrament." It is *"the most theological"* of all Mary's titles, after that of "Mother of God," according to the words of Pope St. Pius X.

At the very beginning of the apparitions of Guadalupe, attention was immediately paid to Our Lord's True Presence. The peasant visionary Juan Diego was on the way to Mass early on the morning of December 9, 1531 (the then-celebrated feast of the Immaculate Conception),when he met "the Lady." Mary's words to Juan Diego were very similar to the request of Our Lady to Bernadette at Lourdes, as the Queen of Heaven immediately asked for a church or "temple" to be built, a place where her Son's Hidden but True Presence would dwell in the tabernacle.

At that time, the Aztec Indians were victims of centuries of bloody sacrifices to the Aztec pagan gods. Thus, historians generally concur that Mary's apparitions to Juan Diego led millions to almost an instantaneous conversion to Catholicism. This conversion taught the Aztec peasants about the bloodless sacrifice of the Mass to the One True God. This was in clear contrast with the daily human sacrifices to the Aztec gods.

Over the centuries, Mary's immaculate image on Juan Diego's tilma stood above the main altar directly over the tabernacle in the old basilica of Guadalupe in Mexico City. This caused her to appear to be adoring the Lord's Hidden Presence.

Francis Johnston in his book, *The Wonder of Guadalupe*, noted that the Mexican people have always had a great love for the Blessed Sacrament. They visit the cathedral at an estimated rate of 15,000 per day. Wrote Mr. Johnston:

> *"Today, as the tourist enters the always crowded Basilica," wrote Henry F. Unger in the early 1970's, "he is amazed by the beauty of the Guadalupe painting high above the main altar. I can remember the intense prayerfulness of the kneeling Mexicans as they crowded around the main altar, banked with great mounds of flowers. I noticed too that scores of Mexicans were moving into the adjoining Chapel of the Blessed Sacrament. The visitor could not but be impressed by the magnificent main altar in this chapel and the many side altars...I could hardly move in this chapel in which Holy Communion was being distributed every fifteen minutes...From all sides, Mexicans moved on their knees over the rough floor towards the Blessed Sacrament. There, often with outstretched arms, they poured out their hearts to the Eucharistic King. Clusters of small children hovered around a praying Mexican mother, her eyes riveted on the Host. Other Mexicans were bringing armfuls of flowers and placing them at the altar rail. Still others were leaving me-*

mentos of some cure obtained through prayers to Our Lord in the Blessed Sacrament..."[3]

It is the same pattern in all the world's Marian shrines. Mary leads the pilgrims to her Divine Son enthroned in the Eucharist. With open arms, she welcomes her suffering children, longing to embrace each one of them and to guide them to the feet of Jesus, who had also once lain in her arms. In this sense she can be called Our Lady of the Most Blessed Sacrament, "the most theological of all Mary's titles after that of Mother of God."[3]

Thus, the miraculous tilma of Our Lady of Guadalupe is, to this day, a mystery that continues to unfold. Curiously, some now believe Mary's image on the cactus fiber cloth was one of a pregnant young girl. If so, perhaps there is more meaning to this than first realized. Attorney Dan Lynch notes in his book, *Our Lady of Guadalupe and Her Missionary Image*, how the presence of Our Lord in Mary's womb again points to the Hidden Presence of the Lord in the Eucharist:

Our Lady appears on the tilma as an olive-skinned young woman, four feet eight inches tall. She is clothed in Middle-Eastern dress of the time of Christ. However, the colors of the clothing are of an Aztec royal virgin. But she is pregnant, which is physically obvious and which is symbolized by the four-petaled flower (Nahui Ollin) over her womb and the sash which is wrapped around her body and tied above her womb. The Nahui Ollin symbolizes the center of the universe; the One True God and Christ Himself who was born through Our Lady. Recent gynecological measurements have determined that Our Lady's image on the tilma has the physical dimensions of a pregnant woman![4]

With this discovery, the mystery of Our Lord's Hidden Presence and His rightful veneration is evident right from the onset of the Guadalupe apparitions. Indeed, Bishop Zummaraga and his aides fell to their knees instantly when the image of the Virgin on Juan Diego's cloak was revealed. Unknowingly, like Saint Joseph, they were adoring the Hidden Lord in the womb of Our Lady of Guadalupe.

In the last two decades, the Virgin of Guadalupe has come to be a powerful symbol of the faithful's efforts to stop abortion. Two missionary images of Our Lady of Guadalupe circulate around the globe, and are often venerated at events drawing tens of thousands. Photographs of these images have produced miraculous signs and wonders. Mary's folded hands have on several occasions revealed her to be holding the Eucharistic Host. In addition, the Virgin's eyes appear to be focused on the Host in adoration. Other miraculous photographs of the missionary images have revealed radiating Hosts in the exact center of the image, slightly to the right of Mary's bowed head.

According to the book, *Mary of the Americas, Our Lady of Guadalupe*, by Christopher Rengers, O.F.M. C.A.P., another phenomenon surrounding Our Lady of Guadalupe and the Blessed Sacrament is taking place. It is the report of one of the longest perpetual adorations of the Blessed Sacrament on record. Writes Rengers:

> *Since 1781, Capuchin nuns in a convent near Tepeyac Hill have been keeping a vigil of perpetual adoration of the Blessed Sacrament. For the first century, the adoration convent immediately adjoined the east side of the old Basilica.*
>
> *It is wonderful, consoling and yet a staggering thought: these hours of uninterrupted prayer, endured through all the minutes of a great country's life. As Presidents came and went, wars were fought, peace treaties signed; as boundaries expanded; as the United States grew from wobbly infancy to unparalleled, mature strength, the patient, adoring prayers have continually ascended.*[5]

After Guadalupe, more reports of the Virgin Mary's miraculous intercessions began to surface. And not surprisingly, Our Lady's actions continued to specifically draw attention to the True Presence of her Son just as they did at Guadalupe. In many of these events, the Blessed Virgin assumes a hidden role, almost as if Mary's defense of the True Presence needs to be veiled and cloaked in mystery, just as Her Son's True yet Hidden Presence is surrounded in mystery. For from Cana to Calvary, Mary has always been the humble and hidden model of disciples.

CHAPTER TWELVE

THE PRISONER OF LOVE

After Guadalupe, the remainder of the sixteenth century witnessed a torrent of heavenly manifestations. From Eucharistic miracles to Marian apparitions, Heaven's many signs and wonders were like a barrage of lightning bolts striking the entire world. In both the New World and the Old, wondrous stories of God's supernatural presence in the lives of the faithful continued to emerge.

In Marseille-en-Beauvais, France, a small town sixty miles northwest of Paris, a Eucharistic miracle was reported to have occurred in the year 1533.

One winter evening, thieves broke into the town church and stole a gold and silver pyx which contained a consecrated Host. Since they had no desire to keep this Host, they hid it in a pouch under a stone by some bushes.

On his way to Mass that day, Jean Moucque kept his head down to avoid the blowing snow and cold wind. Suddenly, he noticed an area that was mysteriously clear of snow, as if the stone in the center of it had melted all the surrounding snow. Jean circled back to see the phenomenon and discovered the consecrated Host under the rock. Heat had radiated from it causing the miraculous melting of the snow.

The pastor, Father Prothais, retrieved the Host, and the miracle became known as the "Miracle of the Host Respected by the Snow." Every year on the second of January, a Mass is still celebrated in thanksgiving for the miracle.

Two years later, on Sunday morning, July 25, 1535, a priest named Father Dominic Occelli celebrated Mass at Saint Secondo Church in Asti, Italy. At the moment of the breaking of the Host, drops of red blood dripped into the chalice, spilling onto the paten. Both the paten and the priest's fingers were stained red by the blood. The entire congregation witnessed the miracle. It was celebrated annually until 1968.

In the small Italian village of Morrovalle, a miracle of the Eucharist occurred on April 14, 1560. At 2:00 a.m. on Easter Tuesday, a fire swept through a church run by Franciscans. The fire was so intense that nothing remained; even metal was melted. However, ten days later, a large, intact consecrated Host was discovered among the ashes of the tabernacle and altar. A papal investigation concurred that it was miraculous, and the Eucharistic miracle of Morrovalle is commemorated to this day.

In 1572, heretics broke into the cathedral of Gorcum in southern Holland. Their goal was to desecrate the church, especially the monstrance that contained the consecrated Host.

In the church, they located the monstrance and threw a consecrated Host on the floor. Then, one of the antagonists stomped on the Host with his spiked boots. Three puncture marks were made in the Host, and three small drops of blood flowed from the Host.

The man was stunned and sought a priest to rectify the situation. Upon retrieval, it was recognized as a miracle by the priest. The miraculous Host was then taken to several cities to escape those who sought to destroy it. Over the centuries, it has survived many dangerous encounters. Today it rests at the royal monastery of El Escorial, Spain, where it is still incorrupt over 400 years later.

In 1597 at the Jesuit church of Alcala de Henares, Spain, a man of Moorish persuasion confessed to have stolen Hosts from churches. He then proceeded to return over twenty-four small, very white Hosts.

Since his story was unverifiable, the priests had no way of knowing if the Hosts truly were consecrated. The Hosts were then ordered to be destroyed by water or fire since they were considered inedible because of spoilage.

Eleven years later, the Hosts were found to be still "like new." In 1619, after years of retaining their original constitution and after numerous scientific tests, the Hosts were declared miraculous.

Over the centuries the Hosts remained incorrupt. However, their whereabouts today are unknown. They were hidden during the Spanish Civil War of 1936 and have not been rediscovered since that time.

In 1583, a rather crude statue of the Virgin Mary and the Child Jesus was fashioned by a young Bolivian Indian named Francisco Tito Yupanqui. The statue was made in order to replace a statue from another Bolivian shrine that was considered miraculous. Soon after, a mysterious light was seen surrounding the statue in the house of a Franciscan friar. Many miracles and cures followed. This statue became known as Our Lady of Copacabana, and the church built for it was elevated to the rank of Basilica in 1920.

In 1586, in Quinche, Ecuador, another statue of Our Lady and the Christ Child was credited with a great miracle. A child who was found dead and badly mangled arose after being placed in front of the statue. Today, this statue is enshrined in a large church.

And it wasn't just in western Europe and the Americas that Church writers detected an increase in the Virgin's presence as a reaction to Luther's attack on the True Presence of Jesus Christ in the Church and in the sacraments. In 1608 in Siluva, Lithuania another miraculous apparition of the Virgin Mary was seen as a direct heavenly intervention in defense of the faith.

Lithuania is one of three Baltic countries that has a long history of turbulence caused by invading neighbors. Over and over, Lithuania has been dedicated and rededicated to the Virgin Mary. At Siluva stands Lithuania's most venerated shrine, Our Lady of Siluva.

In 1551, the effects of Luther's revolution struck Lithuania. While the peasants remained devoted Catholics, many intellectuals and nobles turned to Calvinism. Soon afterward, these nobles began to confiscate all Catholic properties. In 1570, when the Church at Siluva was threatened, the priest, Father John Halubka, removed the church's treasured documents and possessions, as well as a favorite image of the Madonna and Child that hung above the main altar. Father Halubka buried all of these items outside the church beneath a large rock. Not long after that, the Church was seized.

In 1588, a new law decreed that Catholics again had the right to possess church properties providing ownership could be proven. However, the church in Siluva could not prove that a man named Peter Giedgaudas had donated the land in 1457. Thus, the church could not be returned to Catholic hands.

Twenty years later, Heaven intervened. Foreshadowing Fatima in a striking manner, in the summer of 1608, children shepherding their flocks reported an apparition of a beautiful lady standing on a rock, holding a child in her arms and sadly weeping. Even though the Calvinist teacher Mikola Fierra decried it as the devil, news of the apparition spread everywhere.

The following day the area around the rock was surrounded by many curious observers, both devout and doubting. Again, the lady appeared with the child in her arms. This time, everybody could see her.

The teacher ventured forward to inquire of the vision, "Why are you weeping?" The lady sadly answered, *"Formerly in this place, my Son was adored and honored, but now all that the people do is seed and cultivate the land."* With that, the vision vanished.

While an investigation by the Catholic Church commenced, a second miracle occurred. A blind man, upon hearing of the apparition, remembered the metal-covered chest that the pastor had buried under the rock. Upon arrival at the site, the man's vision was immediately restored. He then began to show onlookers the exact location of the chest. Upon its discovery, the painting of the Madonna with Child was found undamaged along with vestments and church papers, which proved the Church's ownership.

The Calvinists returned the land. Over the years several churches were erected on this site; each new one was always larger to hold the crowds. The miraculous painting still exists, and a chapel dedicated to Our Lady of Siluva can be found in the upper basilica of the National Shrine of the Immaculate Conception in Washington, D.C.

Around the same time, at the beginning of the seventeenth century, more Eucharistic miracles were reported.

In La Vilvena, Spain on November 8, 1601, a terrible fire tore through the town's church. Everything was destroyed except a small silver box that contained six consecrated Hosts. Miraculous healings were later reported. Seven years later the bishop visited the town and ordered the miraculous Hosts to be consumed. The miracle is still celebrated.

A different kind of Eucharistic miracle occurred in Faverney, France on May 26, 1608. After special services were held during the day, including exposition of the Blessed Sacrament, two candles were left burning on the altar. This caused a fire to break out in the church during the night.

Upon entering in order to put out the fire, a fifteen-year old boy named Hudelot noticed that the monstrance holding the Blessed Sacrament was suspended in midair above the altar.

Word of the miracle spread quickly, and a great many skeptics came to witness for themselves. After thirty-three hours, the monstrance slowly lowered itself down upon a new altar that had been brought in to replace the fire-damaged original altar.

An inquiry was ordered by Archbishop Ferdinand de Rye. Fifty-four depositions were taken; all swore to having witnessed the miraculous. Two months later, the Archbishop declared that the occurrence was, indeed, a miracle. The original monstrance was destroyed during the French Revolution, but the original Host was preserved and still rests in a perfect replica of the monstrance which had belonged to the church at Faverney.

Almost exactly one hundred years after the apparitions of Our Lady of Guadalupe, Mary appeared again in the western hemisphere. This time the visionary was a woman named Mother Anne of Jesus Torres who lived in the shadow of the Andes Mountains in Quito, Ecuador.

In the year 1634, Mary appeared to Mother Anne as "Our Lady of Good Fortune" and left her several prophetic messages. Most significantly, these Church-approved apparitions were received by Mother Anne while she prayed before the Blessed Sacrament in a church.

Again, a mysterious story unfolded. As Mother Anne prayed before the Blessed Sacrament, the sanctuary light went out. As she tried to relight it, a luminous supernatural light filled the church. Out of this light came the Virgin Mary, and her very first words to the sister called immediate attention to her Son's Hidden Presence. *"The sanctuary lamp burning in front of the Prisoner of Love, which you saw go out, has many meanings,"* said the Virgin to Mother Anne.

Our Lady went on to give Mother Anne three prophetic messages. Miracles followed these apparitions in a series of confirmations from Heaven just as they did at Guadalupe. Centuries later, on April 20, 1906, an image of Our Lady of Quito wept at the Jesuit School of San Gabriel in Quito, Ecuador.

The remainder of the seventeenth century witnessed a significant increase in Our Lady's interventions. Again, more often than not, these appearances were designed to call attention to her Son and His ever True Presence.

In 1600, Our Lady appeared in Cobre, Cuba. Again, Mary came in response to the prayer of three men whose lives were threatened by a storm. In a vision, Mary appeared and promised her help. After their miraculous survival, the three found a statue floating in the water. The statue was sixteen inches tall and depicted the Madonna with the Christ Child in her arms. This event brought many people back to the Church and the Sacraments.

In 1630, a statue representing the Immaculate Conception and another statue of the Madonna and Child were again credited with miracles in Lujan and Buenos Aires, Argentina. Great churches were erected, and over the centuries even more miracles were reported.

In 1697, Our Lady performed another great intercession. In Ireland, where the Catholic Church and the Mass were under restriction, Bishop Walter Lynch of Clonfirt escaped the persecution and eventually fled to Hungary.

He bought with him a much venerated image of the Virgin Mary with the Christ Child, in order to prevent the English from destroying it. Ten years later, the Bishop died, and the picture was bequeathed to the Bishop of Győr, Hungary. The people of

Györ welcomed the image and credited it with a series of victories over the Turks. At the same time, in Ireland the persecutions intensified. In 1697 all priests were ordered expelled from the country by an edict of the Parliament. Churches were confiscated, and all traces of the Catholic religion were to be eliminated. Mass was outlawed.

Meanwhile, on Saint Patrick's Day, March 17 of the same year, the Virgin brought a great miracle to Györ, Hungary. As thousands were participating in Mass in the Cathedral of Györ, the eyes of the image of Our Lady began to shed tears and blood. The people who were attending the Holy Sacrifice of the Mass, as well as other witnesses, took turns in gathering around the Madonna's portrait. At the same time priests wiped the tears from the image of the Virgin with a linen cloth. This cloth is still preserved in the cathedral today.

Not just Catholics, but many Jews and Protestants came to observe this miracle. Many people also signed a document stating that they witnessed this event, an event that was uniquely designed to draw attention to the True Presence of the Lord and to the sadness that all Heaven endured over the events in Ireland at that time in history.

But probably the most significant mystical events on behalf of Christ's True Presence in the seventeenth century were the apparitions and revelations received by St. Margaret Mary Alacoque at Paray-le-Monial in France.

While praying on December 27, 1673, St. Margaret heard the Lord invite her to take the place that St. John had occupied at the Last Supper. Afterward, while in Eucharistic adoration, St. Margaret Mary received four apparitions of Jesus. In these apparitions Jesus specifically referred to his Sacred Heart as being present in the Holy Eucharist. Jesus then gave her His Twelve Great Promises for devotion to the Sacred Heart. The last promise requested celebration of Nine First Fridays of Holy Communion with Him. It was the beginning of a new phase of heavenly efforts to combat the evil that was mounting in the world. Indeed, Heaven's response to this evil was totally supernatural; as it called for souls to embrace such devotions in faith.

During the eighteenth century, Our Lady continued to reveal her presence and to especially draw attention to her Son's True Presence. Again, more Eucharistic miracles were reported.

In 1730 in Siena, Italy, while the entire city attended a feast day celebration of the Assumption, thieves broke into the Basilica of Saint Francis and stole a ciborium and 351 consecrated Hosts. Three days later all of the Hosts were discovered. It was, however, decided they should not be distributed.

As time passed on, it was noticed that the Hosts were not disintegrating. After fifty years, they were tested and discovered to be like new. After 192 years and repeated tests on the incorrupt Hosts, they were officially declared a miracle.

On September 14, 1980, Pope John Paul II traveled to Siena to venerate the Eucharistic miracle. It was the two hundred fiftieth anniversary of the miracle.

In 1740 just outside Rome, Italy, an image of the Virgin Mary and the Christ Child hung over an archway of a tower for almost two centuries. It was left unprotected and exposed to the elements. For reasons unknown, it was credited with miraculously helping a man escape a pack of growling, angry dogs. Soon after, pilgrims came to the site night and day. Many more miracles were claimed. This prompted Pope Benedict XIX to call for an investigation. Again, Mary's miraculous activity led to the rise of a church, and the miraculous image was enshrined as Our Lady of Divine Love.

Over the centuries many more miracles were attributed to Our Lady of Divine Love, including the safe protection of Rome during World War II. Pope Pius XII offered his gratitude for this safekeeping to the Madonna of Divine Love on June 11, 1944.

Once again, the Virgin sought to call attention to Jesus, and this certainly occurred. Pope John Paul II, who visited Castel di Leva on May 1, 1979 declared, *"I also wished to come in pilgrimage to this blessed place, to kneel at the feet of the miraculous image represented enthroned with the Child Jesus in her arms and the dove over her as the symbol of the Holy Spirit."*

Many other miraculous interventions by the Virgin Mary were reported during the late eighteenth and early nineteenth centuries.

Again and again, Mary pointed to her Son's True Presence in the Catholic Church and in the Eucharist.

On January 18, 1772, it was discovered that consecrated Hosts were missing from the tabernacle of the Church of Saint Peter in Paterno, Italy. Days later, strange lights were reported in a field outside the city. At night, the field sparkled in what was determined to be a supernatural way.

On February 24, a great flame was seen in the field. Still, the Hosts were not to be found. Finally, after a bright ball of light came up from a poplar tree, several people began to dig, and the sacred Hosts were discovered. The Archdiocese of Naples still possesses the records and testimonies of those involved in this miracle.

In the year 1793, during the French Revolution, churches were forcibly closed and many priests went into exile in order to save their lives. In the small village of Pezilla-La-Riviere, Father Jacques Perone was forced to leave in September, 1793. Because of the danger, the priest was unable to consume five consecrated Hosts.

Fortunately, certain members of the church were able to hide the Hosts for seven years. Upon his return, Father Perone discovered that not only had the Hosts not decomposed, but they were as brilliant as they had been on the day of his departure. The local bishop recognized the miracle and instituted a feast day. In 1930, because of an unfortunate decision during the construction of a new tabernacle, the Hosts decomposed.

On June 25, 1796 in Ancona, Italy, a painting reportedly wept because of the hardships that Napoleon placed on Pope Pius VI and the Catholic Church during his reign. Again in 1807, Our Lady of the Thunderbolt miraculously brought attention to the Virgin with the Child Jesus in Guadalajara, Mexico. Likewise, in 1809, 1812 and 1814, another statue of the Virgin and the Child Jesus, known as Our Lady of Prompt Succor, is credited with miraculous interventions. The last intervention favored General Andrew Jackson in his defense of New Orleans from the invasion of the British.

Throughout the eighteenth century, Mary came to the defense of many of her children, as the world had shifted far away from

God. Most significantly, the gradual attack on the Church over the centuries had taken its toll. Thus, by the nineteenth century, Mary began to bring to the world a major announcement: *A decisive battle between the Virgin and Satan would soon begin and "her times" were now at hand.*

CHAPTER THIRTEEN

"GRACES WILL BE SHED UPON ALL"

The apparitions and revelations of the Virgin Mary to Saint Catherine Labouré at Rue du Bac, Paris in 1830, officially began an era of Mary. Marian theologians are consistent in their opinion on this point. Also with this apparition, the Virgin Mary especially sought to draw attention to her Son's True Presence in the Catholic Church.

From her earliest childhood, Saint Catherine Labouré led a life that, in itself, revolved around Christ's True Presence in the Eucharist. She ardently longed to receive her First Holy Communion, after which her life totally changed. Even as a child, she sought things of piety and devotion, such as praying daily at fixed times.

Most remarkably, Saint Catherine attended daily Mass and received Holy Communion frequently. Mass was at 6:00 a.m., but this didn't matter as Saint Catherine longed for "complete union with her Beloved in Holy Communion." This was considered heroic at the time, as daily communion for the faithful was not normally permitted. Not until one hundred years later did the practice become more widespread.

At the age of eighteen, Saint Catherine received a special dream in which she was at Mass and a priest spoke to her. The priest told her, "God has plans for you. Do not forget it."[1] A year later, Saint Catherine rejected a marriage proposal, insisting to her sister, "I shall never marry. I am promised to Jesus Christ."[2]

Saint Catherine went on to become a novice in the Paris motherhouse of the Saint Vincent de Paul's Daughters of Charity, sometimes called the Sisters of Charity. It was at this time that Heaven moved powerfully in her life.

She received a series of visions, including one of the visible Presence of Our Lord in the Eucharist. Saint Catherine never fully elaborated on these visions. Therefore, it is uncertain whether they occurred each time she prayed in the chapel or only during Mass. She revealed only that "she saw Our Lord in the Most Holy Sacrament."

Father Joseph I. Dirvin, C.M., in his book, *Saint Catherine Labouré of the Miraculous Medal,* quotes her as saying:

I saw Him (Our Lord) during the whole time of my seminary, except when I doubted; the next time, I saw nothing, because I had wished to penetrate the mystery, and, believing myself deceived, had doubted.[3]

Father Dirvin further adds:

In this straightforward statement of the saint, both her prudence and her discernment are revealed. Strangely enough, she does not seem to have had any doubts concerning the reality of the visions of Saint Vincent's heart. Could it have been the sense of caution urged upon her by her confessor that caused her to examine these visions of Our Lord more closely? At any rate, she felt it prudent to doubt, not the reality of Christ's Presence in the Eucharist (she could never doubt that), but the reality of what she saw. She felt it wise to be afraid lest she suffer illusion—and not once only. Whenever she doubted, whenever she was afraid, she saw nothing.

At the same time, she recognized that the withdrawal of the vision was not a punishment, but a reassurance, a proof of its reality. She understood that Jesus hid Himself when she examined the vision in order to show her that it was genuine, but only to accept it with simple faith. When she had breathed a sigh of relief and gone back to believing and accepting with conscience clear and reassured, He showed Himself again.

This extraordinary favor speaks volumes of the way Heaven cherished this humble little novice. To see Jesus Christ once would be the supreme favor of a lifetime, but to see Him constantly throughout nine months![4]

During the Gospel of the Mass, on Trinity Sunday, June 6, 1830, Saint Catherine Labouré received a special vision of Christ in the Blessed Sacrament. It was a vision of Christ the King. In this vision, Jesus appeared to Saint Catherine robed as a king, with a cross on His breast. Not surprisingly, Saint Catherine said it was an unforgettable experience.

But in the apparitions of the Blessed Virgin Mary to Saint Catherine, we find the greatest evidence that the heavenly manifestations she received were designed to shed light upon the True Presence.

During her initial apparition Saint Catherine first glimpsed Our Lady at the front of the altar. She then witnessed Mary bow before the tabernacle prior to sitting in the chaplain's chair. In the second apparition to Saint Catherine, Mary was seen floating above the tabernacle in the convent chapel. This famous vision has been captured in numerous artistic renditions.

However, in Mary's words to Saint Catherine we especially see the unfolding of Heaven's plan to pay special attention to what would soon happen in the world. Indeed, the Virgin warned Saint Catherine that the Church and priests would soon become victims of evil times.

"My child," Mary told Saint Catherine, *"the Cross will be treated with contempt; they will hurl it to the ground. ... the whole world will be in sadness."[5]* What was Mary's solution? Mary's answer was to focus attention on the True Presence of her Son. *"Come to the front of the altar"* the Virgin urged the saint. *"There graces will be shed upon all, great and small who ask for them. Especially will graces be shed upon those who ask for them."[6]*

Although the Virgin Mary left the Miraculous Medal at Rue du Bac for the faithful, the events Our Lady predicted there quickly began to occur and spin out of control. Beginning in France and then spreading across Europe and the world, the prophesied times were at hand. Indeed, Satan's plan to destroy the Church and the world was becoming visible, and Mary's words to Saint Catherine Labouré specifically confirmed this.

Most significantly, Our Lady revealed that the devil wanted to conquer the world by plunging it into sin. And as Mary indicated, Satan hoped to do this especially by assaulting the faithful's belief in the True Presence of Jesus Christ in His Church.

CHAPTER FOURTEEN

"THE TRUE CHRIST
WHO LIVES AMONG THEM"

Father Charles du Friche des Gennettes, Saint Catherine Labouré's pastor in 1830 (though not her spiritual director), was transferred to the Church of Our Lady of Victories in Paris in 1832.

At one time, it was a glorious church. It was originally constructed in 1629 by King Louis XIII who believed that he had received favors through the Virgin Mary's intercession. However, by the time of Father Gennettes' arrival, the parish had completely disintegrated. Few people attended Mass and received the Sacraments, though the good priest tried everything possible.

On Sunday, December 3, 1836, a distraught Father des Gennettes began to say Mass. Fighting back mental distractions, the weary pastor begged Heaven to free his mind at the moment of consecration so he could worthily consecrate the Eucharist.
Suddenly, Father Gennettes distinctly heard the words, *"Consecrate your parish to the very Holy and Immaculate Heart of Mary."* With these words, a peace suddenly filled him, and he finished the Mass with recollection and devotion.

After the Mass, Father Gennettes began to doubt it all. But again, he heard the same words, *"Consecrate your parish to the very Holy and Immaculate Heart of Mary."* This time he became sure and took action.

At Mass the following Sunday, Father Gennettes announced that special devotions would be held that evening. To his amazement, four hundred or more people attended.

From that night on, the church flourished. People came from all over France and around the world, motivating the Pope to establish the Archconfraternity of the Holy and Immaculate Heart of Mary for the Conversion of Sinners. Affiliated societies then spread throughout the world.

Years later, on November 4, 1887, Saint Thérèse of the Child Jesus (the "Little Flower") visited the Church and later wrote that the graces Mary granted her there *"resembled those of my First Communion."*[1]

Indeed, the miracle of Our Lady of Victories centers around the Virgin Mary's intercession which then led to the conversion of an untold number of souls. But Saint Thérèse's own words which called attention to the graces in the Eucharist, may be most significant of all. For it was at the moment of the consecration that Father Gennettes had heard Heaven speak to him.

The graces given at Rue du Bac in 1830 and then at Our Lady of Victories in 1836 continued to mount, especially in France. In Blangy, France in 1840, Our Lady appeared to Justine Bisqueyburu, a young sister in the novitiate of the Daughters of Charity in Paris, who was praying at the time. Again, Mary came with a gift of supernatural benefit to souls.

To Sister Justine, Our Lady brought the "Green Scapular" and promised that those who wore it would receive special graces through her intercession with her Son. Once again, the apparition was connected to Rue du Bac, since both Sister Justine's and Saint Catherine Labouré's spiritual director was the same priest, Father Aladel.

Six years later at La Salette, France, the Virgin Mary returned again. This time her words, though never fully approved by the Church, were designed to forewarn the faithful of exactly what Satan desired to do to the Catholic faith, and especially to its teachings concerning the True Presence of Christ in the Eucharist. It was a message that appeared to elaborate on her words given at Rue du Bac in 1830. (Note: While the apparitions at La Salette were approved by the Church, the secret message given to Melanie, which was released later, has not been approved.)

The Church Militant on earth truly needed to be militant, the Virgin's message urged. Indeed, in her long and detailed secret Mary told fifteen-year old visionary, Melanie Mathieu, that this was the only way the true faith could survive:

The priests, ministers of my Son, the priests, by their wicked lives, by their irreverence and their impiety in the celebration of the holy mysteries, by their love of money, their love of honours and pleasures, the priests have become cesspools of impurity...

God will strike in an unprecedented way...

...The Society of men is on the eve of the most terrible scourges and of gravest events... Priests and religious orders will be hunted down, and made to die a cruel death. Several will abandon the faith, and a great number of priests and members of religious orders will break away from the true religion; among these people there will even be bishops...

Everywhere there will be extraordinary wonders, as true faith has faded and false light brightens the people. Woe to the Princes of the Church who think only of piling riches upon riches to protect their authority and dominate with pride.

The Vicar of my Son will suffer a great deal, because in a while the Church will yield to large persecution, a time of darkness and the Church will witness a frightful crisis.

The true faith to the Lord having been forgotten, each individual will want to be on his own and be superior to people of same identity, they will abolish civil rights as well as ecclesiastical, all order and all justice would be trampled underfoot.

The Holy Father will suffer a great deal. I will be with him until the end and receive his sacrifice.

All the civil government will have one and the same plan, which will be to abolish and do away with every religious principle, to make way for materialism, atheism, spiritualism and vices of all kinds...

The righteous will suffer greatly. Their prayers, their penances and their tears will rise up to Heaven and all of God's people will beg for forgiveness and mercy and will plead for my help and intercession.

...I make an urgent appeal to the earth. I call on the true disciples of the living God who reigns in Heaven; I call on the true followers of Christ made man, the only true Savior of men; I call on my children, the true faithful, those who have given themselves to me so that I may lead them to my divine Son, those whom I carry in my arms, so to speak, those who have lived on my spirit. Finally, I call on the Apostles of the Last Days, the faithful disciples of Jesus Christ who have lived in scorn for the world and for themselves, in poverty and in humility, in scorn and in silence, in prayer and in mortification, in chastity and in union with God, in suffering and unknown to the world. It is time they came out and filled the world with light. Go and reveal yourselves to be my cherished children. I am at your side and within you, provided that your faith is the light which shines upon you in these unhappy days. May your zeal make you famished for the glory and the honour of Jesus Christ. Fight, children of light, you, the few who can see. For now is the time of all times, the end of all ends...

All the universe will be struck with terror and many will let themselves be led astray because they have not worshipped the TRUE CHRIST WHO LIVES AMONG THEM.[2]

CHAPTER FIFTEEN

AT LOURDES:
THE LORD'S TRUE PRESENCE

The Virgin Mary's apparition at La Salette was later characterized by Pope Pius XII as the "Madonna in tears." The Holy Father, echoing Pope Pius XI's words, saw how Mary was calling Catholics to resist indifference and free-thinking regarding the Church.

Indeed, the world was beginning to suffer the symptoms of moral decay and degeneracy. And visionaries and mystics insisted that this condition would worsen.

Two years after Our Lady's weeping visions at La Salette, more of her prophetic words came to life. In Rome, upheavals swept the city. On November 15, 1848, the Pope's Prime Minister, Count Pellegrino Rossi, was stabbed to death, along with the Pope's secretary Monsignor Palma.

Nine days later on November 24, 1848, the Pope was forced to flee from Rome. A new era for mankind was promised by the enemies of religion and the Church. As the Virgin Mary foretold at Rue du Bac, the cross was indeed being *"held in contempt."*

Across Rome, the Holy Eucharist was defiled in public ceremonies of desecration. In 1849, a French army led by Louis Napoleon marched against Rome. Afterward, the Pope returned to the city on April 12, 1850. But the times had worsened. In Italy, the masses forged together to again attempt to topple the Church. Elsewhere, it was the same. Catholics in Russia, Prussia and Switzerland were besieged with turmoil and persecution.

But amidst it all, the Church managed to move forward. On December 8, 1854, Pope Pius IX proclaimed the dogma of the Immaculate Conception of the Virgin Mary. Heaven had laid the groundwork for this proclamation at Rue du Bac; as the Miraculous Medal given to Saint Catherine Labouré proclaimed, *"Mary conceived without sin, pray for us who have recourse to thee."*

The proclamation of the new dogma was a move that Heaven appeared to be anticipating. For four years later at Lourdes, France, the Virgin Mary solidified the Church's new dogma in a bold and profound way.

With Mary's words at Lourdes to Saint Bernadette Soubirous, **"I am the Immaculate Conception,"** the entire story of Christian redemption was addressed. From the fall of Adam and Eve which plunged mankind into sin, to the Incarnation, and finally the Redemption, the great mysteries of salvation were implicit in Mary's announcement.

Most of all, it was implicit that if the Virgin Mary's body was immaculately conceived, then Mary truly was worthy to bear the all pure and sinless Son of God, whose own Body was to serve as the **"bread of life"** for all who would **"eat His Body and drink His Blood."**

In Lourdes, four separate churches have flourished on the site at Massabielle where Bernadette witnessed the eighteen visions of Our Lady in 1858. Since then, the Virgin has drawn millions to her Son's True Presence in the Eucharist. Indeed, as many as 350,000 people a day visit Lourdes to worship or to find healing.

However, it is most significant that the greatest number of the miraculous healings at Lourdes do not occur at the baths, but during the daily blessing of the people with the Blessed Sacrament. One such healing at Lourdes involved a man named John Traynor. His doctors had given up on him as a hopeless case. After receiving a head wound in World War One, he was left a paralyzed epileptic. His body was a mass of sores, shriveled up to just skin and bones. One arm had no function and he also had a gaping hole in his skull.

In the summer of 1923, Traynor was taken to Lourdes, where he was completely cured after being blessed by the Blessed Sacrament. In his own words, he describes what happened:

The archbishop of Rheims, carrying the Blessed Sacrament, blessed the two ahead of me, came to me, made the sign of the cross with the monstrance and moved on to the next. He had just passed by, when I realized that a great change has taken place in me. My right arm, which had been dead since 1915, was violently agitated. I burst its bandages and blessed myself - for the first time in years. (Immaculata Magazine).[1]

Indeed, Saint Bernadette later implied that it was Our Lord in the Eucharist who first called her back to the grotto, several months after the final apparition. On the feast of Our Lady of Mount Carmel, as Saint Bernadette left the altar after receiving Holy Communion, she felt an irresistible urge to go to the shrine and pray. Though Saint Bernadette never saw Our Lady again, the Virgin Mary's ultimate goal of bringing the faithful to her Son's True Presence was never more apparent than in this small anecdote concerning the miracle of Lourdes.

Though Mary said little for public disclosure at Lourdes, Our Lady continued to alert the world of the dangerous times. *"Penance, penance,"* she exhorted Saint Bernadette, who in turn relayed this message to the faithful. But the times were very turbulent in France, as social changes were sweeping Europe bringing with them the winds of war.

Seven years later, on February 5, 1867, an apparition of Christ in the Blessed Sacrament was witnessed by the people of a parish in the small village of Dubna, Poland.

Coming at a time of great persecution of the Polish people by neighboring Russia, the miracle occurred during a Forty Hours Devotion. However, because of the danger, the local bishops requested silence on the subject. Still, news of this miracle spread throughout suffering Poland.

Indeed, the warnings of La Salette became increasingly more evident as revolutions, crop failures, famines, and wars broke out.

In France, impiety became epidemic as Prussia began to bombard the country. However, hundreds began to turn to Mary at her shrines in Paris, La Salette and Lourdes.

The Barbedette family of Pontmain, France was especially afflicted by the times. The eldest of their three sons, Auguste, was with the army defending against Chancellor Bismarck and the invading Prussian army. Through it all, the Barbedette family retained pious devotion.

The two remaining sons, Eugene who was twelve and Joseph who was ten, rose each day at six o'clock in the morning to recite the Rosary for their enlisted brother. After breakfast, the brothers went to the village chapel to perform the Way of the Cross and to serve Mass. After Mass, they participated in public prayers for the French army.

Thus, it was to these boys that Heaven again sent the Virgin Mary to France to help bring peace. On the evening of January 17, 1871, the two brothers suddenly witnessed a beautiful lady above a neighbor's home. Instantly, they knew who it was. It was the Virgin Mary, dressed in a dark blue dress and wearing a golden crown. Our Lady appeared to be no older than eighteen years, as she did at Lourdes. In her arms Mary held a child.

As the evening progressed, crowds of people came to observe. Suddenly the visionaries beheld a plain white band unfolding itself in the sky near the Virgin. Next, letters began to appear on the scroll spelling: **"MON FILS SE LAISSE"** (My Son permits Himself to be moved).

As the crowd sang, a second vision unfolded. A red crucifix appeared near Our Lady. Mary then took it in her hands and held it toward the children. At the top of the cross appeared the words **"JESUS CHRIST."** Suddenly, a star shot up from the Virgin's feet and the crucifix disappeared. The vision then assumed the attitude of Our Lady of the Miraculous Medal.

The powerful message was understood by the people. Their country and especially their town would be saved from the invading Prussians. The next day the Prussian army unexpectedly retreated, only a few miles from Pontmain. Ten days later an armistice was signed; the war was over.

The Virgin Mary had again come at a crucial moment. Her Son, Jesus Christ, was Lord of all, and no prayer was too great for Him to answer. Mary's words in the sky made it clear that the Prince of Peace truly reigned over all Heaven and Earth.

The message of Pontmain is especially meaningful today. As author Don Sharkey points out in his book, *The Woman Shall Conquer*, "the world today, like France of 1871, is half-conquered."

But, there should be no fear or terror, for The Virgin Mary's widespread presence reminds us that Jesus Christ is in command of all history, great and small.

Not long after the apparitions at Pontmain, Mary came again to France. This time her message left no doubt about what grieved all of Heaven, and especially its queen: Faith in our Lord's True Presence was continuing to be eroded!

The visionary was a thirty two year-old woman named Estelle Faguette, who in May 1875 was diagnosed with a fatal condition. The doctors gave her no hope, and Estelle returned from a Paris hospital to die at her home in Pellevoison. But Estelle rejected the thought of death. Instead she choose to beseech the Virgin Mary through a petition presented to her at a newly erected statue of Our Lady of Lourdes in Pellevoison.

On February 10, 1876, the doctors gave Estelle only hours to live. Yet five days later, the dying woman was still alive and she reported that the Virgin Mary had appeared to her!

Estelle said that Mary told her she would either be cured or dead by the following Saturday. Five days later Estelle was healed! Estelle then reported that a series of apparitions of the Virgin Mary had occurred each night of that week, including one that had also brought Satan. Our Lady also told Estelle, *"If my Son restores your life, I wish you to publish my glory."*

At Pellevoison, the Blessed Mother appeared to Estelle a total of fifteen times. Mary left with her the Scapular of the Sacred Heart and promised great graces to those who wore it in faith. Most of all at Pellevoison, Mary left a series of messages that formed an important link between her past revelations at Rue du Bac and La Salette with what she would later announce at Fatima in 1917.

At the core of the messages was Heaven's prevailing theme: The resurrected Christ is a living God that wishes through His Presence in His Mystical Body, the Church, to shower graces and gifts upon all who ask!

Indeed, the message of Pellevoison is one that holds a special place in the history of Marian apparitions. Here Mary specifically called upon the faithful to treasure her Son's True Presence. Among the many revelations Our Lady gave at Pellevoison were the following:

> *If my Son has allowed Himself to be prevailed upon, it is because of your resignation and patience.*
> *I am all merciful ... Your good works and fervent prayers have touched my mother's heart.*
> *One can be saved in every state (of life).*
> *What afflicts me most is the want of respect shown by some people to my divine Son in Holy Communion and the attitude taken for prayer when at the same time the mind continues occupied with other things. I say this for people who pretend to be pious.*
> *His heart bears so much love for me, that He cannot refuse me any requests.*
> *I have come especially for the conversion of sinners.*
> *For a long time the treasures of my Son have been open; let them pray.[2]*

Mary said of the Scapular of the Sacred Heart, *"I love this devotion."[3]*

But Mary also again brought with her a warning:

> *And France, what have I not done for her? How many warnings, and yet she has refused to listen! I can no longer restrain my Son. France will suffer.[4]*

In May, 1894, Pope Leo XIII approved the Archconfraternity of Our Mother All Merciful of Pellevoison.[5] Likewise, on April 4, 1890, the Congregation of Rites approved the Scapular of the Sacred Heart.

But just three years after Pellevoison, Mary brought what some say is the most profound message that Heaven ever delivered concerning Christ's True Presence. And it was a message containing no words.

CHAPTER SIXTEEN

BEHOLD THE LAMB OF GOD

The Virgin Mary's interventions continued during the 1870's, as reports of apparitions and miracles were frequent. Yet no apparition more clearly showed Heaven's efforts to focus the faithful on Christ's True Presence as the silent apparition that took place on the rainy, foggy night of August 21, 1879 in Knock, County Mayo, Ireland.

Indeed, Our Lady's apparition at Knock has been analyzed in its meaning so often that some say it is truly the most compelling statement of why the Virgin Mary bears the title of "Our Lady of the Eucharist."

The Knock apparition is as mysterious today as it was over a hundred years ago, for historians and theologians continue to debate its significance. No words were left by Mary at Knock, but the story of her appearance there is perhaps Heaven's most definitive statement concerning the Holy Sacrifice of the Mass.

By 1879, the forces of humanism and secularism had cut deep inroads into the governments and leadership of European nations. In Ireland, the hardship was compounded by famine and religious persecutions. An alien government stifled the claim of the Irish people to worship and educate their children in the Catholic faith.

Nowhere was it worse than in County Mayo, the hardest hit region during the potato famines. An overall tyranny prevailed in the entire country, as Catholics were subjected to crushing rents and extreme taxation. But while the times were hard, many Irish faithful preferred starvation to renouncing or compromising their faith in the Church, especially in the Holy Sacrifice of the Mass.

It was a windy and rainy evening, around seven o'clock, when Margaret Beirne noticed a brightness over the church in Knock. Mary McLoughlin, the priest's housekeeper, thought she saw statues of the Virgin Mary, Saint Joseph and a bishop along with an altar. But like Mrs. Beirne, she rationalized her observations as being objects recently acquired by the priest.

But in minutes, as both women approached the church, they realized they were wrong. *"The statues are moving!"* exclaimed Mrs. Beirne. *"They are not statues, they're moving! It's the Blessed Virgin!"*[1]

From the Blue Army pamphlet, *Our Lady of the Eucharist, Marian Eucharistic Lessons from Knock and the City of God*, we are given this account:

> *She (Margaret Beirne) dashed back to her home to tell her mother and Dominic to come up to the church and see the lovely sight, "the Blessed Virgin was at the church gable."*
>
> *This in brief, was what they actually saw, at about half past seven that summer evening, and in daylight, at the south gable wall of the church.*
>
> *The Blessed Virgin was clothed in white garments, wearing a large brilliant crown. Her hands were raised as if in prayer and her eyes were turned heavenward.*
>
> *On her right was Saint Joseph, his head inclined towards her. At her left stood Saint John the Evangelist, vested as a bishop, his left hand holding a book and his right arm raised as if preaching. To the left of Saint John was an altar on which stood a cross and a lamb, about eight weeks old, around which (according to Patrick Hill, one of the witnesses) hovered wings of angels.*
>
> *The gable wall which formed the background of the tableau was bathed in a cloud of light.*
>
> *This vision, seen by fifteen persons, lasted for fully two hours. The rain was falling heavily all the while, yet the figures and the spot where they were seen to stand, were perfectly dry.*[2]

The testimonies from the witnesses were consistent and compelling. A commission was established and fifteen witnesses appeared. One of them was Mr. Patrick Walsh whose testimony was remarkable, for he claimed to see the glowing vision from one-half mile away on his land. It was, Mr. Walsh insisted, *"a globe of glowing light."*[3] This testimony did much to debunk the mass hysteria arguments that critics presented.

But the main mystery surrounding Knock has always been the reason why the apparition was silent. Many writers emphasized that the silence was meant to promulgate the deep mystery which is silently present during the sublime moments within the Holy Sacrifice of the Mass. Likewise this silence was the perfect expression of Our Lady's meditation which centered around her Son's sacrifice on the cross.

Thus, some Church authorities conclude that Heaven's mission at Knock was of the highest importance, especially because of the silence. It is a message, they explain, that supersedes words.

Father Patrick O'Carroll, C.S.Sp.D.D., Provincial of the Holy Ghost Fathers, stated at a conference in Knock in 1942, that indeed, the apparition was meant to focus the believers' attention on the Sacrifice of the Mass:

> *I have said that a little to the left and in the rear, there was an altar on which stood a lamb against a cross, part of which was visible above him. Immediately we are reminded of Him, Whom Jeremias spoke of, "a meek lamb that is led out to be a victim"; Whom Isaias predicted of "that he shall be dumb as a lamb" during the excruciating torments of His Sacred Passion; Whom Saint John the Baptist pointed out to his first disciples (one of whom was Saint John the Evangelist) with this exclamation: "Behold the Lamb of God, behold Him who takes away the sins of the world." Saint Peter writes: "Knowing that you were not redeemed with corruptible things but with the Precious Blood of Christ, as of a lamb unspotted and undefiled." But the writer par excellence of the Lamb, is the beloved disciple, the author of the Apocalypse, where in that work full of mystery he mentions Him twenty-seven times in all.*
>
> *A meditation on Knock, then, will ultimately lead us to the Lamb of God, Who for us was slain on Calvary, and by*

Whose Precious Blood our souls that have been defiled by sin are washed white as snow. Our attention is above all turned to the same Lamb of God that is mystically immolated on every altar when the Holy Mass is celebrated. Knock, then, calls for a fuller appreciation of the Holy Sacrifice of the Mass.[4]

In Ireland, devotion to the Mass over the centuries has been almost miraculous. Indeed, no country has ever been so persecuted for such a specific aspect of its faith. Many saintly men suffered martyrdom for their fidelity to the Holy Sacrifice of the Mass. Many others were exiled; vanquished as slaves, starved to death or even slain on altars.

But the vision at Knock delivered a message for the world: Christ's True Presence in His Church and in the Eucharist will never be destroyed. Heaven itself came to defend it. Furthermore after the Knock apparition, it was apparent that Heaven would not hesitate in any way to repeatedly come in defense of Christ's True Presence.

CHAPTER SEVENTEEN

INFINITE LOVE

The second half of the nineteenth century saw Heaven "circling the wagons," as God boldly amplified His message. Many great saints surfaced to lead the flock through the turbulent times, and they focused their attention on Christ's True Presence.

Saints Peter Julian Eymard and John Vianney, known as the Curé of Ars, were especially devoted to the Eucharist. St. Peter Julian Eymard founded the Blessed Sacrament Fathers and the People's Eucharistic League for the laity. Indeed, it is said that he looked at the world through the "divine prism of the mystery of the Eucharist."

In his encyclical *Sacerdotii Nostri Primoria* commemorating the death of St. John Maria Vianney, Pope John XXIII proposed the Curé of Ars as a model for all priests to imitate.

Wrote Pope John XXIII:

The prayer of the Curé of Ars who, it could be said, spent the last 30 years of his life in church, was above all a Eucharistic prayer. His devotion to Our Lord, present in the most Blessed Sacrament on the altar, was truly extraordinary.

"He is there," he used to say. "He who loves us so much." Why should we not love him? And he certainly loved him and felt himself drawn irresistibly toward the tabernacle. "To pray well, there is no need to talk a lot," he explained to his parishioners. "One knows that the good Lord is there in the holy tabernacle. One opens one's heart to him, one rejoices in his presence. This is the best prayer."

Likewise, Pope Pius XII said:

> *The admirable example of the holy Curé of Ars still has today its complete value.. In the life of a priest, nothing could replace the silent and prolonged prayer before the altar. The adoration of Jesus, our God; thanksgiving, reparation for our sins and for those of all men, the prayer for so many intentions entrusted to him, combine to raise that priest to a greater love for the Divine Master to whom he has promised faithfulness and for men who depend on his priestly ministry.*
>
> *With the practice of this enlightened and fervent worship of the Eucharist, the spiritual life of the priest increases and there are prepared the missionary energies of the most valuable apostles.*

Saint John Neumann, known as the "Little Bishop" and Saint Thérèse of Lisieux, known as the "Little Flower," also came forth during this period to exemplify how God wished His children to imitate His Hidden Presence with humility.

Saint John Neumann was especially committed to the Sacraments as the source of the necessary strengths he felt his flock needed. He established the Forty Hours Devotion of the Blessed Sacrament, which spread from Philadelphia throughout the United States.

Saint Thérèse of Lisieux wrote in her book, *The Story of a Soul*, concerning the True Presence:

> *During three long weeks of trial I was able to have the tremendous consolation of daily Holy Communion. How sweet it was! Jesus spoilt me for a long time, much longer than He did His more faithful brides, for, after the influenza had gone, He came to me daily for several more months and the rest of the community didn't share this joy. I had not asked for any special treatment, but I was most happy to be united each day with my Beloved. I was also allowed to handle the sacred vessels and to prepare the altar linen which was to receive Jesus. I felt that I must be very fervent and I*

*often recalled the words addressed to a deacon: "Be holy,
you who carry the vessels of the Lord."*

*What can I tell you, Mother, of my thanksgiving after
Holy Communion—both at that time and always? I have
less consolation then than I ever have! And it's very natural, for I don't want Our Lord to visit me for my own satisfaction, but only for His pleasure.[1]*

Other great mystics and visionaries arose during this period,
many of whom disclosed revelations from Jesus and Mary concerning the True Presence.

Mother Louise Margaret Claret de la Touche (1868-1915) of
Saint Germain de Laye, France began to receive mystical favors
from Our Lord as a young girl. Her revelations formed a treatise of
God's infinite love, a love God wished to pour out upon mankind
through His priests.

Succinctly summarizing the prophecies of La Salette in purely
spiritual terms, Mother Louise Margaret Claret was given to understand how the world played havoc in souls. She wrote in her
book, *The Book of Infinite Love*:

*As a matter of fact, in the society in which we live, ev-
erything conspires to turn souls away from Faith and Charity. Material cares, the search after pleasures, intellectual
activity often badly directed; and false allurements of
pseudo-science still more injurious to mental equilibrium
than ignorance itself; all these contribute to ruin supernatural life in souls.[2]*

Her answer was: the True Presence of Christ in the Word and
in the Eucharist, a presence of infinite love. Wrote the holy nun:

*The Word became man to come in Person to conquer
men's hearts for Love. He formed His Church to make a kingdom for His Love; He gave the Blessed Eucharist to be the
food of Love; He founded His Priesthood to propagate the
reign of Love throughout the centuries; He showed His Heart
to the world to rekindle Love; He gives It today to His priests
as a weapon of love. God is Love, He must reign by love![3]*

On October 16, 1902, Mother Louise Margaret Claret put into words what the Lord had revealed to her concerning the infinite source of grace available through the Eucharist. Expanding on the revelations of Saint Margaret Mary, she wrote:

The devotion to the Blessed Eucharist and the devotion to the Sacred Heart are not only two sister devotions, in reality, they are only one and the same devotion. They complete each other and develop each other; they blend so perfectly together that one cannot stand without the other, and their union is absolute. Not only can one of these devotions not be prejudicial to the other but, because they complete each other and perfect each other, they also reciprocally increase each other.

If we have devotion to the Sacred Heart, we will wish to find It, to adore It, to love It, to offer It our reparation and praise, and where shall we look for It but in the Blessed Eucharist where It is found eternally living?

If we love this adorable Heart, we will wish to unite ourselves to It, for love seeks union, we will wish to warm our hearts by the ardour of this divine fire, but to reach the Sacred Heart, to take hold of It, to put It in contact with our own, what shall we do? Shall we scale heaven to bear away the Heart of Jesus Who reigns triumphant in glory? There is no need to do so.

We will go to the Blessed Eucharist, we will go to the tabernacle, we will take the white Host, and when we have enclosed it in our breast, we will feel the divine Heart truly beating beside our own.

Mother Louise Claret further added:

The devotion to the divine Heart infallibly brings souls to the Blessed Eucharist, and faith in and devotion to the Blessed Eucharist necessarily leads souls to discover the mysteries of Infinite Love of which the divine Heart is the organ and the symbol.

If we believe in the Blessed Eucharist, we believe in Love. It is the mystery of Love. But in itself love is immaterial and imperceptible; to fix our minds and our senses, we seek an outward form for love. This form, this sensible mani-festation, is the divine Heart.

The Sacred Heart, the Blessed Eucharist, Love are one and the same thing. In the tabernacle we find the Host; in the Host Jesus; in Jesus His Heart; in His Heart, Love, In-finite Love, divine Charity, God, the principle of life, living and life-giving.[4]

Also, the saintly nun insisted that the Blessed Eucharist is the completion of the love of Jesus for man. She wrote:

But still more: the ineffable mystery of the Eucharist can only be explained by Love. By the love of God, yes, but by the Love of Jesus, God and man. Now the love of Jesus is the love of His Heart; to sum up all in one word, it is His Heart; therefore the Blessed Eucharist is explained only by the Sacred Heart.

The Blessed Eucharist is the sublime completion of the love of Jesus for man; it is the highest, the last expression; the paroxysm, if I may so express myself, of this incompre-hensible love.

Nevertheless, without the Blessed Eucharist we could have believed in love; the Incarnation would have sufficed for that; a single drop of the bitter chalice of Passion would have been more than superabundant to prove to us that love.

We would have been able to love the Heart of Jesus, we would have been under the obligation of loving It, of believ-ing that It is sovereignly good, even if It had not gone to this divine excess of the Blessed Eucharist. But, because It has invented this marvel, how we should love this Sacred Heart so divinely tender, so inexpressibly delicate and liberal; so—shall I dare to say it—so madly and so passionately fond of its creatures!

Yes, the Blessed Eucharist augments and inflames our love for the divine Heart. But because we know that we shall find that Sacred Heart only in the Blessed Eucharist, be-cause we are thirsty for union with this Heart so tender and so ardent, we go to the Blessed Eucharist, we prostrate our-

selves before the Blessed Sacrament, we adore the Host ra-
diating its influence from the monstrance. We go to the Holy
Table with ardent avidity; we lovingly kiss the consecrated
paten on which the divine Host reposes each day. We sur-
round with honour, respect and magnificence the tabernacle
in which Jesus, living and loving, makes His dwelling.

Oh! It is impious to say that the worship of the Sacred
Heart can injure devotion to the Blessed Eucharist. What!
Will the knowledge of Him Who gives the gift, make us de-
spise the gift? No, the more we love the divine Heart, the
truer our worship of It is, the more extensive and enlight-
ened it is, the more also will our worship and our love for
the divine Eucharist develop and grow strong.[5]

Around the same time, an English mystic named Teresa
Higginson also was brought up and called by God to continue His
revelations of mercy and love. Complementing the Sacred Heart
devotions given to Mother Louise, Teresa forwarded revelations
about devotion to the Sacred Head.

Teresa was given to understand that the ruling powers of the
Sacred Heart were seated in the Sacred Head. Wrote Teresa
Higginson:

And as the head is the seal of the reasoning powers, and
the faculties of the mind repose therein, so from the Sacred
Head shine forth in a blaze of resplendent light all knowledge,
wisdom, understanding and a guiding power to direct and gov-
ern the Will and Affections of the Sacred Heart; and in this is
seen the connection of the desired Devotion—the ruling pow-
ers of the Sacred Heart are seated in the Sacred Head.[6]

With this understanding, Teresa was led to realize how all
mankind, through adoration of the True Presence of Jesus Christ
in the Blessed Sacrament, can directly access the infinite wisdom
of the Sacred Head. Indeed, she was told that the future of her
country, England, and the Holy Church was to be guided by this
light, a light that revealed Christ's True Presence in his True
Church. Wrote Teresa:

When I knelt to adore the Thrice Blessed Trinity for all the Glory of the Sacred Humanity, I was caught up as it were and dissolved in the excessive heat and glory of the Sun of Divine Justice, and I heard sounds of praise and songs of joy in the heavens which echoed and reechoed from the earth, and they were hymns of thanksgiving and admiration of the Seat of Divine Wisdom.

Then I saw reflected in the large crystal the glory which the ever Blessed Trinity would receive from the Devotion of the Sacred Head and the numberless souls that would be guided by its light to the bosom of the True Church and eventually to the throne of God.

I understand too that this should be the one great means of the conversion of poor dear England, and that it was not far distant when she would bow her understanding to the obedience of faith and repair in some manner through this Devotion the great evil of her apostasy, and that Mary's name and Mary's Son should be more honoured than ever they had been dishonored by our people.[7]

At the end of the nineteenth century, another renown mystic and stigmatist, Marie-Julie Jahenny of Blain, France also disclosed a series of startling revelations concerning the demise of civilization and how God deemed to save it.

Again, supernatural graces available through the Church were to be the answer. Tribulation and chastisement were also strong themes of the revelations, since the entire world was continuing to slip into the pitfalls of secular humanism. Indeed, the world was moving far away from God. The Cross, as foretold at Rue du Bac, was being scorned and trampled upon.

The Virgin Mary told Marie on July 13, 1882:

My children, within a short time the tree of salvation, the Cross, will no longer be lifted up on earth under the gaze of Christians. Already the very hands which desecrated and offended my Divine Son are plotting about fated and deadly projects against the adorable Cross.[8]

Furthermore, Our Lady told Marie, *"The Holy Cross shall be overthrown, trampled underfoot covered with outrages."*[9]

What was the cause of such woe? Again, the Lord emphasized to Marie-Julie Jahenny that it was *"unsound doctrine."* The world, Jesus said, was moving away from His True Presence. The Lord even went so far as to foretell Marie that, *"for a time ... even the Holy Sacrifice will be prohibited. ...no remains whatsoever will be left of the Holy Sacrifice, no apparent trace of faith. Confusion will prevail everywhere."*[10] It was a profound message, one which Mary and Jesus would later bring to other visionaries, especially toward the end of the twentieth century.

Likewise, Jesus told Marie-Julie Jahenny on June 1, 1880:

> *All the works approved by the infallible Church will, at a certain moment, cease existing such as they are at present time. They will have lost nothing of their greatness, but they will be as if non-existing. The mourning of the Church will enwrap everything invigorating the faith of the unfaithful.*
>
> *That period will not last for long, but it will seem like an eternity for the children of the Church will have become like orphans.*
>
> *In that mourning of annihilation, signs striking with wonder will be manifested on earth. If, because of men's wickedness, the Holy Church turns out like darkness, the Lord will also send out darkness which will bring the wicked to a stand on this rushing to evil-doing. If the Church is to suffer, her enemies will suffer...*[11]

With all these revelations, it appears that Heaven was preparing the Church for the climax of something which Satan had begun centuries before. Indeed, by the twentieth century, the evil one's plan was now more than apparent; it was slowly coming to fulfillment. But as God revealed to His chosen ones, it was a fulfillment that would never see the light of day.

CHAPTER EIGHTEEN

THE INVENTION OF LOVE

No one really knows exactly how many nineteenth century visionaries and mystics disclosed revelations that warned of the enemies' growing assault on the True Presence. But by the twentieth century, there were many such voices.

Around the turn of the century, an array of cloistered nuns and stigmatists surfaced with additional admonitions. Paralleling the revelations received by Marie-Julie Jahenny, their divine messages show that Heaven was still trying to awaken the faithful so they would see how serious and dangerous the times were becoming. It was now more than half of a century since Mary's powerful warnings at Rue du Bac and La Salette, France. Also, with the onset of the Industrial Revolution, the world had moved further and further away from God.

But again, at the beginning of the twentieth century, a powerful Eucharistic miracle took place at Saint Andrew's Catholic Church on the French island of Réunion in the Indian Ocean. This story surfaced in 1905.

During a Mass which was preceded by a Forty Hours Devotion, the priest, Father Lacombe, looked up at the Host in the monstrance and observed the face of Christ. Christ's eyes were closed, His head was bowed and a tear was running down His cheek.

After Mass the vision continued. One by one, more and more people came to witness the miracle. As word spread, numerous people from throughout the village came to see the Holy Face. At approximately two o'clock in the afternoon, the vision changed. A crucifix slowly appeared on the monstrance, replacing the Holy

Face. An immense crowd gathered, but the vision eventually vanished at the end of the services for that day.

The miraculous Host was ordered preserved by the bishop. Altogether, several thousand people witnessed the miracle with hundreds attesting to it in writing. In 1904, Father Lacombe testified before the Eucharistic Congress at Angouleme on behalf of the miracle which had taken place at his parish.

During the first quarter of the twentieth century, three victim souls, Sister Josefa Menendez (1890-1923), Sister Mary of the Trinity (1901-1942) and Sister Consolata Betrone (1903-1946) came forth. They later reported extensive and profound mystical lives in union with Christ.

Most significantly, their revelations reveal powerful proof that the Lord wanted His Church to know and to defend the great gift of the True Presence of Jesus Christ in the Sacrifice of the Mass. Indeed, Heaven's revelations to these three nuns are like diamonds of unparalleled quality, as the True Presence of Jesus Christ in the Church is the predominant and consistent theme. These revelations are priceless and must be examined to appreciate their significance.

Jesus said to Sister Josefa Menendez:

> *It is love for souls that keeps Me a Prisoner in the Blessed Sacrament. I stay there that all may come and find the comfort they need in the tenderest of Hearts, the best of Fathers, the most faithful of Friends, who will never abandon them.*
>
> *The Holy Eucharist is the invention of Love...Yet how few souls correspond to that love which spends and consumes itself for them!*
>
> *I live in the midst of sinners that I may be their life, their physician, and the remedy of the diseases bred by corrupt nature. And in return they forsake, insult and despise Me!*
>
> *Poor pitiable sinners, do not turn away from Me...Day and night I am on the watch for you in the tabernacle. I will not reproach you...I will not cast your sins in your face...But I will wash them in My Blood and in My Wounds.*

No need to be afraid...come to Me...If you but knew how dearly I love you.

And you, dear souls, why this coldness and indifference on your part?...Do I not know that family cares ... household concerns ... and the requirements of your position in life ... make continual calls upon you? ... But cannot you spare a few minutes in which to come and prove your affection and your gratitude? Do not allow yourselves to be involved in useless and incessant cares, but spare a few moments to visit and receive this Prisoner of love!...

Were you weak or ill in body surely you would find time to see a doctor who would cure you? ... Come, then, to One who is able to give both strength and health to your soul, and bestow the alms of love on this Divine Prisoner who watches for you, calls for you and longs to see you at His side.

When about to institute the Blessed Sacrament, Josefa, these were My feelings ...[1]

Five days later the Lord told Sister Josefa Menendez:

The Blessed Sacrament is the invention of Love. It is life and fortitude for souls, a remedy for every fault, and viaticum for the last passage from time to eternity. In it sinners recover life for their souls; tepid souls true warmth; fervent souls, tranquility and the satisfaction of every longing ... saintly souls, wings to fly towards perfection ... pure souls sweet honey and rarest substance. Consecrated souls find in it a dwelling, their love and their life. In it they will seek and find the perfect exemplar of those sacred and hallowed bonds that unite them separately to their heavenly Bridegroom.

Indeed, O consecrated souls, you will find a perfect symbol of your vow of Poverty in the small, round, light and smooth host; for so must the soul that professes poverty be: no angles, that is to say no petty natural affections, either for things used nor for her employments, nor for family or country ... but she must ever be ready to leave, or give up, or change ... Her heart must be free, with no attachments whatever.[2]

Jesus told Sister Mary of the Holy Trinity that the souls who lived a Eucharistic life were His favorites. His words were deliberate outpourings of Divine Love:

I desire an army of apostolic souls consecrated to Me by the vow of victim, not to expiate the sins of others by extraordinary trials; no, that is not My desire.

I desire a great army of victim souls who will join Me in the Apostolate of My Eucharistic Life, who bind themselves by the Vow of Victim to choose the methods which I chose.

Silence—immolation—radiating the triumph of the life of the Spirit.

So that My Spirit may spread and so that they may reveal something of My Kingdom, where every soul is called and awaited.[3]

The Lord also told Sister Mary of the Holy Trinity:

Listen to My silence: it is thus that one worthily adores God.

Look well at the Host—how frail it is! So is My grace. I am living there, an invisible but real Presence. So does your soul live in your body.

I live there in a state of obedience, of patience, of dependence, so should all souls live who are vowed to religion, and all victim souls.

Tirelessly day and night I intercede before the Father and I attract souls; so should you live in the tabernacle which is your convent.[4]

Jesus also told Sister Mary of the Holy Trinity that these souls carry a special place in His heart:

...And the most favored souls? Oh, there are many! They are those whom I call to join Me in the Apostolate of

*My Eucharistic Life. They are the richest in grace because
I give them the strength they need to respond to what I ask
of them. And it is as if I hide them in the deepest depths of
My Heart; their life is all in Me.*[5]

Through Sister Consolata Betrone, Jesus also sought to teach
His Church how valuable it was for a soul to seek Him out in the
tabernacle:

*You think you do not know how to pray?...What prayer
is more beautiful and more acceptable to Me than the act
of love? Do you know what Jesus is doing in the tabernacle? He is loving the Father and He is loving souls. That
is all. No sound of words, nothing. Only silence and love.
So, do the same! No, my dear, do not add any prayers; no,
no, no! Gaze upon the tabernacle, and love in that way!*[6]
Jesus also told Sister Consolata Betrone:
*Tell all souls, Consolata, that I prefer an act of love and a
Communion of love to any other gift which they may offer
Me! Yes, an act of love is better than the discipline, for I
thirst for love. Poor souls! They think that in order to reach
Me it is necessary to live an austere, penitential life!... See
how they misrepresent Me. They make Me out as one to be
feared, whereas I am kindness itself! See how they forget
the precept which I have given them, the very essence of
the entire Law: "Thou shalt love the Lord thy God with
thy whole heart, with thy whole soul..."*
*Today, as yesterday and tomorrow, I ask only and al-
ways for love from My poor creatures!*[7]

Indeed, by the end of twentieth century, these were the words
being heard by visionaries throughout the world. The key to Heaven
for every soul is already found in each person's heart; all one has to
do is open it through prayer. And according to so many of Heaven's
messages, this was exactly what God was calling all souls to do.

Mother of the Secret

CHAPTER NINETEEN

TRULY FOOD

H er name was Theresa Neumann. She lived in Germany and is said to be the "most visited stigmatist" in the history of the Church. It is reported that millions saw her either at her home or in public.

Although gifted with visions and many other mystical graces, Theresa's life was primarily a testament to the True Presence of Christ in the Eucharist. Theresa Neumann, like various other "chosen ones" throughout history, did not have to consume food or drink. She subsisted and was nourished for years by nothing except the Holy Eucharist!

According to the book, *Catholic Mystical Life*, this has happened before to saintly Catholic men and women. Saint Nicholas of Flue, the Patron Saint of Switzerland, lived without food or water, only on the Eucharist, for twenty years. Venerable Anne Catherine Emmerich reportedly lived for twelve years on just the Eucharist. Marthe Robin lived on the Eucharist for thirty years. Luisa Piccarreta, a twentieth century Italian victim soul and mystic, reportedly lived on the Eucharist for sixty-five years!

According to accounts, Theresa Neumann felt no urge to eat food or drink water. She lived only on the Eucharist for forty years (1922-1962). She also ingested water only when necessary to swallow the Host or when brushing her teeth.

Many other Eucharistic miracles were reported during Theresa Neumann's life. On one occasion, Theresa miraculously received Holy Communion when she was unable to receive at the regular time. In front of witnesses, she reportedly consumed a visible levitating Host from out of the air. Adalbert Vogl, in his book, *Theresa Neumann, Mystic and Stigmatist*, writes:

> *I had heard reports that sometimes when Theresa was about to receive Holy Communion, the Host left the priest's fingers and was carried through the air onto her tongue. Anxious to clear this up in my own mind, I asked Father Naber about it. His answer was that to his knowledge this had never happened, but that, as in the instance related above, the Host at times reached Theresa's tongue without being placed there by a priest. When the priest approached Theresa with the Host, she was ready to receive, with eyes closed and lips parted.*
>
> *At communion time she often had a vision in which she saw the Savior in bodily presence. Clothed in white and smiling, He benignly moved toward her. Theresa's arms were outstretched, and she was almost lifted from the chair as she reached toward the Lord. Entirely absorbed in the vision, she did not see the priest, the chalice, or the Host. Her lips remained open while the priest placed the Sacred Host on her tongue. Without any perceptible movement of swallowing, the Host immediately disappeared. I have spoken to a number of priests who have seen Theresa in ecstasy at Communion time and have also marveled at the disappearance of the Host as it rested on her motionless tongue.*[1]

For Theresa Neumann, her survival on merely the Eucharist was not without explanation. Writes Vogl:

> *"One very important reason which leads us to believe in the unquestionable genuineness of Theresa's total abstinence from food is the fact that Theresa is deeply grounded in a peculiar phenomenal relationship with the main ecclesiastical Sacrament, namely, the Holy Eucharist or the Last Supper."* So wrote a priest who was present on the eve of a Palm Sunday.
>
> An assistant priest once asked Theresa the question, *"Don't you feel any hunger?"* She answered immediately,

*"You know that I don't eat!" The priest continued, "Do you want to be greater than the Savior? While on earth He ate like we do." Theresa laughed out loud and answered unswervingly, "The Savior is able to do everything. Or don't you know that He is almighty?" Then she turned to the priest once more and continued with great emphasis: "Father, the result from nothing remains nothing. I do not live on nothing. I live on our Savior. He revealed to us: 'My Body is **truly a food.**' Why should this not truly be the case, if it is His will?"*

Despite the fact that Theresa ate no food except Holy Communion from the spring of 1922, she steadily gained weight. When she was investigated in July of 1927, Theresa weighed 121 pounds. In 1935 she weighed 140 pounds. During my visit with her in 1945 she weighed in excess of 185 pounds; in 1950 she weighed over 200 pounds, and in 1953 her weight had reached over 215.[2]

There were other incredible souls during this time whose lives in a special way pointed to the Lord's True Presence.

Another stigmatist, Marie-Rose Ferron (1902-1936) of Quebec, Canada began to report mystical experiences of the Child Jesus at the age of three. The Virgin Mary, Saint Joseph, Saint Anthony of Padua and Saint Gerard Magella also appeared to her. At a young age she began to suffer, and by the age of twenty-five she bore the stigmata. Most of all, her life revealed once more the results of the True Presence of Jesus Christ, for she carried an incredible wound in her heart and received Holy Communion miraculously. Marie, who suffered from a form of lockjaw, would force a crucifix into her mouth in order to open it to receive the Holy Eucharist.

Alexandrina da Costa (1904-1955) was another victim soul that Heaven sent to defend the truth. Again, her life was marked by suffering and prayer. It also centered around the Eucharist.

Reportedly Alexandrina, through her sufferings and prayers, was instrumental in shortening World War II. Like Theresa Neumann, Alexandrina lived on the Eucharist for thirty-six years!

Most amazingly, Alexandrina de Costa's life was so committed to the Eucharist that her last directions for her burial included a profound mystical request. Wrote Alexandrina:

I desire to be buried, if it is possible, with my face turned towards the tabernacle of our Church. As in life I always desired to unite myself with Jesus in the Blessed Sacrament and to look at my tabernacle as often as possible, so after my death, I wish to continue my watch, keeping myself turned towards our Eucharistic Lord. I know that with the eyes of my body I will not see Jesus again, but I want to be placed in this position to demonstrate to Him the love I have for the Adorable Eucharist.[3]

And then there was Little Nelly of God (1903-1908). She is known as "The Violet of the Holy Eucharist." Little Nelly was born in the village of Portlow, County Waterford, Ireland. Although she died before the age of five, her short life is a heroic testimony to the True Presence of Christ in the Eucharist.

Orphaned at the age of two because of her mother's death and the resulting separation of her family, Little Nelly came to live with the Good Shepherd Sisters at Sunday's Well, Cork. Then Nelly began to experience a series of physical ailments that eventually led to her death. But during her brief life of suffering, she was quickly seen to be a chosen soul for she received great graces that drew her to love the Lord, especially in the Blessed Sacrament.

At three years of age, Little Nelly often reported speaking to *"Holy God."* She also reported an unexplainable urge to receive the Eucharist, which by the local bishop's decree, occurred when she was four.

Prophetic statements, ecstasies, and once again, surviving on only Holy Communion, characterized her brief life. Little Nelly died on February 2, 1908. Not long after Pope Pius X began a review of her life. To this day, she is still known for her powerful intercessions, as people throughout the world turn to the saintly child for her help with *"Holy God."*

CHAPTER TWENTY

FATIMA: A EUCHARISTIC CALL TO GRACE AND MERCY

The apparitions of the Blessed Virgin Mary in Fatima, Portugal in 1917 to three shepherd children are most remembered for the incredible signs and secrets given there. Yet it must be said that Heaven truly marked the events with a significant thrust to focus the attention of the faithful on the True Presence of Jesus Christ in the Eucharist. Indeed, this thrust is noted in Fatima's very first moments.

In 1916, one year before the Virgin Mary's first apparition to Jacinta Marta, Francisco Marta and Lucia Dos Santos, the children received an apparition of an angel holding a chalice in his left hand. A Host was suspended above the chalice and some drops of blood from the Host fell into the chalice.

Leaving the chalice suspended in the air, the angel knelt down beside the children and told them to repeat three times the following prayer:

O Most Holy Trinity, Father, Son and Holy Spirit, I adore thee profoundly. I offer Thee the most precious Body, Blood, Soul and Divinity of Jesus Christ, present in all the tabernacles of the world, in reparation for the outrages, sacrileges and indifference by which He is offended. By the infinite merits of the Sacred Heart of Jesus and the Immaculate Heart of Mary, I beg the conversion of poor sinners.

Then rising, the angel took the chalice and the Host in his hands. He proceeded to give the sacred Host to Lucia, and shared the Blood from the chalice between Jacinta and Francisco. As he did, the angel said:

> *Take and drink the Body and Blood of Jesus Christ, horribly outraged by ungrateful men! Make reparation for their crimes and console your God.*

After this, the angel once again prostrated himself on the ground and repeated with the children three times more, the same prayer *"Most Holy Trinity ..."* and then disappeared.

With the angel's appearance and words, we see that Fatima's most visible mysteries are essentially related to God's continued effort to warn His Church of a great danger. This danger was the loss of its sacred and holy mysteries, the core and heart of its existence.

By 1917 beginning in Russia, a new era of atheism in the world was about to take hold. Thus, Fatima's message from the very beginning was a response to this threat.

The truth of this is especially seen in the well-known Secret of Fatima (parts one and two). After revealing a series of prophetic revelations, the Virgin Mary urged the Communion of Reparation on the First Saturday of each month as the remedy for the coming times of distress.

With this, we see how Mary prescribes a supernatural remedy for the troubles and dangers of the world. Like the Nine First Fridays requested of Saint Margaret Mary, it is a remedy that requires belief in the True Presence of Jesus Christ in the Eucharist to be effective. It is a remedy that one can fulfill only as a practicing Catholic who believes and receives the Church's Sacraments in the practice of the faith.

Most significantly, with this remedy, we find Heaven countering the problem with the solution. The problem was that the world was disintegrating and in mortal danger because of its loss of belief in the True Presence. The True Presence allows souls to obtain supernatural gifts through the Sacraments. The solution was a return to the belief in God's True Presence through reconciliation and Holy Communion. As Mary reveals at Fatima, this solution saves not only souls, but also the world.

John Haffert in his book, *To Prevent This*, reveals this understanding. Writes Haffert:

> *The conditions of the Five First Saturday devotion seem simple enough: Rosary, meditation, confession, Communion, all offered in reparation to the Immaculate Heart of Mary.*
>
> *Communion is the most important element. Our Lady said at Pellevoisin that what most offends Her Immaculate Heart are careless Communions. But even more, there is no greater source of Grace than the Sacrament by which Jesus Himself, the Incarnate God, unites with us.*
>
> *Another reason why we know that Communion is at the center of the First Saturday reparation is that Our Lady spoke simply of "Communion of reparation on the First Saturdays" when She said She would ask for this devotion "to prevent" the catastrophes which threaten the world. And in her third memoir Lucia also refers to this as simply the "Communion of reparation on the First Saturdays." The three other requests are seen as aids to the Communion of Reparation. But also they are more than that.*

At Fatima another special prayer was given to further confirm Our Lady's mission to restore the sacred and the holy. It reads: **"O Most Holy Trinity, I adore Thee! My God, My God, I love Thee in the Blessed Sacrament."**

Again, this prayer is intended to deliver the essence of the message of Fatima: that Fatima is a call to the Eucharist. Indeed, four years before the apparitions of the angel, Lucia received a very important manifestation at her First Holy Communion.

John Haffert in his book, *Her Own Words to the Nuclear Generation*, gives us this account:

> *On the eve of her First Communion, the priest to whom she had made her first confession was somehow enlightened as to her special vocation. "My child," he said to her,*

115

"your soul is the temple of the Holy Spirit. Always keep it pure so that He can continue His Divine Action in it."

"And how can I do that?" Lucia asked.

As she tells us in her memoirs, the confessor told her to go and kneel before the statue of Our Lady. *"Ask Her trustingly,"* he said, *"to take care of your heart, to keep it always pure and to prepare it to receive Her beloved Son worthily tomorrow and to keep it for Him alone."*

This was the advice given by the great Doctor of the Church, Saint Alphonsus Ligouri. And it was the usual practice of saints like Thérèse of Lisieux, who begged Our Lady to prepare her heart before every Communion. Saint Alphonsus also advised visits to Our Lady (by going to kneel in front of her statue) after we visit Our Lord in the Blessed Sacrament.

In her childlike simplicity, Lucia (like most Catholics) understood that in the Eucharist we have Our Lord really present, while in a statue we have only an image of Our Lady before which we seek the effect of Her presence as we pray to Her. Thus it was perfectly natural for Lucia to "visit Our Lady" by going to kneel before Her statue.

She knelt in front of the statue of Our Lady of the Rosary (because it was the statue before which her family kept fresh flowers). She repeated the prayer suggested by the confessor several times and the statue came alive and smiled at her.

In the memoirs she mentions only the smile, but in the letter to her confessor of May 13, 1936, she said that: "The statue smiled...and with a kind gesture and look said, '"Yes." Lucia was so filled with joy, she recalled: "I could hardly speak. At night I could sleep little or not at all. At last the time came. After asking my father's, mother's, and older brother's pardon, off I went to the Church as happy as a queen. At the moment when Jesus came into my poor heart, I believe I felt the happiness of Paradise!"*

*And then for the second time in her life Lucia experienced a profound communication from Our Lady who said, **"In the depth of my heart and my inmost soul: My child, the grace that has been granted to you today will always*** *remain alive in your breast, bringing forth fruits of eternal life."* And these words engraved themselves so indelibly on Lucia's mind that years later she said: "Still now I feel them to be a bond of union of my soul with God."

Our primary intention here is to call attention to the fact that the first manifestation of Fatima was through a statue. But we cannot help remarking here, as in absolutely every facet of Fatima, the Hearts of Jesus and Mary working together ... Our Lady of the Eucharist bringing the awareness of Jesus truly present to those who truly seek Him.

Most significantly, Fatima's call to the True Presence of Jesus Christ in His Church and in the Eucharist is not only seen at the beginning of the revelations but also at what some Fatima experts consider to be the end.

Although Sister Lucia is still alive as of this writing and has reported other experiences with Our Lady and Our Lord over the decades, the vision she received at Tuy, Spain, is considered the culmination of the revelations that began in 1916.

On June 13 Sister Lucia received what is known as "The Last Vision." Many Fatima experts say that this vision appears to be a synthesis of the Fatima message.

Sister Lucia described the vision in her own words in a letter to Pope Pius XII:

Suddenly the whole chapel was illumined by a supernatural light, and a cross of light appeared above the altar, reaching to the ceiling.

In a bright light at the upper part of the cross could be seen the face of a man and his body to the waist (Father), on his breast there was a dove also of light (Holy Spirit), and nailed to the cross was the body of another man (Son).

Somewhat above the waist, I could see a Chalice and a large Host suspended in the air, onto which drops of blood were falling from the face of Jesus crucified and from the wound in His side. These drops ran down onto the Host and fell into the Chalice. Our Lady was beneath the right arm of the cross (it was Our Lady of Fatima with Her Immaculate

Heart within a crown of thorns and flames). Under the left arm of the cross large letters, as of crystal clear water which ran down over the altar, formed the words Grace and Mercy.

I understood that it was the Mystery of the Most Holy Trinity which was shown to me, and I received lights about this Mystery which I am not permitted to reveal.[1]

With this vision, Fatima's Eucharistic message was firmly confirmed. But after Fatima, it appears that Heaven wanted to shine even more light on this mystery. And this happened through a series of revelations given to a chosen soul from Cracow, Poland named Sister Faustina Kowalska.

CHAPTER TWENTY-ONE

"YOU ARE A LIVING HOST"

Moses' departure from Egypt with the Israelites for the land flowing with milk and honey marked the end of Egyptian enslavement. Likewise, God's words spoken at Fatima through the Virgin Mary also hold the promise of historic fulfillment. Indeed, Fatima may mark a change unlike anything the world has ever seen. Only this time, the Lord promises to free mankind in many ways from the bondage and slavery of sin.

The Mystical Body of Christ placed its seal on the message of Fatima in 1930 when the Church fully approved Fatima's apparitions and revelations. Now, only the actual passage of time and events is necessary to move God's words from prophecy to fulfillment.

Yet, arrival of the proper time for the fulfillment of the Fatima promises is dependent upon the Church's call to resist the present onslaught against its supernatural character. And this "supernatural character" is found most significantly in the heavenly graces which the Church offers and upholds through the Sacraments.

Indeed, the Church bases its teachings on the belief that its mysteries are holy and sacred. Not surprisingly then, denying the sacredness of these mysteries is the core of the onslaught against the Church, as the world blatantly rejects there truths.

Therefore, Fatima's message, excluding its prophetic element, is a message that is fundamentally Scriptural. It is a recapitulation of the principles upon which the Church was founded, the call from God to His people to respect the sacred and to hunger for what is holy.

Not too long after Fatima, God granted the world another significant revelation that has almost gone hand-in-hand with Fatima.

The revelations of an Era of Divine Mercy to Sister Faustina Kowalska at Cracow, Poland during the 1930's are seen by some experts as a companion revelation to the prophecies of Fatima of the coming Triumph of the Immaculate Heart and an Era of Peace.

Indeed, through numerous visionaries, Jesus and Mary have reportedly revealed that these two revelations are deliberately interwoven and are, in essence, one. As Our Lady told Father Stefano Gobbi of Italy by interior locution:

This is the hour of the Triumph of the Immaculate Heart of your heavenly mother; it is the hour of the great miracle of Divine Mercy.

While Fatima's call for Communions of Reparation indicates how God wished to transform the world through the faithful's response to Christ's True Presence in the Sacraments, the promises of Divine Mercy given to Sister Faustina are much the same. Sister Faustina's visions indicate that the fulfillment of God's promises are, once again, dependent upon faith and trust in Christ's True Presence.

Like Fatima, these revelations indicate that the salvation of numerous souls is to come through the faithful's recourse to the supernatural graces available in the Mystical Body of Christ, the Church. Indeed, Sister Faustina's revelations of mercy are almost a teaching on the graces Christ wishes the faithful to receive through belief in His True Presence.

All of this appears to indicate that God chooses not only to defeat Satan as He has promised, but also to defeat him in exactly the same way as Satan sought to defeat God.

For centuries, Satan's assault on the supernatural character of the Church has been consistent and damaging. Indeed, Pope Leo XIII's eighteenth century claim of hearing Satan boast to God that he could lead the entire world away from any faith now means more than just the fact that Satan wanted to lead mankind away from recognition of its Creator.

Rather, it may be inferred that the challenge was to be directed at the highest level: a specific confrontation with the Church's claim to possession of the True Presence of Jesus Christ.

Indeed, from Mary's warnings, it is implicitly apparent that Satan meant more; his plan is actually designed to eradicate people's faith by eroding their belief in the True Presence. Only by doing this could Satan be totally successful.

In response, God moved to demonstrate that not only would a remnant of His faithful maintain belief in Him, but through increased devotion and surrender to Him in His invisible Presence in the Sacraments, God would bring about Satan's total defeat and usher in the Era of Peace. As He did at the battle of Jericho, God will use only a remnant of the faithful in order to show that victory is due to Him and Him alone.

Like Fatima's revelations, Sister Faustina's disclosures uphold the truth of this plan, for the Divine Mercy revelations call the faithful to a total immersion of themselves in Christ's True Presence. This immersion allows souls, through faith, to totally surrender their wills to God's Will. By this means, their will then unites with the Divine Will which crushes evil and further develops the virtues which souls need to spiritually mature.

The truth regarding God's plan to bring the world into His merciful arms through His revelations to Sister Faustina is evident right from the beginning of those revelations, just as it was at Fatima.

Sister Maria Faustina of the Blessed Sacrament was the holy nun's full name. True to that name, the key to her entire existence was the Holy Eucharist. In her Diary, *Divine Mercy In My Soul- The Diary of Sister M. Faustina Kowalska*, numerous pages of her writings refer to her life in the Holy Eucharist. She once wrote:

> *The most solemn moment of my life is the moment when I receive Holy Communion. I long for each Holy Communion, and for every Holy Communion I give thanks to the Most Holy Trinity* (Diary 1804).

In a vision during Holy Hour, Sister Faustina was shown the institution of the Holy Eucharist. She described this vision:

> *At the moment of the consecration...the sacrifice was fully consummated...Now, only the external ceremony of death will be carved out—external destruction, the essence*

is in the Cenacle. Never in my whole life had I understood this mystery so profoundly as during that hour of adoration (Diary 684, 757, 832).

And the saintly nun wrote in her diary concerning the Eucharist:

All the good that is in me is due to Holy Communion. I owe everything to it. I feel this holy fire has transformed me completely. Oh, how happy I am to be a dwelling for you, O Lord! My heart is a temple in which you dwell continually.

Most appropriately, Jesus once told Sister Faustina: *"You are a living Host"* (Diary 1826).

God's careful choice and nurturing of this instrument furthers our understanding of the mystery of the Divine Mercy Revelations and their Eucharistic foundation.

Indeed, Father George Kosicki, C.S.B., an expert in the Divine Mercy Revelations and the author of numerous books on the subject, steadfastly proclaims this truth. In his book, *Now is the Time for Mercy*, Father Kosicki outlines this opinion:

The Holy Eucharist is central to devotion to the Divine Mercy, so much so that Our Lord specifically asks, through Sister Faustina, that we all receive Communion on the Feast of The Divine Mercy, after preparing for it through the Sacrament of Reconciliation. In the Eucharist, Jesus (Mercy Incarnate) is present Body and Blood, Soul and Divinity. The Eucharist is God's sacrificial gift of mercy, offered in atonement for our sins and those of the whole world; and in receiving it in Holy Communion, we are strengthened and consoled by the Lord Who is Mercy itself.

Like the Virgin Mary's requests at Fatima for Communions of Reparation on the First Saturday of five successive months, the Lord told Sister Faustina that the whole world can receive the graces necessary for its survival through Holy Communion. In this way the world will find true peace. Again, Heaven is calling the faithful to believe in the power available in the True Presence of Jesus

Christ in the Eucharist. Echoing the Fatima revelations, Jesus told
Sister Faustina that *"peace"* will come no other way:
The Lord said to Sister Faustina:

> *My daughter, tell the whole world about My incon-*
> *ceivable mercy. I desire that the Feast of Mercy be a ref-*
> *uge and shelter for all souls, and especially for poor sin-*
> *ners. On that day the very depths of My tender mercy are*
> *open. I pour out a whole ocean of graces upon those souls*
> *who approach the fount of My Mercy. The soul that will*
> *go to Confession* [within 8 days before or after "Mercy Sun-
> day"] *and receive Holy Communion shall obtain complete*
> *forgiveness of sins and punishment. On that day all the*
> *divine floodgates through which graces flow are opened.*
> *Let no soul fear to draw near to Me, even though its sins*
> *be as scarlet. My mercy is so great that no mind, be it of*
> *man or of angel, will be able to fathom it throughout all*
> *eternity. Everything that exists has come forth from the*
> *very depths of My most tender mercy. Every soul in its*
> *relation to Me will contemplate My love and mercy*
> *throughout eternity. The Feast of Mercy emerged from My*
> *very depths of tenderness. It is My desire that it be sol-*
> *emnly celebrated on the first Sunday after Easter. Man-*
> *kind will not have peace until it turns to the Fount of My*
> *Mercy* (Diary 699).

With this revelation, Christ asserted to Sister Faustina that Holy
Communion was central to the promised times of Mercy. These
times are a precursor to the times of Justice. Jesus also promised
through Sister Faustina:

> *I want to grant a complete pardon to the souls that will go*
> *to Confession and receive Holy Communion on the Feast*
> *of My mercy* (Diary 1109).

Again, Father George Kosicki elaborates from the same book
on this message. Writes Father Kosicki:

Jesus made it clear to Sister Faustina that He was very serious about this Feast of Mercy—His desire and plan is to have mercy on all:

This morning during Holy Mass, I saw the Suffering Jesus. His Passion was imprinted on my body in an invisible manner, but no less painfully. Jesus looked at me and said, **"Souls perish in spite of My bitter Passion. I am giving them the last hope of salvation; that is, the Feast of My Mercy. If they will not adore My mercy, they will perish for all eternity. Secretary of My mercy, write, tell souls about this great mercy of Mine, because the awful day, the day of My justice, is near....Say, My daughter, that the Feast of My Mercy has issued forth from My very depths for the consolation of the whole world"** (Diary 964-965; 1517).

But what about God's words to Sister Faustina concerning His coming justice? These are words that carry with them great mystery and trepidation. For according to numerous writers, they hold the promise of fulfillment of justice if the world does not turn back from its errant ways...

CHAPTER TWENTY-TWO

THE EUCHARIST: AN ANSWER TO THE CULTURE OF DEATH

The Divine Justice repeatedly spoken of to Sister Faustina is believed by many to be imminent. Since the 1930's, the world has continued to move farther away from God. This sad fact is especially evident in the world's all-out attack on life through contraception, euthanasia, infanticide, suicide and abortion which has engulfed society.

Indeed, it is an attack on God Himself, according to Pope John Paul II's 1995 encyclical *Evangelium Vitae* (*The Gospel of Life*). Likewise, numerous visionaries claim that this pro-death stance is the greatest affront to God, the author of all life. Thus, these specific crimes call out loudly for God's justice.

It is believed that at the core of the message of Fatima, there is also a warning of a coming time of sin which would especially target the family and life itself. These sins which would produce such confusion and division that the world could destroy itself.

Indeed, some believe that the two great signs prophesied at Fatima are symbolic and refer to a nuclear danger that would come into the world. In 1945 such a danger surfaced. This danger, combined with man's blindness incurred, especially through sins against life, could certainly cause the world to drift toward annihilation. At Fatima Mary warned of *"the annihilation of Nations,"* and, Fatima writers still say this remains an unfulfilled prophecy.

But the remedy to this terrible scenario, which Mary began to foretell with her prophetic messages at Rue du Bac and La Salette, is still available today. It is Jesus Christ in His True Presence in the Eucharist and Blessed Sacrament.

Father George Kosicki, in his book, *The Living Eucharist, Countersign to Our Age and Answer to Crisis*, confronts this precise scenario head-on and speaks of God's solution. Writes Fr. Kosicki:

> *The present worldwide number of abortions each year is conservatively reported as forty million (Review of Inducted Abortions, Vol. 6), and is possibly as high as sixty million. The impact of this number of abortions was impressed upon me while visiting Auschwitz, the Nazi concentration camp outside of Cracow, Poland.*
>
> *It was the Monday after the celebration of Mercy Sunday, at the Shrine of Divine Mercy at Lagiewniki, where Sister Faustina Kowalska is buried. We drove an hour through freezing rain to the town of Auschwitz and entered the camp, now a historic museum, passing under the arch over the entrance. On the arch, a sign in German greeted us: "Arbeit macht frei!" (Work makes for freedom!) As we gazed at the stockpiles of shoes, suitcases, eyeglasses, women's hair and the reconstructed rooms, I kept praying the words of the Chaplet of Divine Mercy: "Have mercy on us and on the whole world." As I gazed in amazement at the execution wall, at the cell where Saint Maximilian Kolbe was starved and finally killed by an injection of phenol, and then at the gas chambers, I didn't know whether to pray or cry.*
>
> *Then the realization of our present age impressed itself on my mind. Which is worse? Hitler's age in which some four million were killed at Auschwitz and another six million at other camps over a decade—or the decade under Stalin in which he killed, according to Zbigniew Brzezinski (in The Grand Failure of Communism), some thirty to fifty million? In the past decade we have surpassed that age by tenfold; four hundred to six hundred million! More than the population of all of North America, that is, Canada, the United States and Mexico, with Australia and New Zealand added in.*

*This means that some 125,000 abortions are performed
each day! This is one-half the number of conceptions in the
world! We are annihilating the human race. We have broken the body of Christ on earth again!*

We are in a crisis of Eucharist!

*The answer to the crisis is the Eucharist—the ultimate
humility and mercy of God.*

Indeed, the popes of our time have concurred through their
writings with Father Kosicki's views. Pope Pius XII in his encyclical letter *Mystici Corporis (The Mystical Body of Christ)* wrote:

*As then in the sad and anxious times through which we
are passing, there are many who cling so firmly to Christ
the Lord hidden beneath the Eucharistic veils that neither
tribulation, nor distress, nor famine, nor nakedness, nor
danger, nor persecution, nor the sword can separate them
from His love, surely no doubt can remain that Holy Communion which once again in God's providence is much more
frequented even from early childhood, may become a source
of that fortitude which not infrequently makes Christians
into heroes.*

Pope John Paul II is believed to be the prophesied *"spark"*
that would come out of Poland. Sister Faustina's writings foretold:
"As I was praying for Poland, I heard the words: **'I bear a special
love for Poland, and if she will be obedient to My will, I will exalt
her in might and holiness. From her will come forth the spark
that will prepare the world for My final coming"** (Diary 1732).
The pope has also written concerning our times and the Eucharist.

At the beginning of his pontificate, the Holy Father wrote in
his encyclical letter of November 30, 1980, *Dives in Misericordia
(Rich in Mercy)*:

*The Church lives an authentic life when she professes
and proclaims mercy—the most stupendous attribute of the
Creator and of the Redeemer—and when she brings people
close to the sources of the Savior's mercy, of which she is*

the trustee and dispenser. Of great significance in this area is constant meditation on the Word of God, and above all conscious and mature participation in the Eucharist and in the sacrament of Penance or Reconciliation.

The Eucharist brings us even nearer to that love which is more powerful than death: "For as often as we eat this bread and drink this cup," we proclaim not only the death of the Redeemer but also His resurrection "until He comes" in glory. The same Eucharistic rite, celebrated in memory of Him who in His messianic mission revealed the Father to us by means of His words and His cross, attests to the inexhaustible love by virtue of which He desires always to be united with us and present in our midst, coming to meet every human heart.

In preparing the Church for the approaching celebration of the Great Jubilee year 2000, the Holy Father explicitly called attention to what the millennial year will be like in the annals of Church history.

In his apostolic letter, *Tertio Millennio Adveniente (As the Third Millennium Draws Near)*, Pope John Paul II's words focused on the approaching fulfillment of the Fatima-Divine Mercy revelations. Wrote the Holy Father:

The year 2000 will be intensely Eucharistic: in the Sacrament of the Eucharist, the Savior, who took flesh in Mary's womb twenty centuries ago, continues to offer himself to humanity as the source of divine life.

With the Fatima-Divine Mercy revelations, God reveals to the world the direness of its state. The world has drifted far away from Judeo-Christian beliefs, especially the Ten Commandments and Christ's Commandment of Love. Since the world has slowly distanced itself from belief in Christ's True Presence, it has simultaneously distanced itself from believing in the sanctity of life itself. Indeed, Christ Himself stated in Scripture that He was *"the way, the truth and the life"* and *"he who believes in Me has life,"* thus giving and sustaining all life in the world. Thus, with the denial of

Christ's True Presence, the world has embraced, on a massive scale, the denial of life itself. From abortion to euthanasia, the signs are clearly present: the denial of Christ's True Presence may be directly related to mankind's blindness regarding the true meaning and gift of life.

Furthermore, the best supernatural gifts available to the faithful to strengthen their will against evil are not being utilized. In the invisible world of the spirit, the enemy has slowly waged a battle designed to topple the Catholic Church and its mission, and eventually the whole world. But through the Fatima-Divine Mercy revelations, God is leading the faithful back to Christ's True Presence; this path will eventually lead the Church to its ultimate victory.

During the 1930's Mary continued to appear to visionaries throughout the world. Her revelations defined the times and called the faithful back to the messages of the Gospel. Again, the solution was threefold: prayer, the Word of God, and the Sacraments.

In Belgium in 1932-1933, two apparitions of Mary occurred that were both found to be worthy of belief. At Beauraing and Banneaux, Our Lady appeared to children with simple messages that reinforced her call at Fatima and pointed the faithful to the Catholic Church.

Like her revelations at Fatima and Cracow, the messages of Beauraing and Banneaux confirmed God's promises and reminded us of Mary's words in Scripture that God's *mercy is from generation to generation.*

Mother of the Secret

CHAPTER TWENTY-THREE

"RECEIVE THE SACRED HOST"

W hile the Divine Mercy revelations were being given to Sister Faustina, Heaven also silently revealed more of God's plan for the end of one era and beginning of another.

Again, these revelations brought attention to the True Presence. And this was evidenced in a most striking way, for now the Eternal Father, the First Person of the Most Holy Trinity, was the source of the revelations. Like the Fatima-Divine Mercy revelations, the Church fully recognized these messages as worthy of belief.

Mother Eugenia Elisabetta Ravasio was born on September 4, 1907, in San Gervasio d'Adda (now Capriato San Gervasio), a small village in the province of Bergamo, Italy. She came from a peasant background and received only an elementary education.

After working several years in a factory, Eugenia entered the Congregation of Our Lady of the Apostles when she was twenty. By the age of twenty-five, she was elected as Mother General of the Congregation. She served in this position from 1935 until 1947.

While her spiritual work received the greatest focus, her worldly contributions were also significant. In twelve years of missionary work, Mother Eugenia opened seventy relief centers in some of the most distant and removed locations in Asia, Africa and Europe. She is credited with being the first to discover a cure for leprosy, extracting it from the seed of a tropical plant. This process was later advanced at the Pasteur Institute in Paris. She further planned and developed a project for a "Lepers City" at Azopte (Ivory Coast). This center serviced an area of over 200,000 square miles and is still today a leading center for the care of leprosy sufferers. In recognition of this achievement, France conferred upon Mother Eugenia its highest national honor for social work.

But the heavenly revelations given to Mother Eugenia made her life truly outstanding. And after ten years of scrupulous examination by a commission, these revelations were approved by Monsignor Alexandre Caillot, Bishop of Grenoble.

Likewise, it is also noteworthy that the revelations were given to Mother Eugenia in Latin, a language totally unknown by her.

On July 1, 1932, Mother Eugenia began to hear and see angels which she described as "the entire Heavenly Court." According to the book, *God Is Father,* there was beautiful singing, incomprehensible harmony, and then finally the appearance of the Eternal Father Himself. God the Father then spoke to Sister Eugenia and told here He was now coming among men in order to love them and to make them know this love.

Mother Eugenia recorded her thoughts concerning this incredible experience. She said God the Father sat next to her and revealed much to her.

The Eternal Father then outlined to Mother Eugenia the purpose of His coming. It was for a threefold reason: to banish fear of Him, to bring hope to men and nations, and to make Himself known, so all mankind might love and trust Him. His only concern, God the Father told the saintly nun, was to *watch over men* and to *love them* as His children.

While the revelations were prophetic and evangelical, from the beginning the Eternal Father asserted to the saintly nun that the Mystical Body of Jesus Christ, the Catholic Church, truly held within it the supernatural gifts and graces which the Eternal Father wanted to give to all mankind.

The complete revelations to Mother Eugenia can be characterized as no less than unfathomable. Throughout His message to her, the Eternal Father outlines His plan, a plan that entreats all men and all nations to turn to Him. Most significantly, He desires them to turn to Him not in trepidation, but in total abandonment and love.

In His conversations with Mother Eugenia, the Eternal Father touches on various subjects ranging from the story of His love for men as revealed to Moses and Israel in the Old Testament, to acknowledging the spiritual differences among His present-day children. In telling her all this, the Eternal Father conveys to Mother Eugenia the idea that the *time of times* has come. It is a time, He tells her, for the fulfillment of His Son's prayer, the Our Father.

As in the revelations of Fatima and Divine Mercy, the love and peace God wishes His people to have is most accessible to all through the Eucharist. Indeed, the Eternal Father told Mother Eugenia that He, Himself caused the mystery of this Sacrament to be instituted. And He desired this Sacrament to be the means for all people to come to Him. The Eternal Father's words were:

> *What do I desire to achieve with this work of love, if not to find hearts able to understand Me?*
>
> *I am the holiness of which I possess the perfect and full expression; I offer you this holiness, of which I am the Author, through My Holy Spirit and I instill it in your souls through My Son's merits.*
>
> *It is through My Son and the Holy Spirit that I am coming to you and into you, and it is in you that I seek My repose.*
>
> *To some souls, the words "I am coming into you" will seem a mystery, but it is not a mystery! Because, having instructed My Son to institute the Holy Eucharist, I intended to come to you every time you receive the Sacred Host!*
>
> *Of course, nothing prevented Me from coming to you even before the Eucharist, as nothing is impossible to Me! But receiving this Sacrament is an action that is easy to understand and it shows how I come to you!*
>
> *When I am in you, I can more easily give you what I possess, provided that you ask Me for it. Through this Sacrament you are intimately united with Me. It is in this intimacy that the outpouring of My love makes My holiness spread into your souls.*
>
> *I fill you with My love, then you have only to ask Me for the virtues and perfection you need and you can be sure that in those moments when God is reposing in His creatures, nothing will be refused you.*

CHAPTER TWENTY-FOUR

THE DAILY MIRACLE

By the 1940's, reports of Marian apparitions markedly increased. If there was a great danger approaching the Church and the world, mankind would not be able to say that Heaven hadn't warned of it.

While previously apparitions were sporadic, by the 1940's the Virgin Mary's interventions were everywhere. An outbreak of Marian sightings was noted especially in Europe.

In Germany, the most significant apparitions during the 1940's occurred in the cities of Heede and Marienfried, where again the Virgin echoed her words at Fatima, foretelling her Triumph and warning of mounting danger.

Likewise, Mary repeated that the answer to the world's problems lay in the reality of the True Presence of her Son. In Germany, Mary continued to call for the Communion of First Saturdays.

Around the world, in a village called Lipa in the Philippines, Mary reiterated this message a few years later: *"What I have asked here is the same I asked at Fatima."*

According to a published study by the French theologian Father Bernard Billet, from 1940 to 1950 there were eighty-four Marian apparitions reported, most of them in Europe. Perhaps as much as anything, the fact that the apparitions predominately occurred in Germany, Italy, Belgium and France may be viewed as Heaven's way of coming directly to the source of danger.

During this time however, apparitions were also reported in Austria (1948), Lithuania (1943), America (1944), Holland (1945), Yugoslavia (1946), Portugal (1946), Hungary (1947), England

(1947), Czechoslovakia (1947-1948), Romania (1948), Spain (1945), Ireland (1947), Poland (1949), China (1949), Switzerland (1949) and Canada (1949).

Undoubtedly, there were probably even more apparitions reported which escaped Father Billet's investigation. However, the most impressive apparitions of the decade were the apparitions at Amsterdam (beginning in 1945) to the visionary Ida Perleman, and the apparitions at Montichiari, Italy to Pierina Gilli in 1947.

The revelations at Amsterdam contained many unique prophecies concerning the future. Most notable was the foretelling that the Era of Peace prophesied at Fatima was related to the fulfillment of a prophecy concerning a final dogma of Mary as Coredemptrix, Mediatrix and Advocate of all Graces.

In the Amsterdam messages, the Virgin Mary continued to reveal how the world was entering into the culmination of the times she had foretold in her messages to Saint Catherine Labouré at Rue du Bac in 1830 and to the two shepherd children, Melanie Mathieu and Maximin Girard, at La Salette in 1846.

Indeed, Mary said, the times were extremely dangerous, as Ida's visions of Russia and China are hauntingly relevant to today's world.

"The powers of Hell will break loose," the Virgin told Ida. Mary also warned of *"the East against the West."* As she had done at Rue du Bac and La Salette, the Queen of Heaven showed Ida how the cross would be held in contempt. She told her to be *"on guard against false doctrines, especially in what concerns the Eucharist."*

Mary also showed Ida how the Church would come under attack. The problems in the world, Our Lady said, arose because of the loss of the truth, the truth which the Church possessed. Mary told Ida, *"Disasters upon disasters, disasters of nature. This applies not only to your country, but to the whole world."* Then Ida heard Our Lady say, pointing to the cross: *"Do bring Him back to mankind."*

With this, a vision of the world appeared to Ida, with a cross planted in the middle of it. Mary then appeared sitting on a throne with the Child Jesus on her lap and said: *"There must be a return to Him first of all, before true peace can come."*

Although the apparitions at Amsterdam are primarily considered to be a series of fifty-six apparitions from 1945 through

1959, Ida Perleman continued to receive mystical experiences for decades.

However, the predominant theme of the fifty-six apparitions was an urgent appeal for the Church to protect the truth entrusted to it. Mary told Ida that this was necessary for God to win and the Triumph to come.

On February 17, 1952, Mary gave Ida an important message concerning Christ's True Presence:

> *Listen carefully and tell your theologians and all the nations that they should try to understand my message and explain it well.*
>
> *The Lord Jesus Christ came and brought with Him the Church and the Cross as a gift from the Lord and Creator. The Church is and will remain. The Lord and Creator brought the Church into the world through the Son. The Lord and Creator demands gratitude from the creature.*
>
> *The Church is the community of nations whose business is to adore and worship their Lord and Creator—the Father, the Son and the Holy Spirit.*
>
> *All those who are in charge of the Community, should see to it that the Church will continue and expand. This time is Our time. The Lord and Creator deems it necessary to send the Church a warning through the Lady of all Nations. The time has come. Inform the theologians.*[1]

On March 19, 1952, Mary prophetically foretold to Ida that *"Before the year 2000 much will have changed in the Church."*[2] On the next day, Mary added, *"1953 was to be known as the year of the Lady of All Nations,"* and she emphasized that the key to the Church's victory was *"the daily miracle."*[2] Ida reports that Our Lady told her:

> *Before the Lord Jesus Christ returned to the Father— before the Sacrifice of the Cross began—the Lord Jesus Christ gave to the nations of the whole world the daily miracle.*

Now the Lady casts a searching glance over the globe and very slowly and questioningly says, *"How many are there...(pause) who experience this great wonder? They pass this great miracle by. The daily Sacrifice has to have its place again at the center of this degenerate world."*

Ida then reported a startling vision. She writes:

> *Then the Lady seems to look into the distance, saying, "And now I address myself to the Holy Father: you have accomplished much. Now the Lady of all Nations asks you once again to make sure to see everything through what yet remains to be done. He knows what I mean. The Holy Father should prepare the Marian dogma of the Co-Redemptrix, Mediatrix and Advocate. She will do her part in it."*

Our Lady also told Ida,

> *On the High Altar the Sacrifice of the Cross—the "Daily Miracle."* (I now see the High Altar and the Lady indicates the tabernacle and the crucifix). *Adjacent to it, on the Gospel side, will be the altar of the Lady of all Nations, and on the Epistle side the altar of the Father, the Son and the Holy Spirit. Notice well, my child: on the same level with the Sacrifice.* (Here the Lady indicates the High Altar again and I see the three altars adjoining on the same level).
>
> *The Lady continues, "I have chosen the Dominican Fathers for this task. There the donor should place the painting, which must promptly go to Amsterdam. It is Amsterdam I have selected as the seat of the Lady of all Nations. This is also the city of the Blessed Sacrament. Make sure you grasp all this. The work of spreading should be taken in hand by the monasteries and thence go to all the clergy, to all the peoples. Dominicans, remember what has been given into your charge."*[3]

Ida reported that the fifty-sixth and final apparition was a powerful vision which again reinforced Mary's call to defend the True

Presence of Christ in the Church and the Eucharist. Wrote Ida:

> *Suddenly the Lady had gone. In her stead I saw a big host. It was exceedingly large and so I could see quite well that it was a normal host, one like those we see in church, a wafer.*
>
> *Then in front of the host there appeared a chalice. I saw that the chalice was of splendid gold. It toppled over, facing me. Then I saw flowing from this chalice thick streams of blood. All this blood poured upon the globe and spilled over the earth; it was a distressing sight; I began to feel quite sick, all the time streams and streams of blood!*
>
> *This went on for quite a while. Then the scene suddenly changed and all of it became a brilliant, dazzling Sacred Host. It shone so brightly that I shaded my eyes so as not to get blinded, but I was forced to keep looking at it. The Host seemed to be made of white fire. In the center of it was a little opening or hollow; I cannot describe it any better. Then all of a sudden, the Host seemed to burst open, and exposed to my view was a figure, soaring in midair, a person, exceedingly mighty and strong. Forgive me, please, I cannot convey the strength and majesty this person embodied, it was too overwhelming! I hardly dared look. I saw one person, but the thought kept recurring in my mind, "And yet there are two"; and then when I looked, I saw only one. Still my mind kept repeating, "And yet they are two."*
>
> *All at once there came from the two an indescribable light and in it I saw, breaking out from the center—I cannot express it otherwise—a Dove! It shot like an arrow down to the earth, unspeakably bright; and I covered my eyes again so as not to get blind. My eyes hurt me and yet again I was forced to keep them open and look at the vision! What splendour, what magnificence! the soaring figure, majestic, powerful, grand; and the world now all bathed in light from the radiant Dove! And a voice rang out, "He who eats and drinks Me, receives life eternal and the Spirit of Truth."* [4]

Mother of the Secret

CHAPTER TWENTY-FIVE

"I AM THE LIVING MANNA"

Over the decades, Ida Perleman reported more divine experiences, most often associated with the Eucharist. These experiences seemed to imply that the disposition of the times at hand was going to be determined by mankind turning to Jesus Christ, especially in His True Presence in the Eucharist. Jesus implied to Ida, through word and vision, that this was the fate of the world for both individuals and nations.

Here are four reports of Eucharistic miracles that Ida experienced as reported in the book, *Eucharistic Experiences* (Queenship Publishing Co. 1996), edited by Josef Kunzli:

30 August 1959

I received Holy Communion and returned by my place. All of a sudden the Sacred Host began to grow on my tongue, becoming larger and thicker. It seemed to expand and then suddenly it came alive. Truly! Strange though it must sound, I felt it as a living object. It must seem irreverently expressed; yet it may help people to form some idea of it when I say, "It resembled a living fish in its movements." I wanted to take it out of my mouth in order to see what it was; but of course, reverence prevented me from doing so.

As may be imagined, I got a terrible shock—it was awful! Never having experienced anything alike, I could not make out what was happening to me. But at the same time a completely different perception arose in me, something so

*delightful. I may well say, something heavenly. It was a state
such as I had never known. Then suddenly I heard, "**Be not
afraid ... I am the Lord, your Creator ... the Lord Jesus
Christ ... The Giver of Life.**" (The dots indicate a silence.)
"**Just as I live in you now, I want to and shall live among
all nations.**"*

*After this the Sacred Host began to grow smaller and
thinner; it resumed its usual form and I was able to consume it. Subsequently I did not go to church for a whole
week—excepting Sunday, of course—in order to check up
on myself. Nothing out of the ordinary took place.*[1]

25 March 1960, Annunciation Day

*During Holy Communion the Sacred Host suddenly
broke into very small crumbs upon my tongue. All at once I
heard, "**I am the Seed, which was plunged into her womb.**"*

*Upon this, the crumbs assumed a delicious taste and
became fluid. Then I heard, "**I am the living Water.**"*

*Then I was startled by a violent, burning sensation on
my tongue and I heard, "**Fear not. I am the eternal Fire
that was kindled in her womb for all nations.**"*

Then the Sacred Host dissolved on my tongue.[2]
*31 May 1960, Queenship of Our Lady
When I went to Holy Communion, I heard, "**I am the Lord,
your Creator, the Risen Lord, the True Wisdom.**"*

*Then the Sacred Host became alive on my tongue and I
heard, "**I am the Fish; you are the salt of the earth. ...I am
the living Water.**" (At this, flows of fresh water, with an ex-
ceptionally delicious taste, began pouring through my
mouth.)*

*"**I am the living Manna.**" (Now that water changed
back into the Sacred Host.)*

*Then all at once the Sacred Host began to burn so vio-
lently on my tongue, that it seemed as if the latter would be
consumed by a fire within. I got a shock and heard, "**Fear
nothing. I am the Fire that was kindled in the womb of the
Lady. You, priests, do not let this fire go out; but carry it***

with you in your hearts, in your hands and on your lips, so that it may continue to burn and live among all nations. For they must all attain eternal life."

"Pass this on; the signs have been given. Do what the Lady told you to do."

Thus all at once the Sacred Host was back in its usual form on my tongue; and I consumed it.[3]

On May 31, 1965 Ida reported another incredible Eucharistic vision, one of significant consequence and meaning for the Church and the world:

During Holy Communion the Sacred Host became active again on my tongue. I saw a pair of lips with a finger across. The finger made the sign of the Cross at those lips. Then I heard the voice say, **"Thus it is all right. Go to Pope Paul and tell him in the name of the Lady of all Nations:**

'This is the last warning before the end of the Council. The Church of Rome is in danger of a schism.' Warn your priests. Let them put a stop to those false theories about the Eucharist, sacraments, doctrine, priesthood, marriage and family-planning. They are being led astray by the spirit of untruth - by Satan - and confused by the ideas of modernism. Divine teaching and laws are valid for all time and newly applicable to every period.

'Keep the primacy in your own hands. Grasp the meaning of these words: the Church of Rome must remain the Church of Rome.

'Do what the Lord has demanded of you - in sending Me, the Lady or Mother of all Nations. You are the Pope who has been selected for this work. Let the nations say the prayer before my picture and the Holy Spirit will come! A Church or a people without a Mother is like a body without a soul.

'This period is now coming at an end.'"

Five years later on the Feast of Corpus Christi, May 31, 1970, Jesus again came to Ida Perleman in an incredible Eucharistic vision. Ida reported:

During Holy Mass I had the following experience: Shortly before the Consecration I saw a large, black plane.

This plane formed itself into a big, black cross. Then within this black cross appeared a smaller, narrower and shining cross that sparkled on all sides. This cross, ablaze in the midst of the black cross, shone so brightly, that the big cross became wholly bathed in its light.

During the Consecration I saw the Chalice that was being raised, encircled by a halo of brilliant light. From out of the Chalice emerged, in horizontal position, a "Spiritualized, Sacred Host." This Sacred Host was translucent.

After that the Sacred Host came to rest above the Chalice in a vertical position.

I discerned a difference between the Host that was still lying in front of the priest, and the "Spiritualized, Sacred Host." This latter irradiated such splendor in all directions that it hurt my eyes.

Then the priest took the Host that lay before him and held it up. I saw the "Spiritualized Sacred Host" combine with the Host the priest was holding up and with it form one blaze of light. This was a most resplendent sight—words cannot suffice for adequate comment.

The next thing I saw was that the light that shone round about the Chalice and the priest, was tending in the direction of the spot (in our room) where the Lady had always appeared. Then the two lights became one. For in the meantime, the light that always accompanied the Lady had also entered the room. The whole room was now one ocean of light.

The Chalice meanwhile stood on the altar and I now saw that blood was streaming out of it. At the same time I heard the words,

"They have reviled Me again."

"They have nailed Me to the Cross anew."

"Make atonement."

The light stayed in the room all the time. Then it looked as if the light was being parted and presently I saw the priest, ready to distribute Holy Communion.

> *When I had received Our Lord, I heard a sentence in an utterly strange tongue. I asked, "What does it mean?" and heard the answer, "I AM THAT AM."*
>
> *It was not the voice of the Lady. I did not get the sense of this saying. After a pause the voice said, "Make this message known to the whole world."* [5]

The second significant apparition of the 1940's occurred in the spring of 1947 in Montichiari, Italy to a nurse named Pierina Gilli. In a chapel of the local hospital, the Blessed Virgin Mary appeared to Pierina in a wonderful vision. The Virgin was bathed in a magnificent light. Pierina reported that Mary, dressed in mauve, was very sad with tears in her eyes.

As Pierina gazed in awe at the Mother of God, she noticed that the Virgin's heart was pierced with three swords. With this sight, it was revealed that the first sword signified the unworthy celebration of Holy Mass and Communion unworthily received. The meaning of the second sword was being unfaithful to and giving up the vocation as a priest or a religious. The third sword represented the betrayal of the Faith. Our Lady then asked Pierina for *"Faith, Sacrifice and Penance."*

Pierina received six more apparitions at Montichiari. After her final apparitions on December 8, 1947, Pierina withdrew to a convent where, hidden from the world, she served in a kitchen and waited in silence for nineteen years.

In Fontanelle, Italy on April 17, 1966, the Virgin again came to Pierina. Her words to Pierina were directly linked with the message of Fatima: Mary promised a miraculous spring which she then revealed on May 13, 1966. It was the anniversary date of the first apparition at Fatima.

Then Our Lady repeated her request at Fatima, Cracow and elsewhere, for the faithful to commit themselves to receiving Holy Communion in a special manner.

Again, as she had revealed before, Mary said it would be in this way that Heaven would be able to achieve what was necessary for the salvation of the world. During the first apparition on November 16, 1947, Mary warned Pierina that the world was in such a sinful state that Heaven was going to send a *"flood of punishments."*

On August 9, 1966 Mary told Pierina:

My Divine Son, Jesus, has sent me again, in order to request the "World League of Penitential Communion" to be done each year throughout the world on October thirteenth. Those priests and faithful who will spread this devotion will be given the wealth of my graces. I have chosen this place of Montichiari because there is still the humility of poor Bethlehem among my sons who till the soil. Furthermore, this place, where so many prayers are said continuously, will be transformed into a source of rich blessings.[6]

Throughout the 1940's, it seemed that what Heaven requested at Fatima and Cracow was now being urgently repeated throughout the world. While these revelations further confirmed the messages given at Fatima and Cracow, they were also signs of the urgency ever present in Mary's words.

The world had fallen so deeply into sin, Mary kept saying, that it was now essential for those who believed in the True Presence of Christ in the Eucharist, to reach for the supernatural graces necessary to turn the tide.

God wanted to live in His people. And although relatively few would respond to the call of a life centered around the Eucharist, it appeared from Heaven's messages that this would be enough to save the world.

Indeed, the little flock was being assembled. It was a flock of faithful sheep nurtured by the Body and Blood of Jesus Christ. These faithful people were living signs to the world of the Way, the Truth and the Light as outlined in Scripture. And it was to be this remnant of the Church who, through their faith and reparation, would bring the world into the new times.

The 1940's were perhaps in many ways, the darkest days the world has ever known. An estimated sixty million people were killed during World War II, yet amidst it all, stories of Christ's True Presence continued to emerge.

On the Tabor Islands near New Guinea in the South Pacific, the Lord again miraculously demonstrated His True Presence in the mid 1940's.

A young missionary named Michael Murphy of Cork County, Ireland was laboring for the Lord in the hot, steamy jungles when one day the Japanese army landed. They took Father Murphy away and murdered him. But the natives kept waiting for his return.

In August of 1946, the Most Reverend Leo Scharmach, Bishop of Rabaul, returned to the island of Mapua to find the mission church spotlessly clean. In the tabernacle were two ciboriums. One contained a few hosts entirely decomposed. But in the other, a number of the Hosts were perfectly preserved. After four years of intense jungle heat and humidity, not a speck of mold was found on them. It was a miracle. Indeed, the natives of Mapua had not been spiritually deserted.[7]

Another Eucharistic miracle reported during World War II occurred in a Nazi concentration camp named Buchenwald.

On August 23, 1944, Father LeLoir stood in line for his daily inspection by the S.S. troops. In his pocket was an envelope containing six consecrated Hosts. Out of nowhere, the soldiers began to search each prisoner. This brought a feeling of great dread and fear, as several prisoners knew that the priest carried the envelope of Hosts.

When it was his turn, the priest silently prayed as the soldiers pried through his pockets. Suddenly, the envelope was found and torn open. To the amazement of all, the Hosts had vanished!

Again, it was another form of Eucharistic miracle. Whereas many times before Hosts had miraculously appeared, this time in order to prevent desecration and to save the priest's life, the Hosts had disappeared.[8]

But the 1940's also proved to be a demarcation line surrounding the Virgin's warnings of a terrible fate which awaited the world. After this decade, the annihilation of the entire world would be possible through the actions of just one or two men who could decide to press a button. This button could begin a holocaust of unimaginable proportion.

One nation on earth understood this. Almost echoing part of the message of Fatima, Emperor Hirohito told the Japanese people and the world on August 14, 1945, five days after the second atomic bomb was dropped on Nagasaki, Japan, that it must find peace. He stated: *"It is our desire to initiate an Era of Peace for future generations by tolerating the intolerable and enduring the unendurable."*

Likewise, just a few years before, Jesus told the Belgian mystic and stigmatist, Berthe Petit, how crucial the times had become. Jesus revealed to Berthe: ***"A frightful torment is in preparation. It will be seen that a force launched with fury will soon be let loose."***

CHAPTER TWENTY-SIX

"THEY WILL BE FED BY HEAVEN"

The decade of the 1950's continued to reveal an increase in the number of Marian apparitions. In his study, Father Billet accounts for eighty-six apparitions. Again, the apparitions were worldwide with a high concentration of reports coming from Europe. For nonbelievers, the numbers mean nothing. But for the faithful, provided the apparitions are authentic, they can be considered as consistent signs of the increasing urgency of the times.

Most curiously, several compelling reports during this period came from behind the Iron Curtain. These reports are most noteworthy since the Communist nations prohibited the Holy Sacrifice of the Mass and closed thousands of churches throughout Eastern Europe and the Soviet Union.

The most intriguing report of the 1950's came from Czechoslovakia, although this account didn't surface until decades later.

At Turzovka in 1958, a forester named Matous Losuta reported a series of encounters with Mary that were extremely compelling and apocalyptical. Matous's accounts relayed mystical visions of a great spiritual war unfolding in the world. It was a war, he revealed, that evoked images from the Book of Revelation.

Matous reported messages from Mary of how both *"good"* and *"evil"* were having their foreheads marked and how a new era would dawn in the world, prior to a great purification. Most notably, Matous reported how the *"good"* would emerge victorious because of their total reliance on the supernatural gifts they would be given, especially in the Eucharist. *"They will be protected by the good spirits and will be fed by Heaven,"* Mary promised Matous. The Virgin then revealed that after this, *"the earth will be beautiful."[1]*

Matous's accounts are most impressive in view of his personal life. Many miraculous events are associated with his reports. Also, the unlikely nature of the entire affair was highlighted by the intense Communist persecution of Matous, thus adding to his credibility.

Overall, there were too many reported apparitions during the 1950's to begin to examine all of them, but like the revelations of 1940's, a central theme prevailed. It was again a reminder of Mary's call at Fatima: a call for the faithful to return to holiness and to the reality of the sacred through the Sacraments.

In Yugoslavia during the 1950's, a unique visionary named Julka reported incredible visions and messages. Again, her messages foretold the dire times ahead. But most of all, the revelations called the faithful to focus on the Church, for the Church held the answer to the world's troubles.

In one vision, Julka was permitted to see how, through the Mass and the Sacraments, the Church Militant and the Church Triumphant are truly together. Wrote Julka of this vision:

> *On the Feast of Saints Peter and Paul I was on pilgrimage in Diakovo and present at the consecration of the new Bishop Stephen Bäuerlein. During the Holy Sacrifice, the upper space of the cathedral was filled by a host of Heavenly Citizens. The Angels and Saints were flying backwards and forwards in splendid long garments.*
>
> *When the newly consecrated Bishop raised the chalice with the Precious Blood at the Consecration, Jesus, wearing His Crown of thorns, came down from the Cross into His chalice. At the Holy Communion he received Him into his heart. The Heavenly Citizens praised and worshipped God up to the end of the Sacred Celebration. Seeing their joy and rapture, I could scarcely tear myself away from this place.[2]*

In Hungary during the 1950's, another incredible visionary and mystic emerged. Her name was Sister Natalie and her revelations are known as the "Victorious Queen of the World" messages.

These messages echoed the many profound and specific revelations which had been previously revealed, including Amsterdam's foretelling of Mary's final dogma and Fatima's Era of Peace.

But the call to Jesus, through adoration and Eucharistic surrender, permeated the messages. Wrote Sister Natalie:

> *I have called for repentance even with the first of mankind, Adam and Eve. I called for repentance through My precursor, John the Baptist. Did I not Myself show you the example of repentance, reparation and a sacrificial life? This is the reason why I remained in the Tabernacles, to lead the souls to love and penance. Is not this why I still live among you inside the decorated doors of the Churches where I console the greatly offended Heavenly Father? Then if I lowered Myself to you with such a noble gesture, why are you shy of Me?*
>
> *A few days later, after Holy Communion, Jesus told me,* **"If My priests could see the world in the light of truth, they would see that I maintain the world only because of the reparation of the just. The prayers and reparations of the just move My Heart to have mercy on My people and shorten the well-deserved sufferings and chastisement."**[3]

Jesus revealed to Sister Natalie how important it is for a priest to truly believe in His True Presence: Wrote the nun concerning a vision of one troubled priest:

> *It was especially painful for Jesus that for a long time the priest offered the Holy Sacrifice of the Mass unworthily. Jesus told me:* **"My daughter, unfortunately there are many among My servants like that priest. Those who lose My grace sink so deeply!"**
>
> *How Jesus feels when a priest in sin consecrates the host.*
> *He showed me the pain that He suffers when He must ascend to the altar when such a priest is calling Him in the transubstantiation of the Host, and touches Him, and re-*

ceives Him in Holy Communion.

*I saw that when this priest approached the altar, Jesus turned away from Him, and prostrated Himself before the Heavenly Father asking Him, "**My Father, if it is possible, please excuse Me from My obligation to be present on that altar on account of this priest's calling.**" The Heavenly Father bent down to His Son and told Him, "**My Son, just now be patient!**"*

In that moment the three Divine Persons united and the Sacrifice separated from them.

The Lord showed me all this that I might understand how He feels at such a Mass. Or when He sees all the sacrilegious novelties in the Mass, the clear signs of the loss of faith?

*He told me: "**If there would be anything that I regret it would be that I confirmed the priesthood on some who are unworthy of it. It is just as sad that among the sisters there are many similarly sinful souls. Woe to such souls if they do not convert before their death. It is terrible to see the eternal fate of such souls!**"*

*On another occasion - to console me - he showed me what a great pleasure it is for Him to come down to the altar when a priest with a clear conscience calls Him, when He renews His Sacrifice of the Cross for the glory of the Father and the salvation of souls. Concerning such saintly priests He told me, "**They are My pleasure, My pride and consolation, My hope. I redeemed the world partly because of them.**"[4]*

Jesus also revealed to Sister Natalie how the ruin of the world was related to the loss of the belief in the True Presence. Sister wrote:

*From a neglected tabernacle I heard the following: "**My priest, My priest, why have you abandoned Me?**" I saw a priest as he visited a neglected Church. I saw how a great flame radiated out from the suffering Heart of the Saviour, the flame of His joy. I saw also that He similarly rejoiced with those priests and bishops who revered and loved Him in the Eucharist.*

*"**I am thirsty!**"*

The Lord told this to a fervent priest: "I am thirsty! Give souls to Me! Give Me clean churches! Give Me souls that they may experience how good, how wonderful it is to live near My Heart. Let them see how much I love them; how much I long after them, how much I want to be near to them always!"[5]

But Heaven's call to holiness in the 1950's can be best found in the Church itself, for the seeds of Vatican II began during this decade. Indeed, Pope John XXIII declared that the idea for an ecumenical gathering had been inspired by the Holy Spirit. On May 16, 1959, Cardinal Domenico Tardini was appointed the head of the first preparatory commission. While the First Vatican Council (1869-1870) defined the pope's primacy and infallibility, its premature adjournment left significant unfinished business. Vatican II completed what the First Council began. The primary goal for the new council, as outlined by Pope John XXIII (1958-1963), was *"to restore the Sacred in the Church of Peter."*

One of the most significant documents released by the Council was the Dogmatic Constitution on the Church of Vatican II. In this document, an entire chapter is devoted to "The Call of the Whole Church to Holiness." This chapter emphasizes that all Christians are called to holiness. Indeed, the document states that they are called to be saints regardless of vocation.

Likewise, it is important to note that the very first chapter of this document strongly reasserts the supernatural mystery of the Catholic Church.

The Church, Vatican II affirms, is not primarily an institution, but a work of God. The Church is a mystery in the same way that Jesus Christ is a mystery: it is a union of the human and the divine. The Church is also a Sacrament, a visible continuation of its founder in the world, Jesus Christ.

While Vatican II has not always been properly interpreted and implemented, Pope John Paul II has struggled courageously to promote the Council's call to holiness. In his best-selling book, *Crossing the Threshold of Hope*, Pope John Paul II emphasizes Vatican II's call to uphold the mystery of the Divine Trinity, its holy, apostolic Church, and the heart of its Church, the Sacrifice of the Mass. Wrote Pope John Paul II:

The Council explained in great depth the mystery of the Church... At the heart of the Church is Christ and His Sacrifice, a Sacrifice celebrated in a certain sense on the altar of all creation, on the altar of the world. Christ "is... the firstborn of all creation" (Col 1:15); through His Resurrection He is also "the firstborn from the dead" (Col 1:18). Around His redemptive sacrifice is gathered all creation, which is working out its eternal destiny in God. If this process causes pain, it is, however, full of hope, as Saint Paul teaches in the Letter to the Romans (cf. Rom 8:23-24).[6]

CHAPTER TWENTY-SEVEN

ANGELIC COMMUNIONS

According to some apparition experts, the events at Garabandal, Spain beginning on June 18, 1961, constitute one of the most important apparitions of the century.

However, there is great debate surrounding these events, as the Church has repeatedly stated it can not support the supernatural character of the apparitions. A recent bishop's statement upholds this position, although supporters maintain that the Church has also not condemned the apparitions.

The irony of it all has also been noted, for it is the reported extraordinary supernatural element of the apparitions that has been always upheld by its followers.

This opinion is well supported, as both still photography and motion picture photography appear to have captured many of the phenomenal occurrences. Once again, as in the Fatima apparitions, children were the visionaries: Conchita Gonzales (age 12), Jacinta Gonzalez (age 12), Mary Cruz Gonzalez (age 11) and Mari-Loli Mazon (age 12).

These four children reported apparitions of the Blessed Virgin Mary from 1961 through 1965. In substance, the reported apparitions have always been associated with Fatima's messages. Most noteworthy is the fact that they commenced shortly after the Third Part of the Secret of Fatima was expected to be released, but was not. According to some experts, the powerful prophetic element of the Garabandal revelations is viewed as quite apocalyptical; something that was expected to be found in the unreleased Secret.

At Garabandal, the children were observed to fall into incredible "ecstasies," or trance-like states. Often walking while in ecstasy, they moved through the village over different paths, all the while observing the floating Virgin. Remarkably, they would then arrive together at the same spot.

Mr. Stan Karminski, a Garabandal expert, wrote the following account published in the newspaper, *Our Lady Queen of Peace*, Special Edition II:

> *The children describe Our Lady as a beautiful young woman, eighteen years of age. Mary wore a white dress with a blue mantle and a brown Scapular on her right arm. On her head she wore a crown of twelve stars. Her hair was deep brown and parted in the center. Her face was oval shaped with a fine nose. The girls said, "No other woman looks like her or sounds like her."*
>
> *During the apparitions, the girls went into ecstasies that lasted from a few minutes to several hours. They would not always experience the apparition together. Sometimes, Our Lady would appear to only one girl. At other times two or three girls would share the same vision.*
>
> *The apparitions were preceded by three interior calls, which the girls described as joys, each one becoming stronger. After the third call, the girls would come running from different parts of the village and would arrive at the same time in the place designated by Our Lady and they would fall to their knees in ecstasy.*
>
> *During the apparition they were subjected to burns, spotlights in their eyes and stuck with pins without showing any physical response to pain. Reports indicate four adult men had difficulty lifting one twelve year old girl. Yet, the girls could lift each other easily to kiss Our Lady good-bye when the apparitions ended.*
>
> *The apparitions were accompanied by many other phenomena that seemed to defy natural law; such as ecstatic falls and running forward and backward over very rocky terrain. Many religious objects were kissed by Our Lady. The visionaries, while in ecstasy, would return the objects*

to their rightful owners even though they were unknown to them. The seers claimed that Our Lady guided them to the right person.

The reported prophecies of Garabandal foretell that four of the greatest supernatural events in the history of mankind will take place during the lifetime of the visionaries:

1. A WORLDWIDE WARNING: It will come from God and it will be experienced by everyone in the world.
2. A GREAT MIRACLE: God will perform the Greatest Miracle of all time.
3. A PERMANENT SIGN: After the Great Miracle, a Sign, something that has never been seen before upon the earth, will remain forever ("para siempre") in the "Pines" of Garabandal.
4. THE CHASTISEMENT: A punishment that is conditional upon the response of mankind to these messages.

While the alleged supernatural character and prophetic element of the apparitions at Garabandal are noted, its message is interpreted by many experts as being predominantly Eucharistic. This opinion is enhanced by the fact that the visionaries were photographed receiving upon their tongues invisible and then visible communion Hosts from an angel.

Ted and Maureen Flynn, in their book, *The Thunder of Justice,* give us this thorough account of the Eucharistic theme of Garabandal. Wrote the Flynns:

Another remarkable event of Garabandal emphasized the importance of the Eucharist. An angel appeared bearing a golden chalice. The angel asked the children to think of the One whom they were going to receive. He taught them to recite the Confiteor, after which he gave them Holy Communion. He also taught them to say the Anima Christi in thanksgiving. These direct interventions occurred regularly whenever the priest from the neighboring village of Cosio was unable to come to Garabandal.

Many of these "Angelic Communions" were recorded on film, showing the movement of the girls' lips, tongue, and throat. However, since these Hosts were only visible to the girls, many skeptics doubted that they were actually receiving Holy Communion.

When questioned about where the Hosts came from, since only a priest could consecrate, the angel told them that the Hosts were taken from the tabernacles of the church. Therefore, a priest and not an angel had consecrated the Hosts. On June 22, 1962, the angel told Conchita that God would perform a "special miracle." The people would be allowed to see the Sacred Host appear on Conchita's tongue at the moment she received Communion, in order that they might believe. Conchita's diary entry for June 30, 1962, stated: "While I was in the pines I heard a voice which said that the miracle would take place on the eighteenth of July." The angel later instructed her to reveal this message fifteen days in advance. The miracle of the visible Host occurred at 1:40 a.m. on July 19, 1962. Hundreds of witnesses were present. The event was recorded on movie film by Don Alejandro, a businessman from Barcelona. This film was later submitted to the bishop of Santander. Witnesses said that Conchita knelt and put out her tongue to receive the Host. At first, nothing was visible. In a few moments, a white Host, thicker than usual, appeared on her tongue. It remained there for a few moments before being consumed. Conchita refers to this event as the "little miracle." It was chosen to call our attention to the reality of the Real Presence of Our Lord in the Holy Eucharist. [1]

Likewise, Mary's public message at Garabandal was reportedly a specific call to the Blessed Sacrament and the Eucharist. Our Lady is said to have told the girls to announce the following message on October 18, 1961:

Many sacrifices must be made. Much penance must be done. We must pay many visits to the Blessed Sacrament...but first of all we must be very good...If we do

not do this, punishment awaits us...already the cup is fill-
ing, and if we do not change we shall be punished.

On January 1, 1965 the Blessed Virgin reportedly told Conchita
that the Archangel Michael would appear to her on the following
June 18th to deliver a final message in Mary's name for the entire
world. This was because, the children calimed, the Virgin's previous message went unheeded.

On June 18, 1965 Conchita left her home at 11:30 p.m. and
walked to a place called the "Cuadro" (a wooden enclosure). There
she went into ecstasy which lasted about twelve minutes, and was
filmed by cameramen from the Spanish television network "NO
DO" and also Italian television.

At the Cuadro, Saint Michael appeared to Conchita. The archangel reportedly delivered the following message from Mary:

Since my message of October eighteenth has not been com-
plied with and has not been made known to the world, I
will tell you that this is the last one. Before, the chalice
was filling; now it is overflowing. Many Cardinals, many
Bishops and many Priests are on the path of perdition and
they take many souls with them. To the Eucharist, there is
given less and less importance. We should avoid the wrath
of God on us by our good efforts.

If you ask pardon with your sincere soul, He will par-
don you. It is I, your Mother, who through the interces-
sion of Saint Michael, wish to say that you amend, that
you are already in the last warnings and that I love you
much and do not want your condemnation. Ask us sin-
cerely and we will give to you. You should sacrifice more.
Think of the Passion of Jesus.

At Garabandal, Our Lady is said to have appeared wearing
the brown scapular, indicating that the faithful should also wear
the brown scapular. Mary also reportedly taught the children how
to pray the Rosary. But her greatest emphasis, according to
Garabandal supporters, was placed on the Eucharist and prayers
for priests.

At Garabandal the call to the Eucharist was also noted by Mary's specific reference to the feast of a martyred saint which will be, according to the visionaries, the day the Great Miracle will take place. Writes Mr. Karminski:

> Our Lady has promised that a Great Miracle will take place above the grove of the pine trees. It will occur on a Thursday evening at 8:30 p.m. between the eighth and sixteenth of April. The miracle will coincide with an important event in the Church and on the feast day of a martyr of the Eucharist. Everyone in the village and on the surrounding mountains will see it. The sick who are present will be cured. Sinners and nonbelievers will be converted. It will be possible to photograph and televise this event.
>
> Russia will be converted after the Miracle. Conchita, who knows the date of this Miracle, must announce it eight days in advance.
>
> According to Mari-Loli, the Miracle will take place within one year after the Warning. She also said that the Blessed Mother told her, **"A time would come, when it would look like the Church was finished, when priests would have difficulty saying Mass and talking about holy things."** When she asked Our Lady how this would happen, Our Lady called it **"Communism."**

Much has been written herein to bring proper perspective to Mary's reported call at Garabandal. Again, it is a call to holiness, a holiness that can be found in Our Lord's True Presence in the Eucharist.

The late Father Philip Bebie, C.P. took special note of this in his Garabandal booklet titled *The Warning*. Wrote Father Bebie concerning the Eucharist and the Great Miracle foretold at Garabandal:

> We must be ready to receive an unmistakable proof from God, through the Miracle, that the Holy Eucharist is the center of our life in the Church, and that Jesus is truly present to us in the Eucharist, in His living Flesh. We are to avail ourselves of this Sacrament as frequently as we can.[2]

Thus, the reported events and message of Garabandal are well noted. But with the Bishop of Garabandal's most recent statement, it appears that only with the fulfillment of the reported prophecies can Garabandal still be found to be one of the great apparitions and calls to the Eucharist that its devout supporters continue to maintain.

Mother of the Secret

CHAPTER TWENTY-EIGHT

"GOD IS FOOD FOR YOU"

With the implementation of the teachings of Vatican II, a door opened for difficulties that were further influenced by the rapid changes in the world. Almost immediately, individuals took it upon themselves to alter the spirit and teachings of the Council. This resulted in dissension within the Church which has led to confusion and division.

From both the right and the left, various interpretations of the new liturgy developed. Consequently, some of the dangers the Virgin Mary warned of appeared to arise almost overnight.

Around this time, another visionary, whose revelations were approved by her bishop, was born in Kenya, Africa on December 29, 1966. Her name is Sister Anna Ali. Her later revelations from Jesus were direct and to the point: The danger to the Holy Sacrifice of the Mass was growing!

Sister Anna Ali reported apparitions of Jesus, and her revelations focus on the Eucharist. These revelations are described by her as "Divine Appeals." Ted and Maureen Flynn, in their book, *Thunder of Justice*, give us this account:

> In *Divine Appeal Number 35, Our Lord said, **"Pray for the many lost souls and many of My Own consecrated ones. The devil is using them in order to abolish the sacrifice of the Holy Mass"** (November 1, 1987).
>
> In *Divine Appeal Number 46, He said, **"Pray, pray for those who ridicule, abuse, condemn and more than in the**

past, step on Me in order to abolish My Presence in the Sacrament of Love."

In Divine Appeal Number 53, He said, "The devil is giving battle against My Divine Sacrament of Love. I am so abused and blasphemed."

In Divine Appeal Number 54, Our Lord said, "My sacraments are abandoned and despised; My mysteries are blasphemed. Continuously, and more than ever before, the Freemasons attack My Divine Sacrament of Love in the tabernacle."

In Divine Appeal 70, He said, "Time is approaching when My church will be devastated and sacked. My Own ... have become like enraged lions. There are many sacrileges committed against My Presence in the tabernacles. Many have lost their dignity and light of reason. The devil has chained their hearts. Led by him they labour hard to abolish the Holy Sacrifice of the Mass. The chalice is filled."

In Divine Appeal 71, Jesus said, "The Freemasons are abusing Me in the tabernacles and in My very Gospel. The iniquity is repugnant. Unite your heart to My tears of blood. They have all agreed to abolish the Mass... Satan is in the midst of their ranks. I assure you that souls are allied with Satan. My great love for mankind keeps Me day and night in the Blessed Sacrament. How much pain do I receive from their treason and indignity! With many sins, revenge cries out on My Eternal Father's behalf. I desire mankind to be saved."[1]

As in the 1940's and 1950's, Marian sightings continued to be reported in significant numbers. Throughout the decade of the 1960's, numerous apparitions were reported throughout the world. Father Billet reported forty-three in his study, although it appears that his information comes mostly from Europe. With these apparitions, we again find the continued call from Heaven for the Church to protect and defend its sacred mysteries.

In the diocese of Liège in Belgium during the 1960's, a series of profound revelations was given to a wife and mother simply known as Marguerite. The local bishop, while not passing full judgment, issued an imprimatur for these revelations. Likewise, two bishops came forward to issue imprimaturs for the English editions of Marguerite's messages.

The revelations to Marguerite again brought to the forefront the attack taking place on the supernatural character of the Church.

Most significantly, Jesus told Marguerite many things about today's world. The Lord especially revealed how some priests were denying the fundamental dogmas of the Church such as original sin, the fall of humanity, personal sin, the Redemption, the bodily resurrection of Christ, the Immaculate Conception of Mary and her divine maternity.

Jesus explained to Marguerite that for many priests the sacrificial issue of the Mass had become for them simply the commemoration of the Lord's Last Supper. By this scorning of the Eucharist, they were denying the real and permanent Presence of the Savior.

The Lord also told Marguerite how priests were *"engaged in a course incompatible with sane doctrines of the Church."* Our Lord was alluding to the abuses of the Vatican Council teachings, which He said exposed them to *"the world's corruption."*

On October 9, 1968, Jesus gave Marguerite, whose messages are known as the "Messages of Merciful Love to Little Souls," the following revelation concerning the supreme value of the Mass:

> *What, I ask you, do you estimate the price of a single soul to be?*
>
> *Believe Me, had it been necessary, I would have given My life as many times as there are souls on earth.*
>
> *My Sacrifice perpetuates itself through the centuries.*
>
> *My little child, love without measure Him who loves you so tenderly.*
>
> *This love is above everything created, for nothing can satisfy the ardent thirst consuming the Heart of your God.*
>
> *They must come to Him.*
>
> *They refuse to go to Him who calls them.*
>
> *And Love never wearies.*
>
> *But where is Love here below?*

Shut in, hidden, bound by its promise never to leave you orphans.

And Love, being able to live only on love, is hungry.

They do not listen, they no longer hear My Voice.

And the day is coming for many.

And I can do nothing for them.

I, the All-Powerful, I am powerless since, being Love as I am, Love replies only to love.

Children of men, as your God is food for you in the Holy Eucharist, be yourselves the food of mendicant Love.[2]

CHAPTER TWENTY-NINE

AT AKITA: EMPHASIZING THE TRUE PRESENCE

By the 1970's private revelations throughout the world echoed a general alarm of urgency. Whatever Heaven was trying to prevent through its numerous interventions was getting nearer. Indeed, an overall summary of the many messages reveals nothing more than a confirmation of the fulfillment of the secret of La Salette. In summary, the revelations contained the following:

1. A spiritual war was unfolding between good and evil. Sister Lucia, in her famous 1957 interview, stated it would be a "decisive" battle between Heaven and Hell.
2. The Church and the world were falling into a great apostasy. There was a loss of the sense of the sacred and a crisis of faith.
3. The sins of the world were mounting, pushing the world into a danger never before realized.
4. Heaven was about to release a great purification which would culminate with a new era of peace as foretold at Fatima.

Behind all this prophetic revelation was Heaven's implicit message. The only way mankind could save itself was to return to God. Revelation after revelation repeated that the world would not find peace until it turned to Jesus Christ. This return did not just mean recognition of Him; rather the messages repeatedly asked for action. This action in faith could be most demonstrated by the faithful's participation in the Sacraments. For it was through participation in the Sacraments that they could best demonstrate their faith and belief in Christ's True Presence. Through this action believers were, in essence, abandoning themselves to Christ, allowing Him to live in them and they in Him.

It was, indeed, a great call to holiness. Pope Pius XII clearly asked for this same call during World War II in his encyclical letter, *Mystici Corporis (The Mystical Body of Christ).*

Wrote Pope Pius XII:

> *As then in the sad and anxious times through which we are passing there are many who cling so firmly to Christ the Lord hidden beneath the Eucharist veils that neither tribulation, nor distress, nor famine, nor nakedness, nor danger, nor persecution, nor the sword can separate them from His love, surely no doubt can remain that Holy Communion which once again in God's providence is much more frequented even from early childhood, may become a source of that fortitude which not infrequently makes Christians into heroes.*

Likewise, Pius XII's memorable encyclical did not fail to invoke the Mother of God as being the source of the hope the world so badly needed. In essence, the Pope's words reflected the reason why Heaven would send Mary on such a great mission during our times.

Wrote Pope Pius XII, almost in confirmation of Mary's promises of Fatima:

> *May she, then, the most holy Mother of all the members of Christ, to whose Immaculate Heart we have trustfully consecrated all mankind, and who now reigns in Heaven with her Son, her body and soul refulgent with heavenly glory—may she never cease to beg from Him that copious streams of grace may flow from its exalted Head into all the members of the Mystical Body. May she throw about the Church today, as in times gone by, the mantle of her protection and obtain from God that now at least the Church and all mankind may enjoy more peaceful days.*

During the 1970's, Heaven also continued to send great signs. In a small hamlet named Stich in Germany, two Eucharistic miracles were reported within thirty days of each other.

The first miracle occurred on June 9, 1970, when a priest noticed a red spot on the corporal after the consecration. The spot quickly grew in size to that of a coin. At the elevation of the chalice, a second red spot was noticed. No leak of the chalice was detected. Laboratory tests revealed the spots to be "human blood" of a person "in agony."

On July 14, 1970 the same priest again reported red spots on the corporal after the consecration. After Mass, the entire congregation came forward to witness the miracle. Again, laboratory analysis determined that they were spots of blood. After studying the results of the tests and interviewing the witnesses, the matter was referred to Rome.

By 1973, the Virgin Mary's work in the world was not only more visible but more difficult. For the world had exponentially grown in its affinity for evil.

In America, abortion became legal and would soon be promulgated throughout the world as a form of family planning. This crime, the Virgin repeated in many of her messages, was directly related to a potential fiery chastisement. Our Lady explained that God would permit this holocaust from the hands of men for their sins, especially for mankind's attack on life.

Also, by 1973 Communism continued to spread atheism throughout the world. In response, western nations set about to wage an arms race with the USSR. It was a race no one could win.

Thus, it is not terribly difficult to realize why God chose to send the Virgin Mary to Akita, Japan, in 1973, as Japan was the only nation that directly experienced a nuclear attack. This frightening reality the rest of the world could not completely share because only Japan had experienced it. But it was a reality that certainly could bring the fulfillment of Mary's many warnings of a fiery purification from the "sky."

The extraordinary events at Akita, Japan began on June 12, 1973, when a nun, Sister Agnes Sasagawa who took her vows at Nagasaki, reported witnessing a brilliant mysterious light emanate suddenly from the tabernacle in her convent chapel. This same mystery happened on each of the two following days.

On June 28, 1973, a cross-shaped wound appeared on the inside of the left hand of Sister Agnes. It bled profusely and caused her much pain. On July 6, 1973 Sister Agnes heard a voice coming from the statue of the Blessed Virgin Mary in the chapel where she prayed. The statue was carved from a single block of katsura tree wood and is three feet tall. The voice delivered a message to her.

On the same day, a few of the sisters in her convent noticed drops of blood flowing from the wooden statue's right hand. On four occasions, the blood flow repeated itself. The wound in the statue's hand remained until September 29, 1973 when it disappeared. Also on this same day, the sisters noticed that the statue began to "sweat," especially on its forehead and neck. On August 3, 1973, Sister Agnes received a second message and on October 13, 1973 a third and final message.

Two years later on January 4, 1975, the statue began to weep. It continued to weep at intervals for the next six years and eight months; it wept a total of 101 times.

On April 22, 1984, Bishop John Shojiro Ito officially recognized the occurrence of the supernatural phenomena and the Madonna's messages given at Akita. Since then there has been a steady influx of pilgrims from throughout the world. Cardinal Ratzinger received the Bishop's decision and judged the phenomena as credible.

Most significantly, there has always been great interest surrounding Mary's final message to Sister Agnes Sasagawa, given on October 13, 1973:

> *As I told you, if men do not repent and better themselves, the Father will inflict a terrible punishment on all humanity. It will be a punishment greater than the deluge, such as one will never have seen before. Fire will fall from the sky and will wipe out a great part of humanity, the good as well as the bad, sparing neither priests nor faithful. The survivors will find themselves so desolate that they will envy the dead. The only arms which will remain for you will be the Rosary and the Sign left by My Son. Each*

day recite the prayers of the Rosary. With the Rosary, pray for the Pope, the bishops and the priests.

The work of the devil will infiltrate even into the Church in such a way that one will see cardinals opposing cardinals, bishops against bishops. The priests who venerate me will be scorned and opposed by their confreres...churches and altars sacked; the Church will be full of those who accept compromises and the demon will press many souls to leave the service of the Lord.

The demon will be especially implacable against souls consecrated to God. The thought of the loss of so many souls is the cause of my sadness. If sins increase in number and gravity, there will be no longer pardon for them.

With courage, speak to your superior. He will know how to encourage each one of you to pray and to accomplish works of reparation.[1]

Like the messages of Fatima, the apocalyptic aspects of the message of Akita are at the forefront. But again, theological experts emphasize that Akita's primary message concerns the Eucharist and Christ's True Presence in the Church.

Indeed, according to Bishop John Ito, it is a message identical to the message of Fatima: a call to holiness in order to save the world. And although a great apostasy is at hand, the little flock's response to Heaven's invitations will be enough to defeat Satan and bring God's victory into the world.

Most amazingly, even before the apparitions of the Virgin Mary began, an angel taught Sister Agnes the same prayer that the children at Fatima learned. Writes John Haffert in his book, *The Meaning of Akita*:

> *It is interesting to note the first message communicated to Sister Agnes (who is to Akita what Sister Lucia is to Fatima) was given to her by her guardian angel in 1969, long before the appearance of Our Lady in Akita, and it was a prayer taught by Our Lady at Fatima.*
>
> *Sister Agnes was in the hospital in Myoko saying her Rosary when the angel appeared and told her to pray at*

the end of each decade: "O MY JESUS, FORGIVE US OUR SINS; SAVE US FROM THE FIRES OF HELL; LEAD ALL SOULS TO HEAVEN, ESPECIALLY THOSE MOST IN NEED."

A priest who later heard Agnes saying this prayer asked where she had learned it. He recognized it as the prayer taught at Fatima and was amazed that Agnes knew it because it had not yet been published in Japan.[2]

This was only one of the many mysteries that make up the message of Akita. But some believe that this message is perhaps the most profound of Mary's revelations concerning the Eucharist.

CHAPTER THIRTY

THE IMPORTANCE OF AKITA'S MESSAGE

Some writers say the meaning behind the mystical phenomena at Akita is very important. Why? Because it continues to point to the significance of the True Presence of Jesus Christ in the world and in the Eucharist.

Indeed, it is a significance that again reveals why Mary's apparitions are primarily in defense of the True Presence of Her Son in our world. This conclusion is drawn by those who have closely reviewed the events at Akita.

Francis Mutsuo Fukushima, who studied the Akita apparitions extensively, wrote in his book, *Akita! Mother of God as Co-Redemptrix — Modern Miracles of the Eucharist* :

> *The most serious crisis of faith resulted from the decline in the faithful's ability to recognize the Real Presence of Jesus in the Holy Eucharist. As the loss of reverence for the Holy Eucharist took place, it started preventing the inflow of divine graces into the souls of Roman Catholics. In Akita, God and the Holy Mother planned to revive the people's faith in the Real Presence by imparting the Divine lessons about the importance of receiving the Holy Eucharist on the tongue.*[1]

Likewise, on the occasion of the seventy-fifth anniversary of the apparitions at Fatima, dozens of bishops, priests and lay persons gathered at Akita for the Akita International Marian Convention. In conclusion, they declared that the message of Fatima was repeated and completed at Akita.

Supported by the Catholic Bishops Conference of Japan, the Akita Convention's primary aim was to unite Marian bishops, priests, and organizations in formulating a practical and effective means of spreading the Communion of Reparation throughout the world.

In its published report, the Akita International Marian Convention stated:

> *Both messages at Akita and in Fatima give men a warning. They speak of the world heading toward its own destruction and of the coming chastisement that could wipe out humanity if men would not repent and amend their lives. The solution to the annihilation was however specified: CONVERSION...*
>
> *In analyzing the messages of Our Lady of Fatima and Akita, one cannot but marvel at the similarity of the two in many aspects. The messages might have been given in different words but the meaning is essentially the same—both reveal the same solution. Mother Mary's formula for peace...*
>
> *Indeed, the similarities of the revelations cannot be denied. Our Lady of Akita has come to renew the messages she gave at Fatima, but this time, she comes with tears of blood to show the greater urgency of the times.*[2]

Most significantly, the Akita convention concluded that according to the Virgin's messages throughout the world, including Fatima and Akita, *"the Triumph of the Immaculate Heart will occur when everyone recognizes the Real Presence of Jesus in the Eucharist."*

But the question of time hangs over Akita like a storm cloud. For the nuclear element is ever-present in the interpretation of Akita's message. It is an element that invokes fear, yet must be confronted, as the Virgin Mary has always said the world has been given a time of grace, yet that time is running out.

Like Fatima's messages, Akita's message raises for us the entire question of what Mary means when she warns of fire falling from the sky causing *"a greater part of humanity to be annihilated."*

John Haffert in his book, *The Meaning of Akita*, brings to the forefront this haunting question. Again, he insists that the solution will be found in the small number of souls who will turn to Jesus in His True Presence, thus fulfilling Mary's request for the Communion of Reparation. Writes Haffert:

> *In addition, even after World War II, Our Lady of Fatima foretold "further wars" resulting from the error spread from Russia "throughout the entire world ... the good will be persecuted ... the Holy Father will suffer much ... and SEVERAL ENTIRE NATIONS WILL BE ANNIHILATED."*
>
> *How could nations be annihilated? Was there to be another deluge? No, because God said this would not happen. (The atom bomb did not yet exist.)*
>
> *We can imagine with what difficulty the first Bishop of Fatima (after repeated consultation with the Holy See) finally issued the pastoral letter of approval.*
>
> *At Akita Our Lady said: "**The Heavenly Father is ready to inflict a great chastisement on the whole of mankind. If mankind does not repent and amend their lives, the Heavenly Father will send a supreme chastisement ... worse than the deluge. Fire will plunge from the sky ... a great part of humanity will be annihilated. The good will die with the bad. Those who survive will suffer so much that they will envy the dead.**"*
>
> *Next Our Lady spoke of the crisis in the Church and said: "**The loss of so many souls is the cause of my sorrow. If people continue to sin, even the remission of sins will finally vanish.**"*
>
> *And we may ask: How can such a message be reconciled with God's Mercy? How can forgiveness of sin ever "vanish"? And if God's justice requires this punishment, why does Our Lady seek to save us from it? And if Our Lady is speaking of atomic war, is the latter likely now that mankind seems to be facing up to the realization that such a war would indeed destroy much of life on earth. Is it not practically hopeless, since even after all the prophecies made by Our Lady at Fatima came true the world not only did not listen but seems worse than ever?*

> *Our Lady said at Akita that already she has been able to hold back the hand of Divine justice through the cooperation of small groups of souls ... and she is now seeking others who will cooperate with Her to turn back the tide of evil in the world before it is too late.*
>
> *She herself is gathering generous souls together ... like the little community in Akita through whom she has made known this message of warning and of hope! She seeks reparation through these few ... having so far been able to forestall the chastisement and at the same time, certainly, to save many souls.*
>
> *If we do not see much hope in convincing a godless world, we DO see hope in persuading some of the millions who have already responded to the message of Fatima to respond a little further...to give Our Lady the small groups she seeks ...*

Throughout the world, Mary's intercessions during the decade of the 1970's continued to reveal how Heaven was preparing the times.

Three different popes were to reign; the last, Pope John Paul II, was to become a force of unparalleled presence. With his attempted assassination on May 13, 1981, the anniversary date of Fatima, his role in the unfolding of our times continued to be revealed in an even more direct yet mystical fashion. His every action after this, the Pope would come to say, was keenly focused on the approaching fulfillment of the remaining prophecies of Fatima.

Indeed, in his book, *Crossing the Threshold of Hope*, the Holy Father acknowledges his understanding of the times. And the Pope unhesitatingly admits that this understanding is based on his deep attraction to mysticism.

Wrote Pope John Paul II:

> *Mary appeared to the three children at Fatima in Portugal and spoke to them the words that now, at the end of this century, seem to be close to their fulfillment.*

Not surprisingly, the Virgin Mary has repeatedly revealed to Father Stefano Gobbi of the Marian Movement of Priests and numerous other visionaries, that Pope John Paul II is her hand-chosen vicar. He is a man, Mary says, personally shaped and molded by her for the task at hand.

To this day, even the media admire the heroic determination of Pope John Paul II's efforts. The Pope led the fight against Communism and now leads the fight against the secular humanizing of the world. This temporal path which the world has chosen has produced a *"culture of death,"* according to the Holy Father.

In the great struggle of our times, Pope John Paul II has forwarded his "Gospel of Life" through his encyclicals *Veritatis Splendor (The Splendor of Truth)* and *Evangelium Vitae (The Gospel of Life)*, to directly confront and defeat the *"culture of death."*

In his writings, the Pope asserts that the goal of the humanists is to destroy all Christian thought. It is a plan that began centuries ago as Mary's revelations confirm and he understands. Pope John Paul II writes further:

> *Who is responsible for this? Man is responsible—man, ideologies, and philosophical systems. I would say that responsibility lies with the struggle against God, the systematic elimination of all that is Christian. This struggle has to a large degree dominated thought and life in the West for three centuries. Marxist collectivism is nothing more than a "cheap version" of this plan. Today a similar plan is revealing itself in all its danger and, at the same time, in all its faultiness. (Crossing the Threshold of Hope)*

The ultimate objective of this plan is clear. It is the age-old attempt of evil to rule the world. But from a totally spiritual view, it must be recognized that it is Satan behind the human forces of evil and their dangerous ideologies and philosophical systems, for it was Satan who chose to hate God and his laws long before men did.

Thus, it is not difficult to understand that Satan, through men, seeks to destroy everything Christian, especially the Holy Sacrifice of the Mass. For he knows that God's True Presence in the world cannot exist without the celebration of the Mass.

From Medjugorje to Knock, from Fatima to Czestochowa, the Holy Father has been keenly aware of Mary's many intercessions, often visiting her shrines. Likewise, he has not hesitated to encourage the faithful to seek her out.

During the decade of the 1970's, the Virgin Mary was again seen throughout the world in numerous places. In 1970, reports came from such places as Milan, Italy; Ladeira Do Pinheiro, Portugal; Lima, Peru; Belgium; Maropati, Italy and dozens of other locations. Again, through revelations and miracles, Mary continued to point to her Son's True Presence.

In Lima, there were reports of bleeding hosts. At Maropati, the visionary reported apparitions of the Madonna of Pompeii. Mary came, said Mrs. Cordiano, the visionary, with a bleeding heart.

In Rome, Jesus and Mary came to Mother Elena Patriarca Leonardi, who received the stigmata and whose revelations echoed again the messages of Fatima and Akita. Our Lady told Mother Elena:

> *I, Mother of Sorrow, appeal to your families, to your consciences, to the whole of humanity. Pray, do penance, receive Holy Communion, participate in Holy Masses and say the Rosary* (March 6, 1977).

Again repeating her prophetic warnings at Akita, Mary told the nun:

> *The churches will be devastated and sacked, and the Sacred Hosts will be underfoot.*
> *Satan stalks among the bishops, the prelates, lay people and cardinals.*

Indeed, like the Holy Father, Mary continued to warn of what was unfolding. And she continued to tell us what we must do to help God bring His victory into the world - as can be found in Her words to visionary Mama Rosa Quattrini of San Damiano, Italy on May 22, 1970,

> *Visit the Eucharistic Jesus often, make a spiritual communion. Even when you wake up during the night, unite yourself to Eucharistic Jesus and you will console Him for the grave sacrileges being committed.*

CHAPTER THIRTY-ONE

THE EUCHARISTIC REIGN OF JESUS

To some it may appear coincidental, but for others it is obviously intentional. Within a period of less than thirty days, the Virgin Mary initiated two of the most significant heavenly interventions in order to fulfill the times.

Just twenty-six days after the events began at Akita, (which were fully approved by the Church on April 22, 1984), the Mother of God officially commenced her powerful work with Father Stefano Gobbi of Italy. Although Father Gobbi's first inspirations were received at Fatima on May 8,1972, Mary declared to him on July 8, 1973, that the Marian Movement of Priests *"is now born."*

Together with the events at Akita, this intervention can be seen as the second part of Heaven's desire for the message of Fatima to be totally fulfilled.

At Fatima in 1917, Mary warned of an approaching apostasy. Through Mary's revelations to Father Gobbi, it became clearer that this apostasy was directly related to the faithfulness of God's chosen sons, His priests. If Satan's plan to destroy belief in the True Presence was to have any chance at all, his activity had to be intensely directed at the priesthood.

It was a simple concept. As Mary and Jesus related to Sister Ali and Marguerite, if priests didn't believe in the True Presence, then certainly their flocks would not be strong in their faith and convictions. Likewise, the visionaries revealed that Satan ultimately hoped that the Sacrifice of the Mass and belief in the doctrine of transubstantiation could be toppled this way.

Up to this time, most of the Virgin Mary's actions and words were designed to indirectly shine light on the importance of the Eucharist and Christ's True Presence in His Church. But with the revelations given to Father Gobbi, Mary not only continued to shine this light, but also began to explain in great detail exactly what the forces of evil were hoping to achieve. She also revealed to Father Gobbi exactly how Heaven wanted the Church to combat this insidious attack. Most significantly, she began to explain to Father Gobbi the mysteries of the Book of Revelation.

In 1973, Mary presented to Father Gobbi the heroic task of humbly submitting himself to her, so that through him she could form an army of priests molded in her Son's image and in her humility and obedience. By the 1990's, tens of thousands of priests were said to be members of this movement, along with millions of the laity worldwide. It was a stunning intervention by Heaven's Queen. Most of all, some of the most prolific and profound private revelations ever disclosed were given in the reported "interior locutions" which Father Gobbi received and spread as Mary asked.

His book, *To the Priests, Our Lady's Beloved Sons*, reveals a blueprint of God's plan for the fulfillment of the times, as many prophecies previously disclosed in divine and private revelations are confirmed in the hundreds of messages given by Our Lady to Father Gobbi.

The profound nature of these revelations is extensive. For Mary's words reveal not only the crucial significance of this period in history, but also its relationship to the new era, an era on earth that will come to center around the Eucharist. Indeed, the new times have often been described by Our Lady to Father Gobbi as the "Eucharistic Reign of Christ."

What exactly will the Eucharistic Reign of Christ in the world be like? Many visionaries have reported messages from Jesus and Mary that declare and explain what this era will hold. While these revelations can be used like pieces of a puzzle to assemble a greater picture, the revelations received by Father Stefano Gobbi from the Virgin Mary truly are some of the most compelling. These messages confidently depict how the world will come to embrace the mystery of Christ's True Presence in the Eucharist and how this practice will transform all of mankind and our planet.

Here are several of the messages given to Father Gobbi which announce the coming Eucharistic Reign of Christ. (The messages have received an Imprimatur from Cardinal Ruiz of Ecuador.)

But as Jesus is truly in Heaven, so also is He truly present on earth in the Eucharist: with His body, His blood, His soul and His divinity.

His glorious reign will shine forth above all in the Triumph of His Eucharistic Person, because the Eucharist will once again be the heart and center of the whole life of the Church.

Jesus in the Eucharist will become the summit of all your prayer, which should be a prayer of adoration, or thanksgiving, of praise and of propitiation.

Jesus in the Eucharist will once again be the center of all liturgical action, which will unfold itself as a hymn to the most Holy Trinity, through the continual priestly action of Christ which will be carried out in the Eucharistic mystery.

Jesus in the Eucharist will once again be the center of your ecclesial gatherings, because the Church is His temple, His house which has been built above all so that His divine presence may shine forth in your midst. (June 14, 1979)[1]

Because in the Eucharist Jesus Christ is really present, He remains ever with you, and this presence of His will become increasingly stronger, will shine over the earth like a sun and will mark the beginning of a New Era. The coming of the glorious reign of Christ will coincide with the greatest splendor of the Eucharist. Christ will restore His glorious reign in the universal triumph of His Eucharistic reign, which will unfold in all its power and will have the capacity to change hearts, souls, individuals, families, society and the very structure of the world.

When He will have restored His Eucharistic reign, Jesus will lead you to take joy in this habitual presence of His, which you will feel in a new and extraordinary way and which will lead you to the experience of a second, renewed and more beautiful earthly paradise. (August 21, 1987)[2]

Expose once again the Eucharistic Jesus on the altar for hours of solemn and public adoration and reparation, because the rise of the New Era will lead to a general reflowering of the Eucharistic cult in all the Church.

In fact, the coming of the glorious reign of Christ will coincide with the greatest splendor of His Eucharistic reign among you. The Eucharistic Jesus will release all His power of love, which will transform souls, the Church and all humanity.

Thus, the Eucharist becomes a sign of Jesus who, still today, loves you to the end, because He is leading you to the end of these times of yours, to introduce you into the New Era of Holiness and of grace, toward which you are all journeying, and which will begin at the moment when Jesus will have restored His glorious reign in your midst. (April 12, 1990)[3]

Not by bread alone does man live.

Man lives also by the Living Bread come down from Heaven, to nourish the hunger of his heart. How many there are today who live under the terrible slavery of pride, of unbridled egoism, of avarice, of hatred, of violence, of a great incapacity to love! The way which leads to salvation is solely that of communion and of love. For this reason Jesus has made you the inestimable gift of the Most Holy Eucharist.

Jesus becomes present in the Eucharist to be the food of your spiritual life and to form you to a true capacity for love.

Jesus gives Himself to you in the Eucharist to love in you, with you and by means of you.

The Eucharistic Jesus is the Living Bread come down from heaven, the food to eat that one may hunger no longer, the water to drink that one may thirst no longer.

The Eucharistic Jesus wants to become today the Good Samaritan for your Church, so divided and suffering, and for your fatherland, so ill and threatened.

The Eucharistic Jesus wants to lead all of you along the road of love, of reconciliation, of communion, of peace, of mercy and of salvation. Learn of Him who is meek and humble of heart and you will find rest for your souls.

This year, Brazil is celebrating its National Eucharistic Congress. May your Church and your fatherland prostrate themselves in an act of profound adoration directed to the Eucharistic Jesus.

Today I ask all to throw open the doors to Jesus Christ who is coming. I am the Mother of the Second Advent and the door which is being opened on the new era. This new era will coincide with the greatest triumph of the Eucharistic Reign of Jesus.

For this, I invite you, in this extraordinary year, to make flourish everywhere the cult of adoration, of reparation and of love for the Most Holy Eucharist. In your churches, return to the exposition of the Most Holy Sacrament, through solemn hours of public adoration. Let the Eucharist become the center of your prayer, of your life, of your cult and of your ecclesial gatherings.

Thus, again today, the Eucharistic Jesus, with His word, will nourish the hunger of minds; with His grace, will nourish the hunger of souls; with His love, will nourish the hunger of your hearts.

And it will be the Eucharistic Jesus who will finally give you the great gift of the true liberation from every form of physical, spiritual and moral slavery. And thus, in all of you there will shine forth the great dignity of sons of God, created by Him, loved, redeemed, sanctified and saved.

Go forth now, from your cenacle, and become the apostles of this new evangelization in all of Brazil. I accompany you with my immaculate love and I sustain you with my motherly blessing. (February 26, 1991)[4]

The glorious reign of Christ will coincide with the triumph of the Eucharistic Reign of Jesus, because in a purified and sanctified world, completely renewed by love, Jesus will be made manifest above all in the mystery of His Eucharistic presence.

The Eucharist will be the source from which will burst forth all His divine power, and it will become the new sun, which will shed its bright rays in hearts and souls, and then in the life of individuals, families, and nations, making of all one single flock, docile and meek, whose sole Shepherd will be Jesus.

Your heavenly Mother is leading you on toward these new heavens and this new earth, a Mother who is gathering you today from every part of the world to prepare you to receive the Lord who is coming. (November 21, 1993)[5]

[Note: All of the excerpts from the book, *To the Priests, Our Lady's Beloved Sons*, are used with permission.]

CHAPTER THIRTY-TWO

THE HIGHEST FORM
OF PRAYER

In recollection of the 1980's, one word may someday be immediately uttered by the faithful: Medjugorje!

From the beginning of her apparitions at Medjugorje on June 24, 1981, Mary's messages there have repeatedly pointed to her Son's True Presence in the Holy Sacrifice of the Mass.

Indeed, Mary's messages at Medjugorje have urged the faithful to attend Mass in order to receive the graces God wants to give His children, especially in the Eucharist.

At Medjugorje, the Virgin Mary said that the Holy Mass *"is the highest form of prayer"* and should be *"the center of our lives."*

In 1985, Our Lady told the visionaries at Medjugorje, *"You do not celebrate the Eucharist as you should. If you would know the grace and what gifts you receive, you would prepare yourselves for it each day for an hour at least."*

This was a message that the Virgin had emphasized in 1983 at Medjugorje, when she stated, *"Mass is the greatest prayer of God. You will never be able to understand its greatness. That is why you must be perfect and humble at Mass, and you should prepare yourselves for it."*

At Medjugorje Mary also declared that there are five weapons which a soul can use for its spiritual welfare: Prayer, the Bible, Confession, Fasting and the Eucharist.

In author Janice T. Connell's book, *Visions of the Children*, visionary Vicka Ivankovic tells us what the Virgin explained to her about Our Lord's True Presence in the Eucharist:

The Blessed Mother says that during each Mass, Jesus comes in person, in tangible form. We can take Jesus, in physical form, into our body. In this way, we can truly understand what it means to have Jesus in our hearts. This is our way to accept Jesus into our heart. Jesus comes alive to us through the Eucharist. It is up to us. Do we accept Him or do we reject Him?[1]

Like Vicka Ivankovic, all of the Medjugorje visionaries emphasize the Virgin's focus on the Mass and the Eucharist. In fact, the late Father Joseph A. Pelletier, A.A., a noted theologian, writes in his book, *The Queen of Peace Visits Medjugorje*, that the central theme of the Medjugorje apparitions is primarily Eucharistic. Writes Father Pelletier:

As more and more information has come forth, it has become increasingly clear that the Eucharist holds center stage in Medjugorje and that from the very start Our Lady spoke to the six seers about the Eucharist and its importance with more frequency than was suspected. This helps to understand why the parish staff has placed so much emphasis on the Mass and public adoration of the Blessed Sacrament in the church services that have been made available to parishioners and pilgrims.

*It is also a fact that Our Lady herself has brought the Eucharist into her messages and requests in a new and more insistent way as time has gone on. She has done this through the new seers, Jelena and Marijana: through the personal messages she gave them and through the messages intended for the parish. One should recall Jelena's statements to the effect that Our Lady never spoke to her about the rosary but spoke to her about the Mass, saying that it is **"the best"** and that the people should **"go to Mass more and more and to Communion."** Moreover Our Lady recommended that the members of the meditation prayer group go to Mass **"frequently, every day if possible."***

One of the strong signs pointing to the authenticity of the Medjugorje message is its emphasis on the Sacraments of the Church, particularly Reconciliation and the Eucharist.[2]

Father René Laurentin in his book, *Is the Virgin Mary Appearing at Medjugorje?*, concurs with Father Pelletier about Medjugorje and the Eucharist. Writes Father Laurentin:

> *Our Lady of Medjugorje leads to Christ. When she was asked which prayer is the best, she answered:* ***"It is the Mass, and you will never be able to exhaust its greatness. That is why you should be there humbly and prepared."*** *At Medjugorje the Virgin leads to the Eucharist. The Rosary and the apparition flow into the Mass. Mary has sometimes appeared showing Christ, in His childhood (the first apparition and Christmas 1983) or in His passion. In showing us Christ, she continues to say, "Do whatever he tells you." (Jn 2:5)[3]*

But probably the best source of Mary's continual pointing to her Son's Eucharistic Presence is found in the messages themselves. Here are several of the most explicit:

March 15, 1984

This evening, dear children, in a special way I am grateful to you for being here. Adore continually the most blessed Sacrament. I am always present when the faithful are in adoration. Special graces are then being received.

August 8, 1981

Do Penance! Strengthen your faith through prayer and the sacraments.

September 25, 1995

Dear Children!
Today I invite you to fall in love with the Most Holy Sacrament of the Altar. Adore Him, little children, in your parishes and in this way you will be united with the entire world. Jesus will become your friend and you will not talk of Him like someone whom you barely know. Unity with

Him will be a joy for you, and you will become witnesses to the love of Jesus that He has for every creature. Little children, when you adore Jesus you are also close to me.

The Virgin Mary's call at Medjugorje to holiness is especially found in the writings of the Franciscan priests who were stationed there at the outset of the apparitions.

In their words and through their thoughts, we find the deep meaning of Mary's call at Medjugorje. It is a call to Jesus, they tell us, a call to His True Presence in His Church. In a 1987 interview published in the book, *A Man Named Father Jozo*, Fr. Jozo said:

The Holy Mass is the root of our religion, our power, our grace. Through Holy Mass bread and wine are being transformed into God's body and blood, by means of the power of the Spirit, God's Word, and the prayer of the Church. The Church is being transformed. It becomes exactly what God wants, the bread that Jesus sent us saying: "Take it and eat it." The Church which lives the Eucharist becomes food, light and peace for everyone. Therefore, at the end of the Holy Mass, the priest says: Go now the Holy Mass is over. Go. You are filled with peace because you have received peace. Be bread, the food of peace. Be love because you are the food of love. Since you have enjoyed love, be the bread of love. Go and share it through your life.

We do not know how to live the Holy Mass. We are used to "listening" to the Holy Mass. Our Lady does not want that. We have learned to "recite" the prayers, but this is not what Our Lady asks for.

Pray with your heart and live the Holy Mass. Listen to God's Word, which is life-giving. Jesus' heart is present in the Bible, which is God's Word. You have to feel God's power and surrender your heart to be able to feel all that love.

According to my experience, Medjugorje is the place where that happens. And you have asked about my experience. Medjugorje gives that to God's children, to His Church. It renews that feeling and brings the grace to put it in our heart.[4]

Likewise, Father Slavko Barbaric, O.F.M., in his commentary on the Virgin's message of April 25, 1988, emphasized Mary's call to holiness at Medjugorje. Said Father Barbaric:

> *Do you pray every day for the grace of holiness? If not, it could be because we do not understand that holiness is a grace, a gift of God Himself. We have to pray for this grace; and we must, because our holiness is good for others and for ourselves. For to be holy means to grow in love, in peace and in joy. To be holy is to be a good Christian. Our Lady says let Holy Mass be your life. There are two parts to the Mass. In the first part, Christ gives Himself to His Church; He surrenders Himself to us completely, to give us life and love. He wants to be our strength and life. In the second part, He sends us out to go and love people and surrender to them in love. The Eucharist means TO GIVE MYSELF TO GOD AND TO OTHERS IN LOVE.*

At Lourdes, Fatima and other noted Marian shrines, one final and conclusive testimony to Mary's call to the Eucharist is the number of communion hosts that are distributed to the faithful.

At Medjugorje, tens of thousands of communions are given each month at St. James Church. Thus, this is probably the most compelling sign of the truth in Our Lady's words to her children when she says, *"Unity with Jesus will be a joy for you."*

Mother of the Secret

CHAPTER THIRTY-THREE

RESTORE THE SACRED

After the apparitions at Medjugorje began in 1981, Heaven initiated an interesting course. The times of the "big" apparitions began winding down. With Medjugorje, and seemingly because of Medjugorje, dozens and dozens—perhaps hundreds—of smaller apparitions and other supernatural phenomena were reported throughout the world.

An apparent outbreak of local apparitions, visions, weeping statues and voices was being reported. In addition, tens of thousands of the laity reported mystical events happening in their lives, such as their rosaries turning gold or witnessing of the sun spinning and emitting colors. Many claimed dreams and God-created "coincidences" as undeniable signs to them of God's presence in their lives.

Thus, a new period of intense supernatural intervention was emerging. In the little country of Ireland alone, over thirty apparitions were reported, while in the Ukraine, over one-half million people were said to have observed the Virgin Mary floating above a chapel in Hrushiv and in several other small villages.

God was alive, alive in our world and He was not going to let the secular press, or the religious press for that matter, deny Him. It was, again, another sign of the times. As the secular world increased its denial of Christ's True Presence as a Living God among His people, God moved to prove the world wrong, by literally blanketing it with mystical interventions.

No one can deny what he sees and hears. Scripture confirms that Christ was accepted because the people could see what He had done. *"The man stood up and picked up his mat and went outside in the SIGHT of everyone. They were awe-struck; all gave praise to God, saying, 'We have never SEEN anything like this'"* (Mk 2:12).

Indeed, as in the times of Christ, it appears that Heaven knows what makes people respond and believe. Once people see the power of God for themselves, they immediately begin to tell others; and once others hear, they, too, want to come and see. *"Jesus withdrew toward the lake with his disciples. A great crowd followed him from Galilee, and an equally great multitude came to him from Judea, Jerusalem, Idumea, Transjordan, and the neighborhood of Tyre and Sidon, because they had HEARD what he had done"* (Mk 3:7-8).

Since 1981, what has occurred at Medjugorje is seen in this same spirit of truth. Despite the local bishop's opposition, over 25 million people traveled to Medjugorje. Hundreds of thousands even came during the worst war that Europe has endured since World War II.

It has been the same around the world at countless other miraculous sites on all continents. Millions have traveled to an untold number of sites of reported miraculous apparitions, weeping statues and icons and a multitude of other supernatural phenomena. The response by the faithful has been unprecedented.

But on March 13, 1990 the Virgin Mary confirmed to Father Gobbi that the time for the fulfillment of some of the more serious prophecies found in Scripture, which are also found in her words at Fatima, was near. Despite the outpouring of heavenly graces, the world had not abandoned its course of ruin. Mary told Fr. Gobbi:

> *At Fatima, I foretold to you that a time would come when the true faith would be lost. These are the times. Your days are marked by this painful and significant situation, which was foretold to you in Holy Scripture: the true faith is in the process of disappearing in an ever increasing grave number of my children.[1]*

The convocation of Vatican II came as a surprise to almost all of the Catholic Church. But, considering the pastoral background of the Council, it was not surprising that the first of its many documents was the Constitution on the Sacred Liturgy. The Council asserted: *"The liturgy is the summit toward which the activity of the Church is directed; it is also the fount through which all her power flows."* (SC, n. 10)

But if Vatican II strongly endorsed the liturgy, then why have there been so many problems? In truth, it is no secret that right from the start, the spirit of Vatican II was greatly abused and altered from its original intent. Especially with regard to the Sacraments and the liturgy, the Church has witnessed a deliberate undercurrent designed to de-emphasize the sacred and mysterious beliefs it proclaims.

This continued loss of the sacred and holy has certainly not escaped Heaven's eyes, but by the 1990's both the secular and religious press were wondering aloud. On November 28, 1994, *Newsweek*'s cover story and photo confronted the issue: *"THE SEARCH FOR THE SACRED"* was *Newsweek*'s bold headline spread across the cover page. The article emphasized how the world had lost its connection with sacred beliefs.

Not long after, the cover story of the Catholic Italian magazine, *Inside the Vatican* (August/September 1995) read: *"RESTORE THE SACRED."* Again, the conservative publication noted the loss of the mystery of God. Its cover showed a photograph of Pope John Paul II consecrating a host to emphasize the essence of this dilemma.

Nonetheless, in spite of Our Lady's words to so many of her visionaries, the push to strip the Mass of its supernatural character is alive and growing. Thus, we find that Heaven is intensifying its intervention in a most noteworthy fashion.

Most curiously, while Vatican II desired to emphasize the liturgy, it also declared its support for a more active role by the laity in the Church. Heaven seems to have adopted this more active role of the laity in a mystical way, for not too long after the apparitions began at Medjugorje, five lay women from different parts of the world began to publicly report profound mystical experiences. Perhaps this was a special confirmation of the Holy Spirit's moving the Council to act on behalf of the laity.

All five women were married and had children. Likewise, all five were called upon by God to become not only visionaries, but stigmatic mystics of world-renown stature as well.

Like previous visionaries of the twentieth century, their words were consistent with the message of Fatima. But in their visible suffering and their unique missions, a unified plea seemed to be surfacing that was directly associated with the urgency of the times. Mary kept repeating that in these times a danger to the Church was near at hand.

Indeed, the lives and messages of these five women seemed to be uniquely designed by Heaven to point to the True Presence of Christ in the Church, a Presence that cannot be denied, distorted or destroyed. These women's revelations indicate that all efforts to do so will fail. Likewise, any partial success to injure the Church will only bring upon the world great suffering. The messages of these visionaries all confirmed what the great Capuchin mystic and stigmatist, Padre Pio, once declared: *"The world can survive easier without the sun than without the Mass."*

As Heaven had shown with the apparition at Knock, these mystics were led to understand that God is truly in control. Thus, a look at each of these unique messengers of God is in order.

CHAPTER THIRTY-FOUR

"MY LITTLE ONE, I AM THE CHURCH"

By the age of thirty-three, Christina Gallagher was married with two children. At a grotto in western Ireland, in 1985, her first supernatural experience happened. After this day her life would never be the same, for she witnessed a apparition of a living, suffering Head of Jesus Christ crowned with black thorns. Christ's Head was smeared with blood, and He was dying.

Three years later, the Blessed Virgin Mary appeared to Christina at a home in Dublin. This began a series of apparitions and mystical experiences comparable to those of the great Catholic mystics of the Middle Ages.

God's gifts to Christina through message and experience where singular. She came to bear the stigmata of Christ and reported bilocating, discerning the secrets of souls, spiritual visitations to Purgatory, Heaven and Hell, and vast prophetic visions of the future of the world. Some of the prophetic visions included a coming purification.

Through direct revelation and infused knowledge, God revealed great mysteries to her. The True Presence of Jesus Christ in His Church and in the Eucharist was especially involved in these mysteries.

In addition, Christina experienced Eucharistic miracles. On one occasion, the Holy Eucharist changed to flesh while in her mouth. Then, on another occasion, Christina saw and tasted the Precious Blood in the form of actual blood.

These spectacular miracles stand alone, but Heaven's words to her are also of great significance. Mary and Jesus gave her great insight into the infinite value of the Sacrifice of the Mass.

The Blessed Virgin Mary told Christina:

My child, if you could see the world through my eyes and realize the value of the Holy Sacrifice of the Mass and the value of praying the Rosary from your heart, you would go to the Mass many times each day and you would pray the Rosary from your heart constantly.[1]

In the book, *The Sorrow, The Sacrifice and The Triumph*, Christina explained some of what she was told about Christ's True Presence in the Eucharist. Here are her own words from a series of questions and answers.

Q. How do we in our lives stay focused on Jesus?

A. *I know I can be drawn away through every distraction but for the grace of God. We should constantly be petitioning God through prayer, sacrifice, fasting. The Holy Eucharist—above all things—will help us. In receiving the Holy Eucharist, we must receive It worthily. Our Blessed Mother said all these things contribute to the Grace of God that you receive. All of this helps to draw you closer to God and to bring you constantly into an awareness of God.*

Q. What has Our Lady taught you about Our Lord's presence in the Holy Eucharist?

A. *On the second apparition, when Our Blessed Mother came from a distance, there was a Light over her heart. Then, when Our Holy Mother came close up, I could see it was the Holy Eucharist and the Light was radiating from It. Our Lady was joyous and drew my attention to look down as she was looking down.*

After that, I was wondering why the Holy Eucharist was over Our Blessed Mother's heart. It's only been these last couple of months that I thought about it. So I prayed and said, "Holy Mother, if you want me to know the meaning of what that was all about, then you'll reveal it." She didn't reveal it in words; it was revealed inwardly. I was aware that she held Jesus over her heart, meaning that she loved Jesus in the Holy Eucharist. Our Lady would give reverence to Him by carrying Him over her heart, meaning that we should carry Him over our hearts and in our hearts. The Light around it, for me signified the graces we can receive by receiving the Holy Eucharist worthily—in a proper way. Our Holy Mother said we can receive the Holy Eucharist only when we have made a proper Confession. Our Blessed Mother desires her children to unburden themselves of all sin and receive her Son's Body and Blood worthily.

Q. Has Our Lady spoken to you about the Mass and the Holy Eucharist? What has she said about the Mass and the Holy Eucharist?

A. *When Our Blessed Mother spoke about the Holy Eucharist and the sacraments, she was talking about the Mass itself. Mass, with the celebration of the Holy Eucharist, is the Reality of Jesus. It is to love Jesus in prayer and adoration. Our Holy Mother said to come to Jesus and love Him. Our Lady has said this so many times. I didn't write down many things because it was as if she was talking directly just to me on some occasions. But when Our Holy Mother would refer to all of this, it was always to love Jesus more and to love Jesus in the Holy Eucharist.*

Q. Has Our Lord spoken of Confession, the sacraments, and of repentance?

A. *Yes. Jesus requested that we make an act of reparation for the abuse of the Holy Eucharist by receiving on the tongue only. This was not a command. It was a desire. Someone I shared it with later said that I was going against the Church's teaching, but a week later Jesus repeated the same request. When I told Jesus of my plight regarding this person, Jesus then replied, **"My little one,***

Mother of the Secret

I am The Church." Our Blessed Mother has also spoken about it. Our Lady has asked that we be absolved of all sin and receive her Son's Body worthily, in the Holy Eucharist. This is what Our Blessed Mother had said to me in an apparition. We must desire the Holy Eucharist in our heart.[2]

198

CHAPTER THIRTY-FIVE

"THE HOST IS BLEEDING"

Maria Esperanza de Bianchini was born on November 22, 1928, in the town of Barrancas, Venezuela. She was raised by her mother, since her father had died when she was two.

Unlike Christina Gallagher, Maria reported mystical experiences since childhood. At the age of five, she reported seeing St. Thérèse of Lisieux, and at twelve she witnessed an apparition of the Virgin Mary. A second vision of St. Thérèse revealed that the Lord was calling her and that she would find the truth of her mission in Rome. She then traveled there and was given the answer to her prayers.

Maria was married on December 8, 1956. She and her husband, Giovanni raised seven children. While she would have many mystical experiences, it was after moving to Betania, Venezuela that she received apparitions of the Virgin Mary. These apparitions and other experiences, such as the stigmata, brought into view a full-blown mystic.

Like others before her, Maria came to understand the world of the spirit. She was also given prophetic visions and messages. Again, her life was to be a testimony to the True Presence of Jesus Christ in His Church.

On December 8, 1991 a consecrated Communion Host began to bleed at a Mass in Betania. The celebrant during the miracle was Father Otty Aristizabal. From the book, *The Bridge To Heaven,* by Michael H. Brown, we are given this account of the Eucharistic Miracle in Father Aristizabal's words:

Between the 7th and 8th of December of 1991, about 40,000 to 50,000 pilgrims had come. It was just an incredible number of people. It was very beautiful, and the people demonstrated much faith, above all during the Mass. They were full of attention to the Word of God. There was such a silence during the Holy Mass.

I had the big Host that I consecrated, and at the moment of consecration I broke it in four parts. I put it into the dish and I ate one of the parts. I put the other three parts in here [the dish].

I closed my eyes, and when I opened them I saw that one of the pieces of this Host had a drop of blood in it, and I thought at that moment it was because of my fatigue. But then when the nun who was behind me said, "Father, look! The Host is bleeding!" I realized, yes, and I covered it. I didn't say anything.

There were so many people there, I didn't know what would happen. They'd kill each other just to see it. At five in the morning I opened the sanctuary and I looked and I saw the Host. The drop of blood was still fresh. And I told the people what had happened.

It was an incredible moment. Everybody got on their knees. Very emotional. I took the Host in my hand and everybody was taking pictures of it. It was very beautiful. And at two in the afternoon, I went to take a rest and to give it to the bishop. He wanted it handed over to a medical expert in the Institute of Caracas in order to analyze it, and so the Host stayed there for a month at the medical institute, and they examined it very carefully and proved that what was on the Host was human blood, that it had magnesium, iron, that it had red corpuscles and white corpuscles. After, I put the Host in the monstrance so the faithful ones could observe it.[1]

Bishop Pio Bello Ricardo of Los Teques, which is the diocese where Betania is located, also attested to the miracle. From the book, *Apparitions in Betania, Venezuela* by Sister Margaret Latteran Sims, C.S., we are given this account in Bishop Ricardo's words:

For three days the Blood on the Host was fluid, and then it began to dry up. Another small miracle is that the Blood didn't seep through the wafer-thin Host. The opposite side of the Host shows no sign whatsoever of Blood.

The Blood on the Host is not a very large spot. The importance of the miracle is that it is a sign. Miracles are signs. The importance is not in the miracle itself, but in the sign. It is a sign that Our Lord is truly present in the Eucharist. In the miracles of the Bible it is not the miracle, but the sign— the sign of our Lord's mercy and love for His children.

The "Miracle of the Eucharist" has been examined in laboratories and it is human blood; however, we know that we cannot say that this is the Blood of Christ in heaven. The characteristics of the glorified Body of Christ in heaven are different than the Body of Christ before the Resurrection. St. Paul says, "The Body of Christ after the Resurrection is a spiritual body."

Again, it is a sign. It is a sign of the Transubstantiation, and that is what is important for us today. God is trying to manifest to us that our faith in the consecrated Host as the Body and Blood of Christ is authentic.

I intend to construct a special altar in the Cathedral of my diocese of Los Teques for this "Miracle of the Eucharist."

Presently, the "Miracle of the Eucharist" is in the bishop's residence. It is my residence, but I prefer to live here at this shrine and be with the Sisters of St. Joseph.[2]

Most significantly, Maria also told Michael Brown that the Church in America needed to be prayed for and people needed to turn to the Eucharist for the answer. Maria said:

In the next few years the United States will suffer much. There will be problems and certain natural calamities. I see little quakes and certain others. Pray for the leaders of the United States! Pray for the priests in America, especially the seminarians, that they be good and loyal priests. It is important to remain loyal to Rome. People have to pray, to do penance, to meditate very much upon the reasons why *they have to prepare themselves in order to evangelize. But all of that is accompanied by the Eucharist. "**Because,**" says the Lord, "**only My daily food, if it is possible, will be able to save a holy, mortal person from catastrophe.**" I have this. All of this is written down.[3]*

CHAPTER THIRTY-SIX

THREE DAYS ON ONLY THE EUCHARIST

Mirna Nazour is a young, married woman who lives in Damascus, Syria, with her husband and two children. On November 22, 1982 in the old city of Damascus, Mirna prayed over her sister-in-law. As she prayed, a Moslem woman noticed a light coming from Mirna's hands. Then, oil began to exude from Mirna's skin. The sick woman was instantly cured. Mirna was eighteen years old at the time.

Five days later, on the anniversary of the apparitions of the Virgin Mary to Saint Catherine Labouré of Rue du Bac, Paris, a three-inch picture card of the Virgin Mary and the Christ Child began to exude oil. The icon was a copy of Our Lady of Cazan, which exuded oil over 200 years ago. The original is kept to this day in Fatima, Portugal, where someday it will be returned to the Byzantine Catholic Church in Russia.[1]

On this same evening, Mirna heard the Virgin Mary speak to her. What followed was a series of apparitions of the Virgin Mary and later visions of Christ. Again, Heaven came with a message. It was a message designed to alert the world of the seriousness of the times. It was also a message designed to call attention to the True Presence of Jesus Christ in the Church.

Mirna received the stigmata and numerous mystical visions. The primary theme of the messages given to Mirna was a stern warning against division in His Mystical Body, the Church.

On August 14, 1986, Jesus told Mirna: *"The Church is the Kingdom of Heaven on earth. He who divides it has sinned!"*

Like Christina Gallagher and Maria Esperanza, miracles involving the Eucharist occurred to Mirna Nazour.

A few days prior to the second anniversary of the events in Damascus, on November 26, 1984, Mirna heard a voice saying she would lose her eyesight. On the anniversary date she lost her sight. Instead of seeing darkness, though, she saw only light; yet, she could not see any of the people around her.

After losing her sight, Mirna was not able to sleep. During this time, she would answer religious questions by opening the Bible and then revealing the answer to the question on a specific page. All the while she was not able to see! On one of the pages was the account of Saint Paul's trip to Damascus before his conversion, in which he too lost his eyesight for three days.

Finally on the third day, a priest gave Mirna Holy Communion. Mirna said, "Why another Communion? I just had one a few minutes ago." When asked, she said the Communion Host had been round, white and radiated light.

After receiving Communion from the priest, Mirna felt a hand closing her eyes. Those around her denied touching her after she inquired about it. Then, a second time a hand touched her eyes to close them. Immediately afterward Mirna fell asleep. When she awoke she could see again. Oil then again exuded from her in a great quantity. Her trial had lasted exactly three days. After receiving a meal, it was also noted that Mirna had lived for all three days on only the Holy Eucharist.

On another evening, Mirna traveled to Lebanon for a Mass of unity in a schoolyard. It was October 10, 1985. Again, as soon as Mirna received Holy Communion, oil began to exude from her hands. Over 500 people in the church turned away from the Mass to observe the miracle. This attention caused Mirna to become upset, and she fled to a church across the field. Inside, she laid her head under a crucifix of Christ and went into ecstasy.

Undeterred, a crowd of people, including a television cameraman, followed Mirna to the church. There they found her in ecstasy as oil poured down from the crucifix which she was kneeling beneath. The oil flowed from Christ's feet to Mirna's face, as all watched in awe.

CHAPTER THIRTY-SEVEN

"RECEIVE HOLY COMMUNION EVERY DAY"

On September 23, 1983, the Blessed Virgin Mary appeared to a middle-aged housewife in San Nicolas, Argentina, named Gladys Quiroga de Motta. Gladys was born on July 1, 1937, and is married with two children. Her husband is a retired metal worker.

One month before the apparitions, a rosary hanging in Gladys' room suddenly lit up. This illumination was observed by her neighbors.

After the initial apparition, Gladys received approximately 1,900 messages from the Virgin Mary and Jesus. Visions of Christ, miraculous healings and eventually the stigmata became part of her now mystical life.

The Virgin Mary requested that a medal be struck and a basilica be constructed. The local bishop, Monsignor Domingo Salvador Castagna, approved with the imprimatur the publication of Gladys' revelations and consented to the building of the basilica. The location of the basilica was marked by the mysterious appearance of a ray of light.

The revelations received by Gladys denote extreme urgency. The messages, according to French theologian Father René Laurentin, specifically spell out the current world situation and give exact guidelines as to what must be done. Most significantly, the revelations confirm that the Virgin Mary is the "New Ark of the Covenant," the "New Eve," and the "Woman Clothed in the Sun."

But again, the significant aspect of these revelations is that they point the faithful to the True Presence of Jesus Christ in the Church and in the Sacraments.

Indeed, many of the messages focus on the Mass and the Eucharist:

September 15, 1984

Beloved children, value the Holy Mass. Every good Christian ought to oblige himself to take part in the Holy Supper, in the Holy Mass daily, or at least once a week.

That is the moment in which my adored Son conveys the Love of the Father and Eternal Salvation to you. It is also where you can recall that Christ Jesus offers Himself, in absolute obedience to God the Father and trusting fully in Him. A great example which you must follow. I invite you to make it a duty of going to Communion, but a duty with great love for the Lord.[1]

October 3, 1984

The Eucharistic Congress must serve for the children to come to God, including priests and nuns, to turn toward Him with all the love and vocation that priesthood requires. Pray for the Holy Spirit to enlighten them, that they may really see Christ in the Eucharist, that they may find Him and never leave Him.[2]

June 9, 1985

In the morning, the Virgin says to me:

In Holy Mass, one not only receives the Body and Blood of Christ symbolically, Christ Jesus is present, and He offers Himself truly.

May all my children see the Savior in Communion; may they feel that intimate communication with Christ, and that Christ enters in them.[3]

August 3, 1985

My children, I ask you to go to Church and to take part in Holy Mass, because during it, you will feed on the Bread of Life that is Christ Jesus.

Nourished by Him, no plague coming from outside will reach you, since Jesus will destroy it. Go then, in search of fortitude. Know that He waits for you.[4]

June 1, 1986

Tell your brethren, Jesus' Eucharist is Live and Real Body! Adore Him and love Him!

My children, it is in the Eucharist where you can feel how He gives Himself to you; it is in the Eucharist where He again becomes Body and Blood, and it is from the Eucharist that He wants to save the souls prepared to receive Him. With prayer and joy in your hearts receive this day.[5]

November 9, 1986

In this Novena, pray for the Holy Church. Today, as never before, it is suffering the most horrifying persecutions. My children, my heart is not dismayed, because the Holy Church will soon come to shine like the brightest of stars.[6]

April 10, 1988

My daughter, sorry are those who, being able to preach, do not preach. Oh, my daughter, there are so few who really love the Lord! My children should receive Holy Communion every day. Body and Blood of the Lord; a food all should long for, Holy food.[7]

May 25, 1988

You must have love and devotion to Mary; constant prayer of the Holy Rosary, and take part daily in the Holy

Eucharist. By loving the Mother, you will find the love of the Son; in the prayer to the Mother, you will be in union with the Son and in the Holy Eucharist, you will find the Son.[8]

August 2, 1988

Oh, my dear daughter! How Jesus loves their souls!

He loves them so; there is no greater love than the Lord's Love! Love that gives itself: Divine love, burning love, love that can be received by all souls through the Holy Eucharist.

It is love offered by Him in the Eucharistic Sacrifice, love wanting to be union, love that human knowledge is unable to understand.[9]

September 12, 1988

Adore the Body and Blood of my Son in the Blessed Sacrament of the altar. Wonderful Mystery, that not all understand, wonderful Mystery of love, offered daily in the Holy Eucharist. A moment in which pain and happiness, suffering and joy, conjugate. Pain, at knowing of His death; happiness, of knowing He defeated death.

Souls must draw near to Christ; souls must unite daily with Christ and nothing better than through Holy Communion. Nourishment of the soul, for life.[10]

May 15, 1989

I tell all of you: Go to meet Jesus in the Eucharist with love, receiving Him worthily. Already my Son is offended too much; that is why you must be fervent Christians and be interiorly prepared to go to His encounter in the great Eucharistic Sacrifice. Do not exclude yourselves from so wonderful a proof of Love.[11]

May 28, 1989
(Corpus Christi Feast Day)

I tell all your brethren: Come, I will show you the Great Love; I will teach you how to adore and to receive Jesus in the Holy Eucharist, so necessary for the soul. Fill your spirit, turning your heart toward Christ. Make the Mother's words known.[12]

August 19, 1989

I say to all my children: This Mother wants you in a growing love for Christ. This Mother wants you fed with the Food of Life—The Holy Eucharist. This Mother wants you beside her Son![13]

Mother of the Secret

CHAPTER THIRTY-EIGHT

"LOOK AT ME"

J ulia Kim was born in 1947. From her earliest years, she endured intense suffering. From trials of war to various chronic physical ailments, her life was filled with misery. In 1972 Julia married Julio Kim and they eventually had four children.

The Kims were Protestant but entered the Catholic Church in 1981 following a miraculous healing of Julia. Not long after, in June of 1985, Julia received a small statue of the Virgin Mary as a gift for her intercessory prayer. It was with this statue that an incredible series of mystical events began to unfold.

On June 30, 1985, the small statue of Mary began to weep. A little less than three weeks later, Julia began to receive messages from the Virgin Mary. What followed is one of the most fascinating stories of a modern-day mystic.

The little statue would continually weep tears, tears of blood and then oil over 700 times. Julia received visions of Christ, Heaven, Hell and Purgatory. Her body began to exude a rose-like fragrance, and she was called to be a victim soul, bearing the physical wounds of the stigmata.

The messages given to Julia Kim were profound. They echoed the same urgent theme of Fatima. They also warned of danger to the Church and, once again, of a fiery chastisement.

Most specifically, Mary gave Julia an in-depth understanding of the sin of abortion. Heaven's justice, Julia was told, cried out for vengeance. In reparation for this sin, Julia often experienced the painful physical suffering of a child undergoing an abortion.

The evil of the world, Julia was told, was pushing the world to a disaster, and the danger to the Church, especially Christ's True Presence in the Eucharist, was real. The Eucharist was emphasized on more than one occasion; as photography at Naju revealed the Eucharist floating in the sky or in the Virgin Mary's hands in some of her images.

As before, the Virgin Mary's messages sought to draw attention to the sacred. Repeatedly, Mary and Jesus spoke about the True Presence and the dangers that threaten the Church today.

The Virgin Mary told Julia:

> *Emphasize to everyone the importance of the Holy Eucharist. By the Holy Eucharist, the Lord will be in you. He will live in you and stay there always, if you open the door of your mind and receive Him with a clean mind.*

In another vision, Julia relayed a revelation which was especially aimed at bringing attention to Christ's True Presence in the Church. It was accompanied by the first Eucharistic miracle she was to receive. Recalls Julia:

> *I received Holy Communion, and when I was standing up to go home supported by Philip and Mark, I felt my mouth being filled with the Body and Blood of Jesus. I was smelling blood, too. Then, I felt as if I was floating in the air and fell down to the floor. At that time, I heard a loud voice of Jesus from the tabernacle.*
>
> *Jesus said: "Look at Me!"*
>
> *I was very surprised when I looked in the direction of the voice. Jesus looked so miserable shedding Blood. The Blood was not falling on the ground, but into the chalice and paten on the altar to be brought to us by the priests. The Blessed Mother, our Mediatrix, was standing by Jesus. She always looks beautiful, and, today, looked particularly anxious and very shiny. She experiences pain, because Jesus is bleeding for His Love for us. But she rejoices, because, by bleeding, He comes to us, sinners, and by our receiving Him, we become renewed and united with Him. For this reason, the Blessed Mother wants and prays that each and every*

one of us renounce the ego and receive the Holy Eucharist with a clean mind. Jesus said: **"I am still bleeding on the Cross to save the whole human race and My Blood will not flow in vain. I am the Transfuser Who washes away your dirty sins. My precious Blood is a special medicine that will open the eyes of the sick souls and wake up the sleeping souls—through priests. I am so troubled that people receive Me out of habit and with indifference.**

I wish to pour down all My Love upon all the souls on this earth. Help them participate in the heavenly banquet (the Blessed Sacrament)."[1] *As the Virgin Mary had done with other present-day chosen ones, she gave many messages to Julia for priests. For priests, Julia was told, hold the key to the defense of the True Presence.*

The Virgin Mary said:

Oh, my beloved priests! My precious ones who perform the amazing miracle of the Sacrament! Do not turn away from my messages, but have complete trust in my Immaculate Heart and entrust everything to my guidance. Rely on my Immaculate Heart totally through unending sacrifices and penances in order to crush the devils who are trying to afflict you with all kinds of cunning means.

My Immaculate Heart will surely triumph. You will certainly see the victory, if you accept my words. *(July 5, 1989)[2]*

The Virgin Mary's call to the priests in this message was followed just days later with a serious warning of the dangers that threaten the Church. Repeating Mary's words, Julia wrote:

The priests, who represent my son, Jesus Christ, must be discreet and do their best to lead a life based on the teachings in the Gospels and within the orders of the Church.

You must understand well what kind of sacrifice my Son Jesus made for you and through what kind of pains your salvation has been won. (October 14, 1989)[3]

Throughout the 1990's, Mary's messages to Julia Kim continued to warn of danger to the Church. Then in 1994, a new series of events began in Naju with eight Eucharistic miracles being reported through 1995. And one of these miracles occurred in the presence of the Apostolic Pro-Nuncio.

CHAPTER THIRTY-NINE

THE EUCHARISTIC MIRACLES OF NAJU

Julia Kim is reported to have experienced fifteen Eucharistic miracles since 1988. The locations and dates of the first twelve of these miracles, as well as the celebrants of the Mass (if known), are as follows:

1. Holy Rosary Church in Naju on June 15, 1988 (a Korean priest).
2. Holy Rosary Church in Naju on May 16, 1991 (Father Jerry Orbos and Father Ernie Santos from the Philippines).
3. At Mass in a hotel room in Rome, Italy on June 1, 1992 (Father Jerry Orbos) (Julia was in severe pain and was not able to go to church.).
4. The church in Lanciano, Italy on June 2, 1992 (Father Jerry Orbos).
5. Holy Rosary Church in Naju on September 24, 1994 (Father Jerry Orbos).
6. St. Anthony's Church in Kailua, Hawaii on November 2, 1994 (Father Martin Lucia).
7. The chapel in Naju on November 24, 1994.
8. Naju Parish Church on June 30, 1994.
9. The chapel in Naju on July 1, 1995.
10. The chapel in Naju on July 2, 1995.
11. On a mountain near Naju in the presence of Bishop Roman Danylak of Toronto, Canada on September 22, 1995.

12. The Chapel of the Holy Father in Rome on October 31, 1995. (see Epilogue)

On May 16, 1991, Julia Kim's second Eucharistic miracle occurred while she participated in Mass with pilgrims from the Philippines Wrote Julia:

> *There was a Mass at 6 p.m. in the Naju parish church celebrated by two priests who came from the Philippines. Some parishioners of Naju and thirty-three pilgrims from the Philippines participated. When I received the Holy Eucharist, I immediately tasted blood in my mouth. When I came back to my pew and showed it to Lubino, the Chapel Administrator, he saw the Host on my tongue being of a yellow-to-light brown color at first and, soon, turning into the red, blood color starting from the edge. This was reported to the priests, and all the faithful present there were able to see it. They were surprised and began crying. The two priests also prayed and cried in front of the tabernacle. The Host continued bleeding and soon my mouth was filled with blood.*
>
> *At that moment, I saw a vision. The weeping Blessed Mother of Naju was wearing a blue mantle, holding a rosary in her right hand and smiling beautifully. With tears in her eyes, she embraced the two priests. Soon there was the merciful but anxious voice of Jesus.*

Here is an excerpt of the message Julia received that day:

> **Daughter! Teach the Mystery of the Holy Eucharist fervently to the children who do not understand it so that the numerous people living in ingratitude may be saved through your bloody sacrifices combined with My Love. However hard I may try to give Love to them, I cannot force them to accept it, as I gave them a free will. I, Who am present in the mystery of the Holy Eucharist, am a spring that never dries, a medicine that can save the sick souls, and a doctor to the patient.[1]**

A little more than a year later, Julia experienced her third Eucharistic miracle in Rome on a trip to visit with the Holy Father, Pope John Paul II. Julia wrote:

June 1,1992 - in Rome

The Mass was scheduled in a church, so, I thought I could not go to Mass today. But I had a strong desire to attend Mass and thought, "How wonderful it would be, if Mass can be celebrated in the hotel." What a surprise! Someone told me that Mass would be celebrated in the hotel.

So, I attended the Mass, supported by others. When I received Holy Communion, I smelled blood. My husband, Julio, the priest and others saw the Host bleeding in my mouth.[2]

The very next day, Julia Kim participated in another Eucharistic miracle. This time it was in the very same church where the most famous Eucharistic miracle in history occurred centuries ago, Lanciano.

Reported Julia:

June 2, 1992 - in Rome

We attended Mass at the church in Lanciano, where a miracle of the Blessed Sacrament had occurred during a Mass about 1,300 years ago. The Host changed to heart muscles and the Blood of Jesus in the cup in the form of wine changed to human blood in form also. They are still preserved in that church.

When Father Orbos consecrated bread and wine and lifted them up to God the Father, there was light pouring down on him and, then, on me and everyone else attending the Mass. I prayed after the Holy Communion:

"Too many people are committing sins with their tongues causing wounds to each other. Give special blessings on their tongues so that they may praise the Lord..."

Then I swallowed the Host. But a tiny piece of the Host remained on my tongue and began growing. I was so sur-

prised that I showed it to my husband, Julio. Other people also came and saw the small piece of the Host growing bigger and becoming bloody. They were crying loudly. At that moment, there was the warm but stern voice of Jesus from Heaven: "I am Light, I am the Light of Love that chases away all the darkness. I intend to let all of you receive My Light of Love and, thus, to repel the darkness in this world that is turning into a vast desert."[3]

On November 24, 1994, the seventh Eucharistic miracle of Naju occurred through Julia. This one was different from the previous ones and truly the most amazing. The Apostolic Pro-Nuncio in Korea, an Archbishop from the Vatican, was present in Naju with Father Raymond Spies, Julia's spiritual director.

The Archbishop made it clear to Father Spies that he was visiting Naju not as a private pilgrim, but as the official representative of the Holy Father. We are given this report from Mary's Touch by Mail of Oregon:

While the Apostolic Pro-Nuncio, Julia and others were praying in the Chapel, the Blessed Mother gave messages to Julia and also gave a most amazing miracle. First, Our Lady asked Julia to receive blessings from the Archbishop and Father Spies on her hands. Then, she had St. Michael the Archangel bring the Holy Eucharist to the Apostolic Pro-Nuncio through Julia. As the Archbishop was representing the Holy Father, this miracle was actually intended for the Holy Father, Pope John Paul II, and, therefore, the whole Catholic Church. This reminds us of the miracle in Guadalupe four and a half centuries ago, because the miracle and the accompanying messages in Guadalupe were also given to a bishop representing the Church.

The first Sacred Host that the Archangel brought was a large-sized one, the kind priests often use during Mass. The angel was not visible to the people in the Chapel except Julia, but everybody was able to see the Holy Eucharist suddenly appearing between Julia's fingers. The Host had images of a cross in the middle and two letters: "A" and "_" just as in the miraculous photograph that Our Lady gave on June 27, 1993. The Host was already broken into two when Julia received It, with one half in Julia's right hand and the other half in her left hand. Julia fell on the floor because of a powerful light from above.

The Apostolic Pro-Nuncio and Father Spies received the Sacred Host from Julia's hands and broke the Host into smaller pieces to give Communion to people in the Chapel who were in total amazement and awe. Even though it was just one Host, everyone in the Chapel received Communion. Some of them later testified that it was an experience that simply defied human description. The Apostolic Pro-Nuncio and Father Spies put a piece of the Host in a pyx for preservation. Our Lady told Julia that the Sacred Host the Archangel brought was about to be consumed by a certain priest, but brought to the Chapel instead, because the priest was in a state of sin and Jesus could not live in him.

Then, Julia wanted to go to her house next door to write down Our Lady's messages for the Archbishop. As she was walking out of the Chapel supported by others because of her continuing pains, the Blessed Mother called her again in a hurry. Julia came back toward Our Lady's statue and held the hands of the Apostolic Pro-Nuncio and Father Spies as the Blessed Mother requested. Our Lady asked Julia to receive the Holy Eucharist for the second time.

This time, the Host was smaller, the same as those lay people receive. Julia received this Sacred Host on her tongue. The Host was standing upright on Julia's tongue. The Archbishop picked up the Host. After showing the Host to people in the Chapel and some photos were taken, Father Spies received the Host from the Archbishop and put It in a pyx. He is preserving the Host at his residence and is expected to bring the Host back to Naju later for exposition in the Chapel so that pilgrims may pray before the Eucharist that was miraculously brought to us.

The Apostolic Pro-Nuncio reviewed what had happened in Naju for the past ten years and was totally amazed. He was so overwhelmed with joy and hope that he was not able to sleep for the next three nights. In the meantime, Arch-bishop Victorinus. of the Kwangju Archdiocese, which cov-ers the Naju Parish, formed a committee to open the formal investigation process for Naju.[4]

CHAPTER FORTY

BEHOLD THE LAMB OF GOD

In August 1988, a tragic accident left three year old Audrey Santo of Worcester, Massachusetts in a coma-like state. Since then, Audrey Santo, though bed-ridden, has been surrounded by reported miracles and mystical phenomena.

Although she is unable to speak or move, thousands of people have visited her and many healings have been reported. But beginning in 1994, a new series of mystical events began to unfold.

On four different occasions in the Santo home, consecrated hosts have mysteriously changed in appearance and have begun to bleed. Likewise, brownish stains have been found on the white doily on the floor of the tabernacle in Audrey's room, as has a red fluid in cups beneath a small crucifix in the chapel.

By 1995, the number of these kinds of events escalated. A red fluid was discovered at the base of a large crucifix in the chapel. A red substance was found outside the door and inside on the floor of the tabernacle and down the left side of a chest.

Then, on May 22, 1996, at the moment of consecration of the Mass, Fr. George Joyce, one of Audrey's spiritual directors, noticed upon the raising of the chalice that the chalice's base, as well as the paten, had myseriously acquired a red substance.

Because of all these unexplainable events, scientific experts were asked to investigate. H.S. Research Laboratory of Cambridge, Massachusetts, issued the following report on its analysis of the first of the bleeding hosts.

H.S. RESEARCH LABORATORY
100 Inman St..
Cambridge, MA 02139
Telephone & Fax: 617-661-4370

REPORT ON PRELIMINARY INVESTIGATIONS OF BLOOD STAIN WHICH APPEARED ON THE BLESSED SACRAMENT IN AUDREY SANTO'S ROOM ON MARCH 28, 1995.

On Wednesday March 29, 1995 I arrived at Audrey's home at about 11:45 AM. Sometime after 1 PM Linda Santo, Audrey's mother, showed me and three Catholic priests present in Audrey's room the Blessed Sacrament which was kept in the tabernacle inside a golden-plated reliquary. This approximately one inch size Host had an irregular stain of what appeared to me as blood occupying about half of the Host's surface. The stain on the Host was brownish similar to dried blood, but on the inside surface of the reliquary glass I could see a smear of what looked like a fresh bright-red blood. After this visual observation, I decided to look at it under the microscope which I brought from my home. The idea was to examine the glass without touching the host. However, when the back cover of the reliquary was opened and a ball of cotton ball removed which held the Host in place, it was found that the Host was stuck to the glass. Not to destroy it I have just removed some cotton wool to which some tiny red spot was adhered. When moistened with physiological saline the red spot appeared under the microscope as coagulated blood with red cells attached tightly to each other.

To demonstrate that this stain was really blood, the same piece of cotton ball was transferred from a microscopic slide to a reagent pad of a commercial kit for detection of occult blood. After adding a drop of developer, instantaneously a blue color developed which is indicative of the presence of blood. Five people who were witnessing all stages of these investigations placed their signatures on the reagent pad, which was wrapped in a plastic foil and placed in the taber-

nacle together with the Host secured in the reliquary. The whole process of investigations was also recorded on video tape.[1]

Boguslaw Lipinski, Ph. D.

Laboratory analysis on each occasion that a red substance has appeared in the Santo home have been positive (+) for the presence of human blood. In addition, on different occasions, some hosts were discovered within pyxes to have changed from their naturally hard composition to a soft and wet, almost *"bubbly'* texture. Fr. George Joyce remarked that one such host felt *"like tissue dissolved in water."*

In early 1996, the miraculous presence of oil also began to become increasingly more present. Out of nowhere on Wednesday, April 24th, oil appeared on seventeen pages of the Sacramentary Book. These are the pages that contain the Eucharistic Prayers of the Mass.

On May 1st, several statues began weeping oil during Mass in the chapel. This phenomena repeated itself on May 8th, as again statues weeped oil and a miraculous odor of flowers occurred on the altar. On May 15th, not only did some statues weep oil, but this time oil miraculously appeared on the paten and on the hosts during Mass. This phenomena repeated itself two more times on May 22nd and May 29th, not only in the chapel, but also in Audrey's room.

Finally, on Wednesday June 5, 1996, as a Mass was celebrated at the chapel of the Santo family home in Worcester Massachusetts another incredible miracle took place. And like before, it shocked everyone.

On that day, three priests concelebrated the Mass: Father George Joyce, Father Tom McCarthy C.S.V. of Chicago and Father Leo Potvin of Newport, New York. Together they had contributed more that one hundred years to the priesthood of the Catholic Church.

At the moment of the consecration, as Father Joyce elevated a large host, he suddenly noticed a smaller host on the paten had changed colors. When he examined the host, Fr. Joyce found there was blood in the center of the small host.

Amidst the shock of all in attendance, the three priests were left shaken, as it undoutably appeared to be a Eucharistic miracle.

In respect to the diocese, the Santo family wishes that the bleeding hosts be not called "Eucharistic miracles" unless the Church rules. But in light of the results from the laboratory tests, it has been hard to deny this apparent reality to the many faithful that come to the Santo home each week.

While many well-respected theologans have not been reluctant to offer their opinion in support of the mystical events surrounding little Audrey, perhaps the best source for testimony concerning these apparent Eucharistic miracles comes from Fr. George V. Joyce, the senior spiritual advisor for the Santo family.

Fr. Joyce is a diocesan priest from Washington, D.C., who retired in Springfield, Massachusetts. His almost day to day interaction and witness to the events surrounding Audrey Santo validate him as a most credible expert witness to the events.

The following is an indepth interview with Fr. Joyce. It is intended to present his findings and opinions based upon his subjective and objective experiences.

Q. How long have you been involved with the events surrounding Audrey?

A. *Since 1991, approximatly five years.*

Q. On Wednesday, June 5, 1996, there was apparently a Eucharistic miracle that occurred during Mass at approximately two (2) o'clock in the afternoon at the Santo's home. You were the main celebrant of the Mass, along with Father McCarthy and Father Leo. Can you tell me what happened?

A. *We were into the Mass. I don't recall whether it occurred before the consecration or not. But I know that when I looked down at the consecration, I saw something that was not on top of the Host, but apparently was "in" the Host. So I sensed that something was going to happen. But something had already happened so I went ahead with the consecration. And when I came to the "Behold the Lamb of God," I lifted the Host up and the first two rows of people said, "A-h-h!" I knew then something happened. I looked down and there was a small drop of blood on the Host.*

Q. What did the people say?

A. *The people in the first rows of the chapel gasped.*

Q. So, when you raised the Host up, these people had already seen the blood.

A. *Yes, they saw it on the large Host because it had rubbed off. The Blood had rubbed off.*

Q. How many Hosts were there?

A. *There was a large Host and small Hosts*

Q. Was blood on the small Host?

A. *There was. That's where the blood was concentrated.*

Q. Did the blood on the small Host rub onto the Large Host?

A. *Yes. So that when I lifted the large Host up — It was on the side.*

Q. What else did you see?

A. *I looked down and I saw the small Host. The blood was concentrated on the center of the Host. The Host has a cross, you know, It has an indented cross in it. The blood was right where the beams met in the center. It was quite heavy — so the blood seeped out through the indentures of the cross as it were, you know, to the limbs of the cross and up above. I just looked the Host today, and there is blood on both sides, now. I mean it's penetrated. And there's a hole which you will see.*

Q. Did you consume that portion that had the blood on it?

A. *The three of us did, because we didn't pay attention at the time. We just consumed it. I took my share and then passed the rest over to the other two priests.*

Q. This was the third Eucharistic miracle involved with Audrey Santo?

A. *Yes, absolutely.*

Q. Was this the first Eucharistic miracle in which you were presiding as the main celebrant of the Mass?

A. *This was the first miracle that happened at Mass. The other one, I consecrated and was placed in the tabernacle in Audrey's room.*

Q. Was that the first or the second host that bled?

A. *That was the second. We're talking about the second. That's the host Audrey's mother Linda gives her communion from. She takes just a little fraction of a gragment and gives it to her. She (Linda) noticed it was darkening, just as the preious one, consecrated by Bishop Flannigan of Worcester.*

Q. Did the first Eucharistic miracle, the host consecrated by Bishop Flannagan, the retired bishop of Worcester, occur during a mass or in the tabernacle?

A. *Again, it was similar. It was placed in a tabernacle and then started changing.*

Q. Who first noticed that it changed?

A. *Linda [Santo] noticed it, and we didn't. It was very slight. It wasn't something we would all agree with. We thought it was a defect in the Host. But, Linda was sure it was something else. And it proved that she was right. It was blood and it burst forth one day.*

Q. Whose decision was it to have it tested?

A. *Father Meade and the Santo family.*

Q. Let's go back to the third miracle that occurred on June 6, 1996. What happened next? Describe what your thoughts were when you noticed the host had changed. What did you feel?

A. *You know, it's amazing because after the other bleeding hosts, I'm just overwhelmed by God's mercy. I mean, I just have a great peace with it. Which surprises me. Here I am seeing Jesus, the reality of the Eucharist, coming right out of my hand and right in front of me.*

Q. How does that make you feel as a priest. This miracle has occurred to only a limited number of priests in history?

A. *It's not the honor of it, it's just the solidifying of my belief which is has always been there which again, just fills my heart with joy because everything is confirmed.*

Q. There's a good point. This wasn't a miracle that was used to reinforces the faith of a doubting priest. As has occurred in some Eucharistic miralces, but the opposite occurred here, where it appears the Lord was rewarding a priest who maintained his faith in Christ's True Presence.

A. *Yes, Jesus in the Eucharist is living. I mean, He' there! That's all you need to know!*

Q. What did the other priests at the Mass that day say when they were going through the experience?

A. *They were more overwhelmed because I've experienced the two miracles previously.*

Q. I understand one of the priests was crying.

A. *Father Tom McCarthy. He gave a little talk afterwards and reviewed his experience in coming here. He first came here a couple of months ago. I believe a month ago, he saw Our Lady of Guadalupe painting weeping oil profusely and he was touched. He was impressed. But he said he was not convinced when he went away. I mean, he wasn't overwhelming accepting everything he saw, But he was overwhelmed here. He had no doubts anymore and he was going to spread the news of Audrey and what's happening here. This is now!*

Q. With the Eucharistic miracles, do you think God is especially trying to call Catholics to the reality of the 'True Presence?'

A. *Yes — absolutely — no question about it. We read about Julia Kim in Korea and the four chilldren at Garabandal in the 1960's. There are miracles everywhere. These are very Eucharistic apparitions. We've seen the overwhelm-*

ing presence of the Eucharist in all these apparitions. If a person really responds to the Eucharist, then everything falls in line. After looking at a Host bleeding, then you should go home overwhelmed with the grace of the moment. And from the first to the last teaching of the Church — accept it as it comes. The miracles make it (the faith) alive and easily acceptable. I think it banishes all questions and doubts, you know. It humbles you to accept what the Church has been teaching. Even it we don't understand what is being taught. We cannot grasp and comprehend it, but we must accept it.

CHAPTER FORTY-ONE

AN OLD PROPHECY

From the events at Lanciano to the miracles surrounding little Audrey Santo, the reality of God's True Presence in the Eucharist has been repeatedly presented to the world to strengthen faith. But these great miracles, along with Jesus' and Mary's words to us through their apparitions over the centuries, have been given at different times for different reasons.

Some of the miraculous events were in direct response to a specific crisis. Others, it appears, were designed to confirm to the faithful that the Church's sacred and holy mysteries are real. Still others were given perhaps as singular graces for chosen souls.

However, these events which span many centuries seem to carry with them a hidden meaning that links them all together. In particular, some visionaries repeatedly state that Jesus and Mary have given them this message: The Sacrifice of the Mass and the True Presence of Jesus Christ are in danger of being suppressed!

But what does this mean? What exactly is this "danger"? And how could this happen ? It is a documentable fact that many visionaries foretell that some form of specific attack on the Church's sacred mysteries, especially the Holy Sacrifice of the Mass, will eventually occur. Yet, at the same time, many of these visionaries also report that the Sacrifice of the Mass will never be "totally" suppressed and that a great victory by God is near. Indeed, it is to be a victory that will especially solidify Christ's Eucharistic Presence throughout the world.

However, visionaries tell us that if some form of suppression of the Sacrifice of the Mass does eventually occur, unlike other times in history, such as the French Revolution of late eighteenth century or the Communist tyrannies of the twentieth century, it will have a very significant affect on the Church and the world. According to some visionaries, it will definitely be worldwide to a degree.

Some writers believe that this prophecy may be connected to the apostasy foretold at Fatima and Akita, an apostasy that is still growing and unfolding. But most significantly, some say it will be the climax of the assault on the Church, which has been building for hundreds of years.

Rev. Msgr. Richard L. Carroll, V.F. gives us this summary in his 1993 book, *The Remnant Church*. Writes Fr. Carroll:

> *It must sadden the heart of Our Lord Jesus at the indif-*
> *ference of so many Catholics. Constantly, Our Lady has urged*
> *us to make the Mass the central act of our life. I believe one*
> *of the trials during the purification will center on the Mass*
> *and the Eucharist - its denial of the Real Presence.*

It would not be possible to quote all the visionaries in this century, or even half century that have warned of a coming suppression of the Holy Sacrifice of the Mass. But since, the beginning of the 1990's, two more noted visionaries reported receiving messages concerning the celebration of the Mass and a coming crisis surrounding it. Because of the overall respect they generate as being considered authentic, and because of the previous prophecies emanating from their visions or messages have come to fulfillment, we will focus on only the reported revelations of these visionaries.

On August 11, 1993 in Marmora, Ontario, the Ukrainian visionary, Josyp Terelya, reported that the Virgin Mary told him:

> *Satan shall gain control, for a short time, over certain*
> *parts of the earth, and his rule will extend for forty-two*
> *months. That part of the earth where Satan shall have full*
> *authority over the subjected nations will experience un-*
> *told evil and terror as never before. It will be absolutely*
> *forbidden to celebrate the holy Sunday, the day of the res-*
> *urrection of Christ.*[1]

Likewise, in what is probably the most persuasive revelation ever given concerning this mysterious prophecy surrounding the Mass, Father Steffano Gobbi reported receiving a detailed and profound message on December 31, 1992.

In this message, not only did Our Lady tell Fr. Gobbi that the celebration of the Holy Mass would be suppressed, but she also revealed that this would then be the partial fulfillment of the prophet Daniel's ancient prophecy, a prophecy that foretells that the *"daily sacrifice will be abolished for one thousand two hundred and ninety days."*

The message to Father Gobbi is titled *"THE END OF TIMES,"* and like all of the messages received by Father Gobbi, it has received an imprimatur from Bishop Donald W. Montrose, D.D. of California and his Eminence Bernardino Cardinal Echeveria Ruiz, O.F.M. of Ecuador. Here is the text of the entire message given to Father Gobbi:

> *With docility, allow yourselves to be taught by me, beloved children. On this last night of the year, gather together in prayer and in listening to the word of your heavenly Mother, the Prophetess of these last times.*
>
> *Do not spend these hours noisily or in dissipation, but in silence, in recollection, and in contemplation.*
>
> *I have announced to you many times that the end of the times and the coming of Jesus in glory is very near. Now, I want to help you understand the signs described in the Holy Scriptures, which indicate that his glorious return is now close.*
>
> *These signs are clearly indicated in the Gospels, in the letters of Saint Peter and Saint Paul, and they are becoming a reality during these years.*
>
> *The first sign is the spread of errors, which lead to the loss of faith and to apostasy.*
>
> *These errors are being propagated by false teachers, by renowned theologians who are no longer teaching the truths of the gospel, but pernicious heresies based on errors and on human reasoning. It is because of the teaching of these errors that the true faith is being lost and that the great apostasy is spreading everywhere.*

"See that no one deceives you. For many will attempt to deceive many people. False prophets will come and will deceive very many" (Mt 24:4-5).

"The day of the Lord will not come unless the great apostasy comes first" (2 Thes 2:3).

"There will be false teachers among you. These will seek to introduce disastrous heresies and will even set themselves against the Master who ransomed them. Many will listen to them and will follow their licentious ways. Through their offense, the Christian faith will be reviled. In their greed, they will exploit you with fabrications" (2 Pt 2:1-3).

The second sign is the outbreak of wars and fratricidal struggles, which lead to the prevalence of violence and hatred and a general slackening off of charity, while natural catastrophes, such as epidemics, famines, floods and earthquakes, become more and more frequent.

"When you hear of reports of wars, close at hand or far away, see that you are not alarmed; for these things must happen. Nation will rise against nation, and kingdom against kingdom. There will be famines and earthquakes in many places. All this will be only the beginning of greater sufferings to come. Evildoing will be so widespread that the love of many will grow cold. But God will save those who persevere until the end" (Mt 24:6-8, 12-13).

The third sign is the bloody persecution of those who remain faithful to Jesus and to his Gospel and who stand fast in the true faith. Throughout this all, the Gospel will be preached in every part of the world.

Think, beloved children, of the great persecutions to which the Church is being subjected; think of the apostolic zeal of the recent popes, above all of my Pope, John Paul II, as he brings to all the nations of the earth the announcement of the Gospel.

"They will hand you over to persecution and they will kill you. You will be hated by all because of me. And then many will abandon the faith; they will betray and hate one another. Meanwhile, the message of the kingdom of God will be preached in all the world; all nations must hear it. And then the end will come" (Mt 24:9-10, 14).

The fourth sign is the horrible sacrilege, perpetrated by him who sets himself against Christ, that is, the Antichrist. He will enter into the holy temple of God and will sit on his throne, and have himself adored as God.

"This one will oppose and exalt himself against everything that men adore and call God. The lawless one will come by the power of Satan, with all the force of false miracles and pretended wonders. He will make use of every kind of wicked deception, in order to work harm" (2 Thes 2:4,9).

"One day, you will see in the holy place he who commits the horrible sacrilege. The prophet Daniel spoke of this. Let the reader seek to understand" (Mt 24, 15).

Beloved children, in order to understand in what this horrible sacrilege consists, read what has been predicted by the prophet Daniel: "Go, Daniel; these words are to remain secret and sealed until the end time. Many will be cleansed, made white and upright, but the wicked will persist in doing wrong. Not one of the wicked will understand these things, but the wise will comprehend. Now, from the moment that the daily sacrifice is abolished and the horrible abomination is set up, there shall be one thousand two hundred and ninety days. Blessed is he who waits with patience and attains one thousand three hundred and thirty-five days" (Dn 12:9-12).

THE HOLY MASS IS THE DAILY SACRIFICE, THE PURE OBLATION WHICH IS OFFERED TO THE LORD EVERYWHERE, FROM THE RISING OF THE SUN TO ITS GOING DOWN.

THE SACRIFICE OF THE MASS RENEWS THAT WHICH WAS ACCOMPLISHED BY JESUS ON CALVARY. BY ACCEPTING THE PROTESTANT DOCTRINE, PEOPLE WILL HOLD THAT THE MASS IS NOT A SACRIFICE BUT ONLY A SACRED MEAL, THAT IS TO SAY, A REMEMBRANCE OF THAT WHICH JESUS DID AT HIS LAST SUPPER. AND THUS, THE CELEBRATION OF HOLY MASS WILL BE SUPPRESSED. IN THIS ABOLITION OF THE DAILY SACRIFICE CONSISTS THE

HORRIBLE SACRILEGE ACCOMPLISHED BY THE ANTICHRIST, WHICH WILL LAST ABOUT THREE AND A HALF YEARS, NAMELY, ONE THOUSAND TWO HUNDRED AND NINETY DAYS.

The fifth sign consists in extraordinary phenomena, which occur in the skies.

"The sun will be darkened and the moon will not give its light; and the stars will fall from the sky; and the powers of the heavens will be shaken" (Mt 24:29).

The miracle of the sun, which took place at Fatima during my last apparition, is intended to point out to you that you are now entering into the times when these events will take place, events which will prepare for the return of Jesus in glory.

"And then the sign of the Son of Man will appear in heaven. All the tribes of the earth will mourn, and men will see the Son of Man coming upon the clouds of heaven, with great power and splendor" (Mt 24:30).

My beloved ones and children consecrated to my Immaculate Heart, I have wanted to teach you about these signs, which Jesus has pointed out to you in his Gospel, in order to prepare you for the end of the times, because these are about to take place in your days.

The year which is coming to a close, and that which is beginning, form part of the great tribulation, during which the apostasy is spreading, the wars are multiplying, natural catastrophes are occurring in many places, persecutions are intensifying, the announcement of the Gospel is being brought to all nations, extraordinary phenomena are occurring in the sky, and the moment of the full manifestation of the Antichrist is drawing ever nearer.

And so I urge you to remain strong in the faith, secure in trust and ardent in charity. Allow yourselves to be led by me and gather together, each and all, in the sure refuge of my Immaculate Heart, which I have prepared for you especially during these last times. Read, with me, the signs of your time, and live in peace of heart and in confidence.

I am always with you, to tell you that the coming about of these signs indicates to you with certainty that the end of the times with the return of Jesus in glory, is close at hand.

"Learn a lesson from the fig tree: when its branches become tender and sprout the first leaves, you know that summer is near. In the same way, when you see these things taking place, know that your liberation is near" (Mt 24:32-33).[2]

With these messages from the Virgin Mary to Josyp Terelya and Father Gobbi, we are perhaps given an insight into some of what God has tried to warn us of over the centuries concerning the sacred mysteries of the faith, especially through so many Eucharistic signs and revelations involving Christ's True Presence in the Eucharist and the importance of the Sacrifice of the Mass.

But Mary's revelations carry with them a myriad of questions. Some of whose answers can be found in the Church's own history and writings, and some of whose answers we will never know. But one thing is certain: the Virgin Mary's repeated revelations concerning this prophecy are not meant to be taken lightly.

Mother of the Secret

CHAPTER FORTY-TWO

THE EUCHARIST:
A LINE OF DEMARCATION

The Second Vatican Council's Dogmatic Constitution on Divine Revelation delineated the method by which divine revelation is handed down. The Constitution asserted that the principal intent of the books of the Old Testament is to indicate that the purpose of the Old Covenant was to prepare for the coming of Christ, the Redeemer of all. These books enable us to know God; they also disclose the plan of salvation.

Most significantly, the Dogmatic Constitution defined how the contents of the books of the Old Testament are meant to show their full meaning in the New Testament.

The Council wrote:

> God, the inspirer and author of both Testaments, wisely arranged that the New Testament be hidden in the Old and the Old be made manifest in the New. For, though Christ established the new covenant in His blood (see Lk 22:20; 1 Cor 11:25), still the books of the Old Testament with all their parts, caught up into the proclamation of the Gospel, acquire and show forth their full meaning in the New Testament (see Mt 5:17; Lk 24:27; Rom 16:25-26; 2 Cor 3:14-16) and in turn shed light on it and explain it.

Indeed, as Christ explained to the two travelers on the road to Emmaus, His life and death fulfilled the words of the prophets.

Christ Himself said, *"How slow you are to believe all that the Prophets have announced"* (Lk 24:25). Afterwards, when Christ appeared again, this time to the Apostles, He told them, *"Recall those words I spoke to you when I was still with you, everything written about Me in the law of Moses, and Psalms had to be fulfilled"* (Luke 24:44). Scripture says Christ then *"opened their minds to the understanding of the Scriptures"* (Luke 24:45). Therefore, no Christian can ignore how the words of the Old Testament are enacted in the events of the New Testament.

Likewise, although the mystery of salvation is fulfilled with the completion of Divine Revelation, Christ's own words foretell that which must come before the end of the world. And His words are once again connected to the words of the Old Testament prophets.

Most significantly, the Lord specifically states that some of the words the prophet Daniel spoke are to be fulfilled at a future date. In fact, the Lord refers to no other Old Testament prophet in His foretelling of the future to the apostles:

> *When you see the abominable and destructive thing which the prophet Daniel foretold standing on holy ground (let the reader take note!), those in Judea must "flee to the mountains"* (Mt 24:15).

Scripture tells us that during their lifetimes, the apostles and disciples continued to adhere to Christ's admonition that events would unfold and His words would be fulfilled someday. Most specifically, they especially took into account Daniel's prophecies, just as Christ told them to. In his Letter to the Thessalonians (2 Thes 2:3-4, 8-9), St. Paul parallels, scholars say, the writings of the Book of Daniel as does Saint John in his first Epistle (1 Jn 2:18-23).

In addition, many writers believe that the Book of Revelation cannot be properly discerned without knowledge of the Book of Daniel. Indeed, the symbolism of the images in both books, such as horns and beasts, is overtly apparent.

Over the centuries, many writers have cross-referenced the two books, searching diligently for clues to support their understanding and interpretations of the end times. For the end times will reportedly "fulfill" the writings of both books.

Both the Gospels and the Book of Revelation, as well as the Book of Daniel, assume that the future of the world has been decided. God will rise up to overthrow the powers of the world to then rule forever. All of the books also emphasize God's divine control over the events which ultimately lead to this triumph. Experts tell us that throughout the books, Christ is the central figure who guides believers toward the promised kingdom. However, while Christ's role is apparent in the books of the New Testament, in Chapter Seven of the Book of Daniel He is also clearly discerned to be the mysterious figure whose *"dominion is an everlasting dominion."*

Citing other specific verses of Daniel, theologians agree that the book of Daniel clearly foretells Christ as the coming Messiah. This is especially confirmed by the use of the term *"Son of Man,"* which is repeatedly found in the Book of Daniel, the four Gospels and the Book of Revelation.

In the Book of Daniel (Dn 7:13), we read, ***"One like the Son of Man coming on the clouds of Heaven."***

Likewise, in Scripture Jesus called Himself the ***"Son of Man:"***

> ***To help you realize the Son of Man has authority on earth to forgive sins*** (Mt 9:6).
> ***When the Son of Man comes in his glory, escorted by all the angels of Heaven, he will sit upon his Royal Throne*** (Mt 25:31).
> ***Who do you say the Son of Man is?*** (Mt 16:13).
> ***After that men will see the Son of Man coming on a cloud with great power and glory*** (Lk 21:27).

Finally, in the Book of Revelation (Rv 1:13) we read, *"One like the Son of Man wearing an ankle-length robe, with a sash of gold about his breast."*

Biblical experts have often referenced these verses of Scripture to convey the direct correlation of the events of the New Testament to the events of the Old. But most significantly, these verses by their very words directly connect Daniel's visions and words with Christ's life and words.

Thus, Daniel's words clearly link his prophecies to Christ, and Christ's words establish that some of the meaning of His own prophecies are to be found in the prophecies of Daniel.

Since Christ's words in Matthew 24:15 are clearly intended for a time after His own life, the founders of the early Church interpreted that this prophecy's fulfillment would be directly related to the Church, Christ's Mystical Body on earth, and especially to its liturgical worship.

Father Vincent P. Miceli, S.J. in his book, *The Antichrist*, states that the early founders of the Church foresaw and wrote about an end times scenario involving the Church and especially its liturgical worship. Writes Fr. Miceli:

> *The Fathers of the Church emphasize the corruption of the liturgy that will prevail in the last days.*
>
> *As the end draws near, the Church will be subjected to a fiercer, more diabolical persecution than any previously suffered. There will be a cessation of all religious worship. They will take away the Sacrifice.[1]*

Indeed, this teaching concerning a formidable assault by the Antichrist on the Church's sacred mysteries has spanned the centuries.

The Greek Fathers, who were directly associated with the apostles themselves, established great authority in their writings on this issue. Both Saint Irenaeus (A.D. 135) and Saint Cyril (A.D. 315) of Jerusalem refer to Daniel's visions in their writings concerning Christ's prophetic words, while Clement of Alexandria, Athanasius, Basil the Great, Gregory of Nyssa, Gregory of Nazianzus, and Saint John (Chrysostom) all accepted the traditional teachings on this matter.

St. Hippolytus who lived in the first century, wrote that the Antichrist will order all things that might *remind* men of Jesus Christ to be destroyed and that he will *prohibit* under pain of death, the administering of the Sacraments and the offering of the Holy Sacrifice of the Mass. Hippolytus also wrote that the Mass would have to be celebrated mostly in the forests and in secretive places, as in the early Church.

The Latin Fathers of the Church also referred to Daniel's prophecies in their writing concerning the future of the Church. Saint Augustine especially noted Daniel's words, maintaining that *"whoever reads portions of Daniel even half-asleep"* cannot fail to see that the Church will be greatly assailed in the future. Over the next eight centuries, the same is found in most scholarly writings concerning the "end times" and the Church.

Many of the great medieval writers wrote in depth about the terrifying themes of the apocalypse. Like the early Fathers, their writings were motivated by contemporary predictions of an approaching end to the world. Their writings strongly centered around the early Fathers' writings and Scripture, and emphasized the signs that are to accompany the rise of an Antichrist figure, especially as noted in the Book of Daniel and discerned from Matthew's Gospel and the Book of Revelation.

St Robert Bellarmine, who died in the year 1621 and who was the last Doctor of the Church to specialize in extensive study of eschatology, wrote,

> *"For it must be known that in the divine letters (Scripture), the Holy Spirit to have given to us six sure signs concerning the coming of Antichrist: two of which precede Antichrist himself, namely the preaching of the Gospel in the whole world, and **the devastation of the Roman Empire**: the two contemporaneous men (the Two Witnesses), **which it is to be seen prophesied Enoch and Elias**, and the greatest and last persecution, and also that the PUBLIC SACRIFICE (of the Mass) SHALL COMPLETELY CEASE, the two following (signs) surely, the death of Antichrist after three and a half years (after his rise to power) and the end of the world: **none of which signs we have seen at this time."***

Desmond Birch, in his extensive study of the writings of the Fathers and Doctors of the Church concerning the "end times" (up to and including St. Robert Bellarmine of the 17th century), gives us this general summation of his findings concerning the rise of the Antichrist, and what is obviously the accepted and traditional understanding of Daniel's prophetic words.

> *"Scripture itself speaks of the "abomination of desolations" during which the perpetual "Sacrifice" (the Sacrifice of the Eucharistic liturgy) shall cease. Antichrist shall have outlawed the saying of Mass. Many prophecies state that during this period, the Mass will only be said in the "desert" (wilderness). The Christians will have fled the cities which are controlled by Antichrist. Certain priests will have gone into the wilderness to serve the Christians in hiding."* (*Trial, Tribulation and Triumph* by Desmond Birch, Queenship Publishing, 1997).

From the nineteenth century onward, a wealth of writings is found concerning the end times. Like the writings of the founding Fathers and the medieval writers, the focus continued to be upon the rise of an antichrist figure. Again there is little disagreement that this figure will assail the Church and for some writers, all religion. A look at just one of these writers gives us some insight into the thinking of this era concerning the awaited fulfillment of this prophecy.

John Henry Newman (1801-1890), a Catholic convert and acknowledged scholar, wrote with authority on this topic. Cardinal Newman foresaw the total loss of the Church's temporal power. In particular, he saw signs that Daniel's prophecies were alive in the nineteenth century.

Applying the words of Daniel's prophecies to his contemporary surroundings, Newman became convinced that a great apostasy against the Church was forming. He saw parallels between the Jews repeatedly falling away from the faith and the various heresies which the Catholic Church sequentially experienced over the centuries. From Arianism to the Age of Enlightenment, Cardinal Newman connected the errors of each generation to his own times, foreseeing a climate that would eventually favor the rise of an Antichrist.

It was especially in the peaceful civilized nations that Cardinal Newman suspected danger, for he saw a supreme effort by men toward government without religion. He saw this effort as attempting to rule without truth.

It was also apparent to Cardinal Newman that many countries endeavored to remove all religion from public activities, such as schools, the media and political affairs. Utility would be the principle that societies would be based on, not the principle of truth, wrote Newman.

In the end, Cardinal Newman saw that the objective validity of religion would be denied, as would its historical reality. Rather, people's feelings, experiences and psychological formation would take precedence. - which is exactly what has occurred.

Cardinal Newman also cited what he believed to be the principal cause of all the trouble. It was the *"Evil One,"* Newman said, who was bringing about the apostasy. Wrote Newman:

> *He (Satan) offers baits to tempt men; he promises liberty, equality, trade and wealth, remission of taxes, reforms. He tempts men to rail against their rulers and superiors in imitation of his own revolution. He promises illumination, knowledge, science, philosophy, enlargement of mind. He scoffs at times gone by; at saved traditions, at every institution which reveres them. He bids man mount aloft, to become a God. He laughs and jokes with men, gets intimate with them, takes their hands, gets his fingers between theirs, grasps them and then they are his.*[2]

Cardinal Newman's in-depth perceptions are uncanny in their accuracy; as today the world appears to reflect the fulfillment of his words.

Most significantly, Cardinal Newman wrote that in the final trials of the Church, *"They shall take away the daily sacrifice."* Like the writings of the Fathers and the Doctors of the Church, these words indicate his interpretation of the fulfillment Daniel's words.

Around the same period that Cardinal Newman lived, a saintly mystic and stigmatist, who lived only on the Eucharist for many years, received a prophecy.

The Venerable Anne Catherine Emmerich (1774-1824), an Augustinian nun from Westphalia, Germany, received a powerful vision of the coming times. In this vision, Catherine saw that the Holy Sacrifice of the Mass was the line of demarcation between men in both time and eternity. She saw that the Church would triumph around the year 2000. And Catherine Emmerich said she saw that at a particular moment in history, *"the Holy Sacrifice of the Mass would cease."*[2]

While openly speaking about the existence of the devil and his activities in today's society is rare for fear of loss of credibility, there are contemporary writers who continue to echo Newman's words. Father Randall Paine, ORC in his book, *His Time is Short: The Devil and His Agenda,* concurs that Satan is forging ahead with his plan in our times, a plan aimed at toppling Christ's True Presence in the Church. Writes Father Paine:

> *Satan's sifting will be nowhere so thorough as there where the wheat of the earth has quite literally been lifted to the Cross of Christ. I mean the Eucharist. The Church grew slowly to recognize the full riches the Lord has laid into this mystery, and soon the Sacrifice of the Mass became the central act in the construction of the Heavenly Jerusalem. But Satan came to recognize this too. And he has been working overtime in the last 30 years to find ways to bring the whole, awe-inspiring structure of the Church's liturgy to a ludicrous collapse. His immense success here has bulldozed thousands of Catholic ramparts to dust.*[3]

CHAPTER FORTY-THREE

"THE SACRIFICE
WILL NEVER CEASE"

Shortly before the times of the Venerable Anne Catherine Emmerich and John Henry Cardinal Newman, another great figure in the Catholic Church wrote about Daniel's prophecy and how he believed that this prophecy was directly related to the Holy Sacrifice of the Mass.

Saint Alphonsus Liguori (1696-1787) was the founder of the Redemptorists and specialized in preaching missions and hearing confessions. The author of many books, St. Alphonsus was canonized in 1839, and Pope Pius IX declared him a Doctor of the Church in 1871. In 1950, Pope Pius XII declared him the patron of moral theologians and confessors.

An expert on the Eucharist and the Mass, Saint Alphonsus wrote extensively on the sacrificial aspects of the Mass and how the Mass fulfilled old and new Scripture.

Most significantly, Saint Alphonsus specifically noted in his writings how he believed the meaning of Daniel's words were to be applied to the Holy Sacrifice of the Mass. Wrote Saint Alphonsus Liguori:

> *This offering which our Lord made then did not limit itself to that moment. It began then; it has continued since; it will continue forever. It will cease on earth only at the time of the Antichrist, as Daniel foretold (Dn 12:11).*[1]

In another one of his writings, Saint Alphonsus elaborated on what the prophet Daniel referred to when he spoke of the *"abolishment of the sacrifice."* Wrote Saint Alphonsus:

> *The devil has always managed to get rid of the Mass by means of the heretics, making them the precursors of the Antichrist who, above all else, will manage to abolish, and in fact will succeed in abolishing, as a punishment for the sins of men, the Holy Sacrifice of the altar, precisely as Daniel had predicted.*[2] (St. Alphonsus Liguori, "La Messa e l'Officio Strapazzati" in *Opere Ascetiche*)

Along with the many previous quoted authorities, the writings of Saint Alphonsus Liguori, together with the Virgin Mary's revelations to Fr. Steffano Gobbi concerning Daniel's prophecy, are significant for us in three different ways.

First of all, these revelations call upon Christians to recognize, discern, and dismiss what appears to be misguided interpretations of Daniel's prophecy. Many Christian ministers of various protestant denominations continue to preach that Daniel's prophecy concerning *"the abolishment of the sacrifice"* deals not with the Holy Sacrifice of the Mass, but with the eventual reinstitution of the daily sacrifice of animals by the Jews in the temple on the Mount in Jerusalem. This would then be followed, they argue, by a cessation of the Jews' renewed sacrifices for forty-two months, thus fulfilling Daniel's words in their opinion.

Some televangelical ministries have even traveled to Jerusalem to interview orthodox Jews who hold elaborate plans to rebuild the temple on the Mount, where now sits a Moslem mosque of great significance to the Islamic faith. These Jewish fundamentalists explain that, indeed, they wish to reinstitute the sacrifices of their forefathers. Consequently, they believe this will then fulfill Scripture. They also believe that this will lead them to find the true Messiah.

While there perhaps remains some valid and historically important events to occur concerning the Jewish people, Jerusalem and even the Antichrist, this does not changes the fact that Church Tradition is clear on the true meaning of Daniel's warn-

ing of a coming "abolishment of the Sacrifice," and that this abolishment refers to the Sacrifice of the Holy Mass.

The second important significance of the revelations concerning Daniel's prophecy and the Mass is the understanding of why, theologically, the Holy Mass is really a true and perfect sacrifice. And with this understanding, it is also important to understand how this sacrifice perfectly fulfills the meaning of the Old Testament prophecies that were meant to foretell the coming of the Holy Sacrifice of the Mass, the perpetual renewal of Christ's death on the cross.

Through the words of Saint Alphonsus Liguori, we are given this understanding:

> The Sacrifice of our Lord was a perfect sacrifice of which those sacrifices of the Old Law were but signs, figures and what the Apostle calls "weak and destitute elemental powers" (Gal 4:9). The sacrifice offered by Jesus Christ really fulfilled all the conditions mentioned above.
>
> The first condition, sanctification, or the consecration of the victim, was accomplished in the Incarnation of the Word by God the Father himself, as Saint John reports, "the one whom the Father has consecrated" (Jn 10:36). When the Archangel Gabriel announced to the Blessed Virgin that she was chosen to be the Mother of the Son of God, he said, "The child to be born will be called holy, the Son of God" (Lk 1:35).
>
> This divine victim, who was to be sacrificed for the salvation of the world, had already been sanctified by God when he was born of Mary. From the first moment in which the Eternal Word took a human body, he was consecrated to God to be the victim of the great sacrifice that was to be accomplished on the Cross for the salvation of mankind. Therefore Christ said to the Father, "But a body you prepared for me ... I come to do your will, O God" (Heb 10:5, 7).
>
> The second condition, the oblation or offering, was also fulfilled at the moment of the Incarnation when Jesus Christ voluntarily offered himself to atone for the sins of mankind.

Knowing that divine justice could not be satisfied by all the ancient sacrifices, nor by all the works of mankind, he offered himself to atone for all sins and said to God: "Sacrifice and offering you did not desire ... holocausts and sin offerings you took no delight in. Then I said, 'Behold I come to do your will'" (Heb 10:5-7).

Then Saint Paul adds immediately, "By this 'will' we will have been consecrated through the offering of the body of Jesus Christ once for all" (Heb 10:10). This text is indeed remarkable. Sin had rendered mankind unworthy of being offered to God and of being accepted by him; therefore it was necessary that Jesus Christ should offer himself for us in order to sanctify us by his grace and to make us worthy of being accepted by God.

The third condition of sacrifice—the immolation of the victim—was obviously accomplished by the death of our Lord on the Cross.

Finally, we must look at the consumption and partaking which complete a perfect sacrifice. The consumption is accomplished by the Resurrection, when Christ shed all that was terrestrial and mortal and was clothed in divine glory. He had asked his Father to glorify him (Jn 17:5), but it was not the divine glory which he possessed from all eternity. It was for his humanity that he prayed.

The partaking in the perfect sacrifice was accomplished in Heaven where all the blessed are partakers of the victim's triumph.

The two conditions of consumption and communion are manifestly fulfilled in the Sacrifice of the Altar, which, as the Council of Trent declared, is the same as that of the Cross. In fact, the Sacrifice of the Mass instituted by our Lord before his death, is a continuation of the Sacrifice of the Cross.

Jesus Christ wished that the price of his blood, shed for the salvation of mankind, should be applied to us by the Sacrifice of the Altar. In it, the victim offered is the same, though present there in an unbloody manner. Thus said the Council of Trent:

Although Christ our Lord was to offer himself once to his Eternal Father on the altar of the Cross by actually dying to obtain for us eternal redemption, yet as his priesthood was not to become extinct by his death, in order to leave his Church a visible sacrifice suited to the present condition of mankind, a sacrifice which might at the same time represent to us the bloody sacrifice consummated on the Cross, preserve the memory of it to the end of the world and apply the salutary fruits of it for the remission of the sin we daily commit ...

At his last supper, on the very night on which he was betrayed, giving proof that he was established a priest forever according to the order of Melchizedek, he offered to God the father his body and blood, under the appearances of bread and wine, and, under the same symbols, gave them to the apostles, whom he constituted at the same time priests of the New Law.

By these words, "Do this in remembrance of me," he commissioned them and their successors in the priesthood to consecrate and offer his body and blood, as the Catholic Church has always understood and taught (Sess. 22, c.1).

In the very next chapter the council declares that the Lord, appeased by the oblation of the Sacrifice of the Mass, grants us his graces and the remission of sins. "It is one and the same victim; the one that offers sacrifice is the same one who, after having sacrificed himself on the Cross, offers himself now by the ministry of the priest; there is no difference except in the manner of offering" (Sess. 22, c.2).[3]

Besides St. Alphonsus' explanation of the validity of the perpetual sacrifice of the Holy Mass, scholars note that Scripture also foretold the ceasing of the bloody animal sacrifices.

For example, in the book of Hosea, we read:

For the children of Israel shall sit many days without a king, and without price, and without sacrifice, and without altar, and without ephod, and without teraphim; and after this the children of Israel will return and shall seek the Lord their God and David their king; and they shall fear the Lord and His goodness in the last days.

In his writings, Saint Alphonsus also explained that the prophesied *"abolishing of the sacrifice"* would not be a complete abolishment. The "true Sacrifice" would always continue to an extent, he reminds us, as there will always be the offering of the Holy Sacrifice of the Mass.

Indeed, contemporary visionaries also emphasize that the Sacrifice of the Mass will always continue to be offered. However, much like the early apostles and disciples were forced to conceal their services of worship, it is prophesied that at some point the true offering of the Holy Sacrifice of the Mass may have to be held somewhat clandestinely or apart from what will be considered the mainstream practice of the faith. While all of this is a mystery, the words of Saint Alphonsus again clarify some of this for us:

> *The sacrifice of Jesus Christ will never cease since the Son of God will always continue to offer himself to his Father by an eternal sacrifice, for he himself is the priest and the victim, not according to the order of Aaron of which the priesthood and the sacrifice were temporary, imperfect and inadequate to appease the anger of God against rebellious mankind, but according to the order of Melchizedek, as David predicted: "You are a priest forever according to the order of Melchizedek" (Ps 110:4).*
>
> *The priesthood of Jesus Christ will be eternal, since even after the end of this world he will always continue to offer in heaven this same victim that he once offered on the Cross for the glory of God and for the salvation of mankind.[4]*

Likewise, how and when any partial cessation or suppression of the Mass will ever be legislated by law or occur because of an internal shift in the validity of Church teachings is unclear, but one thing is sure. Even with the fulfillment of this prophecy, many writers emphasize that nothing can occur which would conflict with the promises held within Scripture. This is shown most specifically in Christ's words to Peter, ***"I for my part declare to you, you*** *are 'Rock' and on this rock I will build my Church, and the jaws of death will not prevail against it"* (Mt 16:18), and in Christ's words at the end of Matthew's Gospel, *"And know that I am with you always, until the end of the world"* (Mt 28:20).

With these verses of Scripture, theologians note the implicit guarantee that Christ's True Presence will remain until the end of the world despite the mysterious implications of a period of *"abolition."*

The third significance of the writings of Saint Alphonsus Liguori and the revelations of the Virgin Mary concerning the meaning of Daniel's prophecy of an *"abolishment of the sacrifice"* involves the faithful's need to properly heed these admonitions. Indeed, believers need to understand their responsibility to being vigilant and prepared so that through prayer, reparation and public action they may respond to any challenge to the Church's sacred mysteries.

While a total abolition of the Holy Sacrifice of the Mass is considered impossible, the degree to which some sort of event of this nature may occur must not be understated. Indeed, it would not be such a heralded prophecy if anything less than a widespread impact occurs. Thus, to whatever degree this prophecy may someday be fulfilled, and regardless of when, it will probably produce an unprecedented effect on the world.

Today, an estimated 350,000 or more Masses are offered each day. This continual offering of the bloodless sacrifice of the Mass, according to the great saints, popes and mystics of the Church, is said to allow the world to endure the perils and consequences of the sins that plague it. Withdrawal of this significant amount of grace would consequently have an enormous negative effect on the harmonious function of the world. This effect is not humanly estimable since there is no way of measuring the mystical equation of grace that permits the world to function as it does.

Father P. Huchedé, a highly respected nineteenth century professor of theology at the Grand Seminary of Lavel, France, wrote a timeless work titled the *History of the Antichrist*. In it, he offers an opinion of what would occur if the True Sacrifice of the Holy Mass were in some way altered or interrupted to a degree, and he also concurs with St. Alphonsus and others that this is exactly what the prophet Daniel foretold.

First published in 1884, reportedly the same year of Pope Leo XIII's famous vision of Satan's confrontation with God, Father Huchedé wrote:

> No language can give an adequate idea of the atrocity and effects of this frightful persecution. "I beheld and, lo, that horn made war against the saints, and prevailed over them" (Dn 7:21). "The beast shall make war against the saints, and shall overcome them and kill them" (Rv 11:7). And he "shall crush the saints of the Most High" (Dn 7:25). "And he will put to death all those who will not adore the image of the beast" (Rv 13:15). Then shall the truth be oppressed. The Church shall see her children apostatize in vast numbers, and in the agony of her heartrending grief, she will cry out in the words of her divine spouse, "My God, My God, why hast thou forsaken me?" (Mk 15:34).
>
> "Then by order of the tyrant the continual sacrifice shall be abolished" (Dn 9:27). THE HOLY SACRIFICE OF THE MASS SHALL NO LONGER BE OFFERED UP PUBLICLY ON THE ALTARS. The Church shall be de vastated; the sacred vessels desecrated; the priests shall be scattered and separated from their flocks and be put to death. The beauty of the new Zion has vanished! Her priests sigh; her streets resound with wailings and lamentations because there is no one found to assist at the solemnities of the Lamb. The Church has taken up her abode in the catacombs. (Jerem. Thren-Lamentations)
>
> All the faithful shall be terror-stricken, for there is nothing to equal the ferocity with which the beast will persecute the Church. "The beast which I saw," says Saint John, "was like to a leopard, and his feet were as the feet of a bear, and his mouth as the mouth of a lion" (Rv 13:2). Those who will refuse him obedience, says Saint Gregory (32 Moral., c. 12), shall perish in the midst of the most excruciating torments. They shall be tortured by infernal engines of pain such as had never been thought of before. The persecutors will add

to the terror of punishment the prestige of miracles, which makes Saint Gregory exclaim in a state of bewilderment, "What a frightful temptation for the human heart! Behold a martyr who delivers over his body to torture, and his executioner performs miracles before his eyes!" Where is the virtue that would not receive a profound shock in the presence of such a scene? "Woe, then, to land and sea because the devil is come down unto you having great wrath, knowing that he hath but a short time" (Rv 12:12). "And a time shall come such as never was from the time that nations began even until that time" (Mt 24:21; Mk 13:19).[5]

Thus, based upon Father Huchedé's interpretation of the prophesied coming trials of the Church, and according to many contemporary visionaries' messages, the specific segment of Daniel's words concerning an *"abolishment"* is exactly what the faithful need to focus on.

Indeed, Scripture and the great Church writers have made it clear that the Antichrist's identity is to remain a secret until he appears. Afterward, his reign will be short and futile. But before his appearance, the little flock of the Church must be prepared. They must recognize the Antichrist by his actions, especially if they should see an action that affects the Sacrifice of the Mass or its validity.

Perhaps this is what Heaven has been trying to prepare the faithful for through its many divine interventions. Through Eucharistic miracles, great signs and apparitions, and especially Mary's words, the faithful are being charged and prepared to usher in God's coming triumph, a triumph that will surely come after a considerable trial.

And perhaps this triumph will fulfill Saint John Bosco's famous dream of a great victory. It is a victory, he said, that will be secured through the indomitable efforts of a heroic pope, true devotion to Mary and unwavering faith in the True Presence of Jesus Christ in the Eucharist.

Mother of the Secret

CHAPTER FORTY-FOUR

THE TWO COLUMNS – MARY AND THE BLESSED SACRAMENT

On May 30, 1862, Saint John Bosco prophesied from a dream that after a Vatican Council there would come a great crisis in the Church and in the world. From the dream, St. John Bosco described a mighty, stately ship that was the target of attack by a flotilla of smaller, yet generously armed ships. The stately ship came under great siege by the enemy. The enemy was aided by the wind and waves.

In the middle of the sea, two solid columns, a short distance apart, soared high into the sky. One was capped with a statue of the Virgin Mary, at whose feet were the words: *Help of Christians*. The other pillar, which was far loftier and sturdier, supported a Communion Host of great size. Beneath this was the inscription: *Salvation of Believers.*

The flagship's captain, the pope, called for a meeting of all the ships' captains to discuss their strategy. Meanwhile, a furious storm broke out, causing the conference of ships' captains to disband. After the storm, the pontiff again summoned all the captains, as the flagship stayed on its course. Standing on the helm, the pope valiantly steered his ship between the two columns, from whose summits hung many anchors and strong hooks linked to chains.

Saint John Bosco gives this summary of the climax of his dream:

> *The entire enemy fleet closes in to intercept and sink the flagship at all costs. They bombard it with everything they have: books and pamphlets, incendiary bombs, firearms,*

cannons. The battle rages ever more furious. Beaked prows ram the flagship again and again, but to no avail, as, unscathed and undaunted, it keeps on its course. At times a formidable ram splinters a gaping hole into its hull, but, immediately, a breeze from the two columns instantly seals the gash.

Meanwhile, enemy cannons blow up, firearms and beaks fall to pieces, ships crack up and sink to the bottom. In blind fury the enemy takes to hand-to-hand combat, cursing and blaspheming. Suddenly the pope falls, seriously wounded. He is instantly helped up but, struck down a second time, dies. A shout of victory rises from the enemy and wild rejoicing sweeps their ships. But no sooner is the Pope dead than another takes his place. The captains of the auxiliary ships elected him so quickly that the news of the Pope's death coincides with that of his successor's election. The enemy's self-assurance wanes.

Breaking through all resistance, the new pope steers his ship safely between the two columns and moors it to the two columns; first, to the one surmounted by the Host, and then to the other, topped by the statue of the Virgin. At this point, something unexpected happens. The enemy ships panic and disperse, colliding with and scuttling each other.

Some auxiliary ships which had gallantly fought alongside their flagship are the first to tie up at the two columns. Many others, which had fearfully kept far away from the fight, stand still, cautiously waiting until the wrecked enemy ships vanish under the waves. Then, they too head for the two columns, tie up at the swinging hooks, and ride safe and tranquil beside their flagship. A great calm now covers the sea.[1]

After concluding his account, Saint John Bosco asked a young priest, Father Michael Rua, what he thought of his dream. Replied Fr. Rua:

The flagship symbolized the Church, commanded by the Pope, the ships represented mankind. The sea was an image of the world. The flagships' defenders are the laity, loyal to the Church, the attackers are her enemies who strive with every weapon to destroy her. The two columns were to symbolize Mary and the Blessed Sacrament.[2]

"Very well Father," said Saint John Bosco, *"except for one thing; the enemy ships symbolize persecutions."*
Saint John Bosco then gave this prophecy:

Very grave trials await the Church. What we suffered so far is almost nothing compared to what is going to happen. The enemies of the Church are symbolized by the ships which strive their utmost to sink the flagship. Only two things can save us in such a grave hour: devotion to Mary and frequent Communion. Let's do our very best to use these two means and have others use them everywhere. Good night![3]

Neither Father Michael Rua nor Saint John Bosco mentioned the pope who fell and died. But one other priest, who claims to have heard Saint John Bosco tell the story of the dream, added another dimension. Father John Bourlot insisted for many years that there were actually three popes in St. Bosco's dream, two that had fallen. This point of fact Saint John Bosco reportedly confirmed.

Over the years, Saint John Bosco's dream has been both heralded and awaited in its fulfillment by many.

Many of the prophecies given by the Virgin Mary at Fatima have been fulfilled. Hence, enthusiasts of private revelations have conjectured that Saint John Bosco's dream may be part of the eventual fulfillment of all of Fatima's revelations, especially the remaining prophecies that may concern a great apostasy and chastisement. Indeed, some believe that these prophecies are contained in the unreleased third part of the Secret of Fatima.

Likewise, after examining Mary's apparitions at Akita and Medjugorje, it is apparent that Our Lady and the Eucharist are intended to be the primary vehicles of grace which the faithful will call upon to secure God's victory as foretold at Fatima.

And while the Akita revelations are acclaimed as highly Eucharistic in meaning, the events at Medjugorje are recognized by many theological experts as the quintessential apocalyptic apparition, fulfilling St. John's Book of Revelation which foretells the victory of "The Woman Clothed in the Sun."

Thus, it appears that Saint John Bosco's dream comes closer to fulfillment each day that the world nears the year 2000, the time St John Bosco reportedly foretold Our Lady's victory. It is also apparent that Daniel's prophecy and Saint John Bosco's dream are but two of many prophecies from both divine and private revelations that may be approaching fulfillment in the near future.

Indeed, from Scripture's foretelling of a period of tribulation and apostasy, to Saint Catherine Labouré's promise of a time when the whole world would embrace Mary as its queen, the approaching times appear to carry with them the closing chapters of many foretold events.

In fact, the Virgin Mary's words to Father Stefano Gobbi on December 5, 1994, at the Shrine of Our Lady of Guadalupe in Mexico City, state exactly this:

> *I confirm to you that by the great jubilee of the year two thousand, there will take place the Triumph of my Immaculate Heart, of which I foretold to you at Fatima ...*[4]

CHAPTER FORTY-FIVE

LAST VISION

O ver the last two centuries, visionaries, prophets, mystics and seers have pointed to the year 2000 as a crossroad in the history of the world. It will be a time, they say, when one era will end and a new era will begin.

But complicating all of this future worry is the confusion that has overtaken our present times. For many different groups are making declarations. From millennialists and New Agers to Indians and psychics, the world is deluged with predictions of what may soon take place.

Whether or not God is leaking an across-the-board preview to so many different kinds of prognosticators is unknown. Obviously many of the prophecies are completely invalid. However, even everyday common folk are testifying to mysterious dreams and visions of a coming time of great change in the world, both spiritually and physically.

Thus, it is as if the prophecy of Joel, later echoed by Peter, is truly upon the world:

> *It shall come to pass in the last days, says the Lord, that I will pour forth of my spirit upon all flesh; and your sons and your daughters shall prophecy, and your young men shall see visions, and your old men shall dream dreams. And moreover upon my servants and upon my handmaids in those days will I pour forth of my spirit, and they shall prophesy* (Acts 2:17-18).

But for Christians, especially Catholics, discernment of the times need not be complicated. Many of the prophecies delivered in the past by such voices as the Venerable Catherine Emmerich, Saint Maximilian Kolbe, Saint Catherine Labouré and numerous others were marked by an array of signs and miracles that give affirmation and credibility to their words. Indeed, their lives were characterized by holy and special events intended to confirm that they were of God. From their fulfilled prophecies to their incorrupt bodies, many of the great Catholic voices reveal lives saturated with the supernatural.

Likewise, many of today's most noted visionaries and mystics present a solid array of supporting evidence to legitimize the credibility of their words. Like their predecessors, numerous miracles such as incredible spiritual and physical healings surround their lives. All this lends consistent proof of Scripture's admonition not to despise the signs, wonders and prophetic utterances that mark God's work.

Many of today's visionaries, such as the five female lay-visionaries who emerged in the 1980's, are stigmatists. Their wounds being almost undeniable signs of Christ's True Presence in them and consequently their presence in Him.

But most significantly, the approved apparitions of Fatima give us secure and confident assurance in our prophetic times. For the Church's stamp of approval of Fatima in 1930 confirms its legacy in Church history, both past and future.

Thus, Fatima's prophetic message is a safe source of refuge during our turbulent times. Indeed, Mary promised at Fatima, regardless of the world's response to her call, that *"in the end my Immaculate Heart will triumph and an Era of Peace"* will be granted to the world.

The events at Fatima show us that this peace will be based upon our secure knowledge of Christ's True Presence. For as much as anything else, the Eucharistic emphasis of the message of Fatima is much more revealing of the future than even Fatima's incredible prophecies. Indeed, the depth of this aspect of the message cannot be found in just the Fatima prayers, nor in the apparitions and their revelations. For if we look closely, we will find there is much more and it was given right from the very beginning of the apparitions at Fatima.

At Fatima, the Eucharist was of such great significance to Mary's message that the Virgin Mary's first apparition took place on May 13, 1917, which at the time was the Feast of Our Lady of the Blessed Sacrament.

Years later, after the publication of Sister Lucia's memoirs, theologians began to understand the deeper meaning of this occurrence. For this sign underscored again how much God wants to bring the world to a better and deeper understanding of the True Presence of Jesus Christ in the Eucharist through the Fatima apparitions.

Most curiously, the Eucharistic message of Fatima appears to be a message for the Church that was designed to preempt the approaching times, times that Heaven knew would hold great confusion for the Church, especially concerning Eucharistic adoration and Eucharistic reparation.

With Vatican II's great emphasis on the priority of the Mass, a result was the placing of the tabernacle to one side of the Church. Many initially understood this to be a de-emphasis of Eucharistic adoration. But in reality, the Council was attempting to create special chapels of adoration.

Fortunately, through the efforts of many Fatima apostolates, this situation was rectified. For the Fatima apparitions had especially shown Heaven's desire for Eucharistic adoration.

The 1916 apparition of the angel, who prostrated himself before the Blessed Sacrament in the presence of the three children, was one indication. Then, in Mary's first apparition at Fatima, the children themselves fell also to the ground in adoration before a beam of streaming light in which they "recognized and felt lost in God." The children then repeated the angel's words to them in reparation for offenses against the Eucharist.

Likewise, adoration of the Eucharist as an emphasis of Fatima's message is revealed through Jacinta's words, which relay Our Lady's request for a chapel of perpetual adoration in the Cova da Iria. This chapel stands today just a short distance from where the Virgin appeared, and millions over the decades have adored the Lord here. In fact, it is seen by some as the faithful's response to Our Lord's words at Gethsemane: *"Could you not watch one hour with Me?"* (Mt 26:40).

Some believe that Our Lady prepared the children at Fatima in imitation of her own earthly ways after the Lord's Ascension. For along with the apostles, Mary is believed to have become a model of Eucharistic love.

Indeed, according to the writings of the great mystics, Mary spent her remaining years particularly close to the Blessed Sacrament. Wrote Saint Peter Julian Eymard, *"She found again in the adorable host the blessed fruit of her womb."* The great saint adds: *"She ascended Calvary, but she returned with her adopted son, Saint John, to begin in the Cenacle her new maternity at the feet of Jesus in the Eucharist."*

Through her many intercessions and apparitions today, Our Lady is sent by Heaven to continue to teach and guide her children in accepting the reality of her Son's True Presence in the Eucharist and adoring Him there. As her words reveal to us in so many of her messages, it is a teaching that Mary finds most important for her earthly children.

In fact, when Mary opened her hands over the three children at Fatima and poured upon them the Eucharistic light, writers say that in a mystical way Our Lady was duplicating the moment she first brought forth her Son into this world in Bethlehem. From her flesh, Christ would redeem us and then nourish us in the Eucharist. And all of this began through Mary's Immaculate Heart that first night. At Fatima, the significance of this is reenacted every October twelfth, as thousands adore the Blessed Sacrament in an all-night adoration before Fatima's annual celebration on October thirteenth. The celebration then shifts to Mary and reveals the truth of her words at Fatima: ***"God wishes to establish in the world devotion to my Immaculate Heart."***

Along with the call to Eucharistic adoration there also came at Fatima a strong appeal to the faithful for Eucharistic reparation. This is seen in many of the statements attributed to the children. But theologians say that Sister Lucia's climactic vision at Tuy, Spain in 1929, of a crucified Christ being offered to the Eternal Father, was an especially important sign of God's call to Eucharistic reparation. For this vision, known as the "Last Vision" carried great mystical signifcance, especially Sister Lucia's vivid description of both Christ crucified and the host dripping blood into the chalice on the altar below.

With this vision, Heaven was seemingly telling us that Christ's sacrifice on Calvary is mystically continued through the Mass. Thus, the Church's declarations at Trent and Vatican II concerning the meaning of the Holy Sacrifice of the Mass are corroborated almost perfectly.

From the "Last Vision," we are called to understand that at Mass, we too, like Mary, are to offer ourselves in union with Christ in reparation for the sins of mankind. Like the children of Fatima, each time we receive Holy Communion, we can offer reparation for sacrilegious communions, desecrated tabernacles and the many violations of consecrated Hosts which have occurred over the centuries. With our offering, we too are doing what the angel asked the children of Fatima to do: *"Receive the Body and Blood of Our Lord Jesus Christ, horribly outraged by ungrateful men."*

Perhaps author Francis Johnston, in his book, *Fatima-The Great Sign*, best sums up the intense significance of the Eucharistic message of Fatima and why so many other Eucharistic signs have been given to the world during our times. Wrote Mr. Johnston:

> *Today, we seem to be living in an age of unprecedented Eucharistic manifestations, as if God was going to exceptional lengths to bring home to us the importance of what had been recounted. There is the incorrupt body of Saint Charbel Makhlouf, the great modern saint of the Mass, which is still perspiring a mixture of blood and water; the Eucharistic fasts of Berthe Petit and Alexandrina, to name just two in this century, and the sublime miracle of Lanciano. The case of Alexandrina is especially important since her fourteen year sustenance on the Eucharist alone was confirmed in the hospital by the highest medical authorities as "scientifically inexplicable." She was reputedly told by Christ: "You are living on the Eucharist and the power of My life in souls."*
>
> *Thus, in our de-Christianized twentieth century, a portion of that **"heart burning with love for men,"** as Christ told Saint Margaret Mary Alocoque, "is seen as the seat of that great manifestation of God's love-the Holy Eucharist."*[1]

CHAPTER FORTY-SIX

THE ARK OF THE NEW COVENANT

While the darkness of today's world leaves much to the imagination regarding the glorious era proclaimed to be so near, historians may someday look back in awe at it all. For Heaven has so repeatedly announced the coming of the new times that it may be a wonder to our descendants how so many signs and revelations went unheeded by the majority of the world.

Indeed, the end of this era will probably be seen in clear distinctive steps. These steps will reveal and confirm a divine process begun before and continued after Fatima. But Fatima will be the crossroad.

Like the Israelites' departure from Egypt through the miraculously parted Red Sea, our times may be seen as no different. Fatima is the key milestone which will be recognized as a virtual renewal of God's new covenant with His people. This covenant began with the shedding of Christ's blood on the cross and promised to climax with the glorious resurrection of His Mystical Body, the Church of believers whose names are recorded in the Book of Life.

Most importantly, the significance of the Blessed Virgin Mary in all of this must not be taken lightly. For Mary is the living Ark of the New Covenant, as heralded in the Litany of Loreto.

With the Annunciation, the greatest story in the history of the world begins, as God chooses a divine tabernacle to dwell in order to redeem and restore mankind. The Annunciation was the beginning of the "good news" which God had promised for centuries.

And Mary's "yes" served that promise and also began the end of Satan's tyranny.

Most significantly, when the Angel Gabriel announced, *"The Holy Spirit will come upon you and the Most High will overshadow you"* (Lk 1:35), the Virgin Mary became Christ's unique human parent. No human father is involved, for it is Mary's genetic makeup which solely constitutes Christ's human body.

Thus, the implications from this mystery are endless. At the moment of the Annunciation, the daughter of the Father became the mother of the Son and the bride of the Holy Spirit. This then produced another mystery: a woman became the mother of her own Creator, and the eternal now dwelt in time.

With this, many of the Old Testament's words find their full meaning. Mary, as God has deemed, replaces the Ark of the Covenant and becomes the New Ark.

Just as the ancient Ark was made of incorruptible wood, Mary is conceived immaculate and is also incorrupt. This signifies, according to Mariologists, that Mary was to be preserved from the corruption of the grave. And the Church celebrates this great mystery each year on the feast of the Assumption. Likewise, as the ancient Ark contained the Ten Commandments or Laws; in a similar manner, Mary carried within her the Lawmaker Himself.

Dr. Courtenay Bartholomew, in his book, *A Scientist Researches Mary, the Ark of the Covenant*, unfolds this mystery:

> *As David brought the Ark with the tablets of the Law to Jerusalem from Kiriath-Jearim, so did Mary carry her God from Nazareth to Jerusalem. David leapt with joy in front of the Ark before it was brought to Jerusalem, so did the unborn John the Baptist leap with joy in his mother's womb when Mary arrived at the house of Zacharias (Lk 1:44). Elizabeth's exclamation at the appearance of the living Ark of the Covenant at her doorstep: "Who am I that the Mother of my Lord should come to me?" (Lk 1:43) recalls David's query in 2 Sm 6:9-10 when the Ark came to him from Kiriath-Jearim: "How can the ark of the Lord come to me?" The analogies do not stop there. The Ark remained in the house of Obedom for three months and*

God blessed Obedom. Likewise, Mary brought blessing to the house of Zacharias and Elizabeth, and stayed for three months until John the Baptist was born. As the beautiful Ark was terrible to its foes (1 Sm 5) or to those who treated it with disrespect (1 Sm 6:19), so is Mary fair as the moon but terrible as an army set in battle array (Song 6:10). According to Alphonsus Liguori: "She is called terrible because she well knows how to array her power, her mercy and her prayers, to the discomfiture of her enemies and for the benefit of her servants who in their temptation have recourse to her most powerful aid."[1]

Most significantly, just as the Ark of the Covenant contained a ciborium with some of the heavenly manna that the Israelites ate in the desert, Mary contained in her womb the True Bread of Life which came down from Heaven to feed souls. Jesus' words would later attest: *"I tell you most solemnly, it was not Moses who gave you bread from the desert, the true bread; for the bread of God is that which comes down from heaven and gives life to the world"* (Jn 6:32-34). *"I am the bread of life ... your fathers ate manna in the desert and they are dead; but this is the bread which has come down from heaven. Anyone who eats this bread will live forever"* (Jn 6:48-50).

The apocalyptical significance of all of this for our times is evident. Mary, the Woman Clothed with the Sun whose actions at Guadalupe, Fatima and Medjugorje are so directly linked with the fulfillment of the words of the Book of Revelation, is seen and understood to be fulfilling Scripture's words. Professor Bartholomew explains:

In the time of Christ and Mary, the Holy of Holies was empty. The ancient Ark was not there. However, little did the priests of the Temple know that at the "presentation" of the child by Mary in the Temple, the living Ark of the New Covenant had entered. In the Book of Revelation, the Ark is eventually seen in Heaven. "Then the sanctuary of God in heaven opened, and the ark of the covenant could be seen inside it. Now a great sign appeared in heaven: A woman

> adorned with the sun, standing on the moon, and with twelve stars on her head for a crown" (Rv 11:19; 12:1).
>
> According to Catholic theologians, this certainly could not be the ancient Ark in the desert since that Ark lies hidden somewhere on earth. It can only be the Blessed Virgin the God-bearer.
>
> The Ancient Ark was the most holy object in all of Israel. In like manner, the new and living Ark is the most holy of God's creatures.[2]

Indeed, the Virgin Mary is most holy because by her status she is the Mother of the Eucharist. It was she who gave Christ His Body and Blood, and it is she who now draws her children to the divine grace available in the sacrament of the Eucharist. As Pope John Paul II stated in his encyclical, *Redemptoris Mater* (Mother of the Redeemer): *"Mary guides the faithful to the Eucharist."*

Most importantly, Mary's guidance will be *"intensely Eucharistic"* in the year 2000, the year of the Great Jubilee; even the Holy Father has declared this. Likewise, we see that Mary's many apparitions are meant to prepare the world for the Eucharistic reign of her Son that draws near. As Father Martin Lucia wrote for the journal, *Immaculata*:

> The message of all the Marian apparitions, both past and present, is that the triumph of the Immaculate Heart of Mary will culminate in the Eucharistic reign of the Sacred Heart of Jesus. This Eucharistic reign will come through perpetual adoration of Jesus in the Blessed Sacrament.
>
> Prophetically the Mass for the Feast of Christ the King begins with the opening prayer: "Worthy is the Lamb that was slain to receive honor, glory and praise." Jesus is the Sacrificial Lamb in the Blessed Sacrament. When we give him what he truly deserves, then he will establish his kingdom. What he truly deserves is perpetual adoration. When we profess and express our faith, hope and love through perpetual adoration, we, in effect, proclaim him king by giving him the honor he desires and deserves in the most Blessed Sacrament. Then, by proclaiming him king, he will claim his kingdom by fulfilling his promise to "make all things new."[3]

CHAPTER FORTY-SEVEN

UNTIL THE END OF TIME

Now that the year 2000 is approaching, both the Church and Our Lady foretell a new horizon in the history of man. It is a horizon in which the faithful are called to understand more about the role of their heavenly mother.

Given by Christ to all souls at the foot of the cross on Good Friday, Mary's life and the life of the Church walk hand in hand. She has been the spiritual mother of every soul born over the last 2,000 years. Likewise, visionaries tell us that Mary will again present Jesus Christ to the world for His second coming as she did at His birth.

But first the Church, the Mystical Body of Christ, must suffer. Therefore, Mary's words through her apparitions are to help the faithful to sustain themselves from whatever assault will occur at the height of the apostasy.

Indeed, Mary's words to us now are more than important, they are paramount. For Our Mother reveals that she is the Mother of the Eucharist, a title said to be the most theological of all Mary's titles after that of Mother of God. And it is a title which the faithful need to contemplate in their own imitation of Mary, the perfect disciple.

Through her messages, Mary repeats the words of Jesus: Man cannot live by bread alone, but only by the true bread which is her Son, the bread of life. For in the Eucharist, Mary says, Jesus loves us to the end. And through His love, He teaches us how to love.

Indeed, Our Lady emphasizes that Jesus loves us in our "hearts" so that we may love each other with our "hearts." Mary says that this is why it is in the Eucharist that we find the nourishment which our hearts so badly need.

For believers, this understanding is vitally important today because we live in a world that has lost its capacity to love. It is a world filled with pride, unbridled egoism, avarice, hatred, violence and a great incapacity to love. It is a desolate world devoid of all feelings. But it is only through love, Mary says, that the world will find salvation. The Queen of Heaven tells us that this is why Jesus gave us the Eucharist. He gave it to us for our salvation and the world's salvation!

In the Eucharist, Jesus becomes present to be the food of our spiritual lives and to form in us the true capacity to love. Jesus gives us Himself in the Eucharist so as to love in us, with us and by means of us. He is the True Bread come down from Heaven so that we no longer hunger. He is, Mary says, the Water to drink so that we no longer thirst.

Most importantly, as Our Lady says, the Eucharistic Jesus wants to become the "Good Samaritan" of the Church today. In this way, He will be able to heal the divisions and sufferings of all people and nations. In this way, He wants to lead us to peace, love, reconciliation, mercy and salvation. In the Eucharist, we learn of Him who is humble of heart and in Whom we can find rest for our souls.

Thus, remembering the night the Lord celebrated His Last Supper with the apostles, we find great significance in Jesus' words, *"I have eagerly desired to eat this Passover, with you before I suffer."*

For the Lord was near the summit of every possibility of His love. Indeed, He was about to accomplish on Calvary the sacrifice that would fulfill His own words of love: *"No one has greater love than he who lays down his life for those whom he loved."*

Death: it is the ultimate demand imposed by love. With His sacrifice, Christ was able to fulfill the ultimate desire of love, to be in the constant presence of the one loved. And with His Sacrifice, Christ was able to institute the Eucharist so that He would remain with us always, truly Present with His glorified body and His divinity even though He is hidden under the veil of the Eucharistic species. Thus, His words were fulfilled, *"I am with you always, even until the end of time."*

Indeed, Christ is! In our misery and our poverty, the Sacrament of the Eucharist makes Christ one with us. He becomes the flesh of our flesh and the blood of our blood. In our hearts, He communicates with us, becoming present in our lives every second of the day, ... each day, ... till the end of our lives, ... till the end of all lives, ... till the end of time.

Mother of the Secret

CHAPTER FORTY-EIGHT

MOTHER OF THE EUCHARIST

"*I* am," the Virgin tells us *"the Mother of the Most Blessed Sacrament."*

It is a title Mary received from the moment she said *"yes,"* because at the moment of the Incarnation, Our Lady made it possible for the Word of God to place Himself in her virginal womb. And, while Mary is also truly the Mother of God, because Jesus is true God, her collaboration nevertheless took concrete form, most of all, in giving the Word His human nature. This made it possible for Jesus, the Second Person of the Most Holy Trinity to become man in time.

By assuming human nature, it then became possible for Christ to carry out the work of redemption. This then also made Mary the Mother of the Redemption, a redemption that was carried out from the moment of the Incarnation to the moment of Christ's death on the cross. Thus, the Lord's sacrifice became a perfect ransom to the Father, making a worthy and just reparation to His justice.

Most significantly, Mary is also truly the Mother of the Most Blessed Eucharist. This reality is given her because of her maternal function that first cold night in the Cave in Bethlehem and is relived at the moment of the consecration of the Mass. Because of the powerful action of the Spirit, each time a priest consecrates the bread and wine into the body and blood of Christ, Christ's real presence comes among us. For Jesus, in His Eucharistic presence, is in his divinity and in His glorious body, a body given to Him by His mother, Mary.

In effect, it is the same body which Mary gave Him at birth in Bethlehem. However, it is in a new form. But whether in heaven or in the Eucharist, Christ remains the Son of Mary. Thus, Jesus, at the moment of every Eucharistic consecration, is still the Son of Mary.

Our Lady explained this mystery to Father Stefano Gobbi in detail. On August 8, 1986, the Virgin told the humble Italian priest:

> *"I am therefore the Mother of the Eucharist.*
>
> *"And as a mother, I am always at the side of my Son. I was there on this earth; I am there now in paradise, in virtue of the privilege of my bodily assumption into heaven; and I am still to be found wherever Jesus is present, in every tabernacle on earth.*
>
> *"Just as his glorious body, being beyond the limits of time and space, allows Him to be here before you, in the tabernacle of the little mountain church but at the same time allows Him to be present in all the tabernacles spread throughout every part of the world, so also your heavenly Mother, with her glorious body, which permits her to be both here and in every other place, is truly near every tabernacle in which Jesus is kept.*
>
> *"My Immaculate Heart becomes, for Him, a living, beating, motherly tabernacle of love, of adoration, of thanksgiving and of unceasing reparation.*
>
> *"I am the joyful Mother of the Eucharist.*
>
> *"You know, beloved sons, that wherever the Son is, there too the Father and the Holy Spirit are always present. Just as, in the glory of heaven, Jesus is seated at the right hand of the Father, in intimate union with the Holy Spirit, so also when at your bidding, He becomes present in the Eucharist and is placed in the safekeeping of the tabernacle, surrounded by my motherly heart, close to the Son there is always the real presence of the Father and the real presence of the Holy Spirit; there is always present the divine and Most Holy Trinity.*
>
> *"But, as in heaven, so also at the side of every tabernacle, there is the enraptured and joyful presence of your heavenly Mother. Then, there are all the angels, arranged in their nine choirs of light, in diverse modulations of harmony and glory the omnipotence of the Most Holy Trinity,*

as if to make its great and divine power appear in different degrees. About the choirs of angels are all the saints and the blessed who, from the very light, the love, the unending joy, and the immense glory which issues forth from the Most Holy Trinity, receive a continuous increase of their eternal and ever greater beatitude.

"To this summit of paradise, there also ascend the profound inspirations, the purifying sufferings and the unceasing prayer of all the souls in purgatory. Toward it they strain forward with a desire and a charity which becomes ever greater, the perfection of which is proportionate to their progressive release from every debt, owed because of their fragility and their sins, until the moment when, perfectly renewed by love, they can join in the heavenly song that arises about the most holy and divine Trinity, that is found in heaven and in every tabernacle where Jesus is present, even in the most remote and isolated parts of the earth.

"This is why, there at the side of Jesus, I am the joyful Mother of the Eucharist.

"I am the sorrowful Mother of the Eucharist.

"With the Church, Triumphant and Suffering, which palpitates around the center of love, which is the eucharistic Jesus, the Church Militant should also be gathered together; you should all gather together, my beloved sons, religious and faithful, in order to form, with heaven and purgatory, an unceasing hymn of adoration and praise.

"Instead, today, Jesus in the tabernacle is surrounded by much emptiness, much neglect and much ingratitude. These times were foretold by me at Fatima, through the voice of the Angel who appeared to the children to whom he taught this prayer: 'Most Holy Trinity, Father, Son and Holy Spirit, I adore you profoundly and I offer You the most precious body, blood, soul and divinity of Our Lord Jesus Christ, present in all the tabernacles of the world, in reparation for the outrages, sacrilege and indifference with which He Himself is surrounded....

"This prayer was taught for these times of yours.

"Jesus is surrounded today by an emptiness, which has been brought about especially by you priests who, in your apostolic activity, often go about uselessly and very much on the periphery, going after things which are less important and more secondary and forgetting that the center of your priestly day should be here, before the tabernacle, where Jesus is present and is kept especially for you.

"He is also surrounded by the indifference of many of my children, who live as if he were not there and, when they enter church for liturgical functions, are not aware of his divine and real presence in your midst. Often Jesus in the Eucharist is placed in some isolated corner whereas He should be placed at the center of your ecclesial gatherings, because the church is his temple which has been built first for Him and then for you.

"What causes deep bitterness to my motherly heart is the way in which Jesus, present in the tabernacle, is treated in many churches, where He is placed in an little corner, as thought he were some object or other to be made use of, for your ecclesial gatherings.

"But above all, it is the sacrilege which today form, around my Immaculate Heart, a painful crown of thorns. In these times, how many communions are made and how many sacrilege perpetrated! It can be said that there is no longer any eucharistic celebration where sacrilegious communions are not made. If you only saw with my eyes how great this wound is which has contaminated the whole Church and paralyzes it, halts it, and makes it impure and so very sick! If you only saw with my eyes, you too would shed copious tears with me.

"And so, my beloved ones and children consecrated to my heart, it is you who must be today a clarion call for the full return of the whole Church Militant to Jesus present in the Eucharist. Because there alone is to be found the spring of living water which will purify its aridity and renew the desert to which it has been reduced; there alone is to be found the secret of life which will open up for her a second Pentecost of grace and of light; there

alone is to be found the fount of her renewed holiness: Jesus in the Eucharist!

"It is not your plans and your discussions, it is not the human means on which you put reliance and so much assurance, but it is only Jesus in the Eucharist which will give to the whole Church the strength of a complete renewal, which will lead her to be poor, evangelical, chaste, stripped of all those supports on which she relies, holy, beautiful and without spot or wrinkle, in imitation of your heavenly Mother.

"I desire that this message of mine be made public and be numbered among those contained in my book. I desire that it be spread throughout the whole world because I am calling you today from every part of the earth to be a crown of love, of adoration, of thanksgiving and of reparation, upon the Immaculate Heart of her who is true Mother—joyful Mother but also most sorrowful Mother—of the Most Holy Eucharist."[1]

Many of the Popes have emphasized this reality of Mary, as they have written of how Mary and the Eucharist are intricately linked.

Pope Paul VI, who declared Mary the Mother of the Church at the close of Vatican II, wrote of Mary's special role in the Eucharist. In his encyclical *MYSTERIUM FIDEI*, he wrote:

"May the most Blessed Virgin Mary from whom Christ our Lord took flesh which under the species of bread and wine is contained, offered and consumed, may all the saints of God especially those who burned with a more ardent devotion to the divine Eucharist, intercede before the Father of mercies so that from this same faith in and devotion toward the Eucharist may result and flourish a perfect unity of communion among all Christians."

Likewise, Pope John Paul II has also written extensively of Mary and the Eucharist. In his encyclical, *MOTHER OF THE REDEEMER*, he wrote:

"The piety of the Christian people has always very rightly sensed a profound link between devotion to the Blessed Virgin and worship of the Eucharist. This is a fact that can be seen in the liturgy of both the West and the East, in the traditions of the Religious Families, in the modern movements of spirituality, including those for youth, and in the pastoral practice of the Marian Shrines. Mary guides the faithful to the Eucharist."

Indeed, Mary is the Mother of the Eucharist and God calls the world to this reality. It is a call which God hopes will especially lead the little flock down the road they must now travel, a road to be led by Mary, following her directions, listening to her teachings and expecting everything of her. For we must live the same as Our heavenly Mother did. We must accustom ourselves to do everything, everyday with her. Thus, nothing will disturb our peace.

Like herself, Mary is seeking to lead her "little flock" into a climactic life of love, adoration, thanksgiving and reparation to Jesus present in the Eucharist. With the inspiration of faith which illuminates us, with the flame of love which consumes us, with the strength of God which protects us, we are called to truly experience, like Mary, the Eucharistic Presence of Jesus Christ. For in each consecrated Host, He is truly with us.

It is an invisible presence. But we must not let the fact that our eyes cannot see Him, or that our ears cannot hear Him, prevent us from communicating with Him and Him with us. We must go beyond the senses, beyond the appearances to the powers of our souls. Our Lady says we must especially use our intellects and wills to be with the Lord. And then with our hearts, we must try to learn to love as He did.

Indeed, the power of our intellect can allow us to see Him. It can allow us to see him in His Divinity, in His luminous presence of love and grace. Through the intellect, Our Lady promises Christ will reveal Himself even more to us. And in an even greater way, one more beautiful than our bodily senses would permit.

We must also find Him through our will. For the force of Christ's presence, if we are searching for it, leads us to become absorbed in

His Divine Will. The more we think as Christ did, the ever more enlightened we become. Thus, allowing us to fulfill the mission of doing the will of the Father. A mission we pray for each day in the Our Father and one which Christ Himself requested, *"Not my will, but yours be done."*

Finally, Our Lady says that through love we can find Jesus. In Christ's Eucharistic Heart, we enter into a personal intimacy of life with Him. Our Lord then takes our heart, opens it, expands it and then fills it with His love. Through love, we are led to become like the Apostle John. We are called into a profound intimacy with the Lord, immersed in His perfect and Divine charity.

In the Eucharist, Jesus is truly present in His glorified body, truly present as a victim, as a prisoner of love, hidden under the appearance of consecrated bread, but available in every Tabernacle on the earth. And when we find Him, He blesses us and satisfies all our needs.

Perhaps, Saint Louis de Montfort and Saint Maximilian Kolbe understood these things. Perhaps Saint John Bosco and Saint Catherine Labouré lived such lives. Perhaps Sister Josefa Menendez and Sister Faustina, Saint Margaret Mary and Padre Pio are all telling us that beneath the Cross and in front of the Tabernacle is where they lived and we should too.

The *"Holy Mass,"* Our Lady said at Medjugorje, *"must be our life."*

Indeed, for it is a life centered around the True Presence of God on earth, a True Presence which Saint Louis de Montfort said can be found most easily by having True Devotion to Mary. For in living our consecration to Mary, our Mother of the Eucharist, we can together crush the head of Satan and secure the Triumph of the Immaculate Heart. A triumph that will finally bring "true peace" to our world and to our lives!

Mother of the Secret

EPILOGUE

MORE EUCHARISTIC MIRACLES

The decade of the 1990's has witnessed a considerable number of reported Eucharistic miracles. These reports have been worldwide, with many of them coming from America. As in the past, the stories are quite compelling.

In the Philippines in 1992, a sixteen year-old boy reported that a Host turned into flesh and blood in his mouth after receiving Holy Communion in a convent.

In January 1994, again in the Philippines, two college students reported witnessing a "throbbing or pulsating Host" as they adored the Blessed Sacrament in Eucharistic adoration at a youth cenacle.

In Ogden, Utah, on the feast of Corpus Christi in 1992, Father Lawrence Sweeney felt a sticky substance on his hands while he was offering Mass. A closer look revealed a bright red spot at the bottom of his chalice. This was especially noteworthy since Father Sweeney used only white wine. The Eucharistic occurrences repeated themselves on July 5, the feast of the Precious Blood, when what appeared to be droplets of blood were noticed on the outside of the chalice. The miracles drew widespread attention in the local and national media.

Likewise, on April 10, 1994, at St. Vincent de Paul Church in Yardville, New Jersey, a Host began to bleed instantaneously at the moment of the consecration. It was Divine Mercy Sunday. There have also been two reports in America of Eucharistic Hosts miraculously shedding oil.

All in all, over a dozen Eucharistic miracles have been reported in America in the 1990's, with many more occurring throughout the world. But, probably the most phenomenal reports concerning Eucharistic miracles again came from Naju, Korea.

Indeed, the urgency of Heaven's message at Naju, Korea, regarding the Eucharist intensified in 1995, as five more Eucharistic miracles were reported. Many of them were captured in photographs and on videotape. Three of the miracles were of an extraordinary nature, and one of them reportedly occurred in the presence of the Holy Father in Rome.

The following account is excerpted with permission from the book, *Message of Love, the Mother of the Savior Speaks to the World from Naju, Korea* (Mary's Touch by Mail, 1996).

On October 31, 1995, Julia Kim attended a private Mass with the Holy Father in his chapel in Rome. After receiving Holy Communion, there was a strong fragrance of roses and a strong scent of blood. The sacred Host then became larger in Julia's mouth. Julia was instructed by Monsignor Paik, to go to the back and wait. Julia then witnessed a bright light descend upon the Holy Father and the area around him. In it, Julia saw baby angels dancing and guarding the Holy Father. Our Lady then spoke. Here is an excerpt from part of the message Julia received that day.

"...Hurriedly and with a simple heart like a child, accept the gift (the change of the Eucharist) that God the Father has prepared and make it known to all. Teach the importance of the Mass, the importance of the Sacrament of Confession and the Mystery of the Holy Eucharist to all the children in the world who do not know them and, thereby, perpetually continue the gift of the Paschal Mysteries of the Last Supper and Resurrection.

"The visible change of the Eucharist today was to show that Jesus came to you through the Sacrifice of the Holy Eucharist, which is a repetition of the Sacrifice completed on Calvary, Golgotha, to wash away the sins in the world with His Precious Blood...

"Let all know the Sacred Real Presence of the Lord in the Holy Sacrifice of the Mass where He comes as the Transfuser; help Him wash away the filthy dirt from their souls, and give eternal adoration and praise to the Lord..."[1]

Mother of the Secret

FOOTNOTES

Chapter Five
1. John M. Haffert, T*he World's Greatest Secret* (Washington, New Jersey, A.M.I. Press, 1967), p. 61.
2. Ibid. pp. 66-67
3. Haffert, Op. Cit., p. 79.
4. Venerable Mary of Agreda, T*he Mystical City of God* (Rockford, Illinois: TAN Books and Publishers, Inc., 1978), pp. 635-636.

Chapter Six
1. Pope Pius V., *The Catechism of the Council of Trent* (Rockford, Illinois: TAN Books and Publishers, Inc., 1982), p. 213.
2. Ibid., p. 334.
3. Haffert, Op. Cit, p. 60.

Chapter Eight
1. Nathan Mitchell, osb, C*ult and Controversy - The Worship of the Eucharist Outside Mass* (New York: Pueblo Publishing Company, Inc., 1992), p. 137.

Chapter Nine
1. St. Louis de Montfort, *Secret of the Rosary* (Bay Shore, New York: Montfort Publications, 1984), p. 18.

Chapter Eleven
1. Rev. Edward Carter, S.J., Mo*ther at Our Side* (Milford, Ohio: Faith Publishing Company, 1993), p. 74.
2. Msgr. Patrick F. O'Hare, LL.D. T*he Facts About Luther* (Rockford, Illinois: TAN Books and Publishers, Inc., 1987), pp. 134-135.
3. Francis Johnston, T*he Wonder of Guadalupe*, (Rockford, Illinois: TAN Books and Publishers, Inc.), 1981. p. 99.

4. Daniel J. Lynch, *Our Lady of Guadalupe and Her Missionary Image* (St. Albans, Vermont: The Missionary Image of Our Lady of Guadalupe, Inc.), 1993. p. 16.

5. Christopher Rengers, OFM Cap., *Mary of the Americas Our Lady of Guadalupe* (New York: Alba House, 1989), p. 77.

Chapter Thirteen

1. Father Joseph Dirvin, C.M., *Saint Catherine Laboure of Sister Mary of the Holy Trinity* (Rockford, Illinois: TAN Books and Publishers, Inc.), 1987.

2. Ibid., p. 39.

3. Ibid., p. 74.

4. Ibid., p. 75.

5. Ibid., p. 86.

6. Ibid., p. 84.

Chapter Fourteen

1. Saint Therese Liseux, *Story of a Soul. The Autobiography of Saint Therese of Liseux*. New York: Image Books-Doubleday, 1989) p. 76.

2. ——., *Apparitions of the Blessed Virgin on the Mountain of LaSalette the 19th of September, 1846*. Berlin New Jersey: Gregorian Press (no date), pp. 10-20

Chapter Fifteen

1. Martin Hebert, "Miracles of the Eucharistic Real Presence" in *Eucharistic Adoration* (magazine - no date or publisher given) pp. 32-33.

2. Don Sharkey, *The Woman Shall Conquer* (Libertyville, Illinois: Prow Books/ Fraciscan Marytown Press, 1976), pp. 64-71.

3. Ibid., p. 70.

4. Ibid. p. 71.

Chapter Sixteen

1. ——., *Our Lady of the Eucharist* (pamphlet) (Washington, New Jersey: World Apostolate of Fatima (no date given)), p. 5.

2. Ibid., pp. 5-6.

3. Ibid., pp. 6-8.

4. Ibid., pp. 15-16.

Chapter Seventeen
1. Liseux, Op. Cit., p. 76.
2. Mother Louise Margaret Claret de la Touche, T*he Book of Infinite Love* (Rockford, Illinois: TAN Books and Publishers, Inc., 1979), p. 99.
3. Ibid., p. 80.
4. Ibid., p. 91.
5. Ibid., p. 91-92.
6. Theresa Higginson, M*essages of Our Lord to Theresa Higginson* (pamphlet - no publisher or date given) p. 23.
7. Ibid., p. 26.
8. Jahenny, Marie-Julie, *Prophecies of LaFraudais of Marie-Julie Jahenny* (texts related and presented by Pierre Roberdel) (Montsurs, France: Editions Resiac, 1977) p. 111.
9. Ibid.
10. Ibid., p. 269.
11. Ibid.

Chapter Eighteen
1. Sister Josefa Menendez, Th*e Way of Divine Love* (Rockford, Illinois: TAN Books and Publishers, Inc., 1972), p. 246.
2. Ibid., pp. 252-253.
3. Rev. Silvere Van Den Broek, O.F.M. S*ister Mary of the Holy Trinity* (Rockford, Illinois: TAN Books and Publishers, Inc., 1981, p. 103
4. Ibid., p. 155.
5. Ibid., p. 214.
6. Lorenzo Sales, I.M.C., J*esus Appeals to the World* (Staten Island, New York: Alba House, 1955), p. 164.
7. Ibid. p. 75.

Chapter Nineteen
1. Aldabert Albert Vogel, T*heresa Newman Mystic and Stigmatist* (Rockford, Illinois: TAN Books and Publishers, Inc., 1987), p. 19.
2. Ibid., p. 25.
3. Francis Johnston, A*lexandrena The Agony and The Glory* (Rockford, Illinois: TAN Books and Publishers, 1981), p. 107.

Chapter Twenty

1. John M. Haffert, *Her Own Words to a Nuclear Age* (Asbury, New Jersey: 101 Foundation, Inc., 1993), p. 301.

Chapter Twenty-three

1. Quote is from the pamphlet, *God is Father*. (No Copyright, address or publisher cited.)

Chapter Twenty-four

1. Josef Kunzli, *The Message of The Lady of All Nations* (Santa Barbara, California: Queenship Publishing Company, 1996), p. 99.
2. Ibid., p. 102.
3. Ibid., p. 114.
4. Ibid., p. 115.
5. Ibid.. pp. 148-149.

Chapter Twenty-five

1. Kunzli, Op Cit., pp. 152-153.
2. Ibid., p. 155.
3. Ibid., pp. 155-156.
4. Ibid., pp. 158-160.
5. Ibid., pp. 164-166.
6. Thomas W. Petrisko (editor) *Our Lady Queen of Peace* - Special Edition I. Pittsburgh, Pennsylvania: Pittsburgh Center for Peace, Inc., 1991.
7. Martin Herbert, "Miracles of the Eucharistic Real Presence" in *Immaculata* (Libertyville, Illinois: Immaculata (no date given)), pp. 32-33.
8. Ibid.

Chapter Twenty-Six

1. Petrisko, Op. Cit. p.
2. ——., *Jesus Calls Us* (Appearances and Messages from 1945-1974 to Seeress Julia) (Germany: Neugra-Druck GmbH), p. 138.
3. Sr. Maria Natalia, *The Victorious Queen of the World*, (The spiritual diary of a contemporary mystic, Sr. Natalia of Hungary) (Mountain View, California: Queen Publishing, 1993), pp. 62-63.
4. Ibid., pp. 53-54.

5. Ibid. p. 57.
6. Pope John Paul II, *Crossing the Threshold of Hope* (New York, Alfred A. Knopf, 1994), pp. 136-138.

Chapter Twenty-seven
1. Ted and Maureen Flynn, *The Thunder of Justice* (Sterling Virginia: MaxKol Communications, Inc.), 1993.
2. Father Phillip Beebe, C.P., T*he Warning* (Asbury, New Jersey: 101 Foundation, 1986), p. 42.

Chapter Twenty-eight
1. Flynn, Op. Cit., pp. 249-250.
2. Marguerite, M*essage of Merciful Love to Little Souls* (San Rafael, California: POPE Publications, 1975), p. 401.

Chapter Twenty-nine
1. Petrisko, Op. Cit., p. 17.
2. John M. Haffert, T*he Meaning of Akita* (Asbury, New Jersey: Lay Apotolate Foundation), 1992.

Chapter Thirty
1. Francis Mutsuo Fukushima, A*kita: Mother of God as CoRededmptrix Modern Miracles of Holy Eucharist* (Santa Barbara, California: Queenship Publishing Company, 1994), p. 4.
2. —— A*kita International Marian Convention* (Metro Manila, Phillippines: Two Hearts Media Organization, Inc.), 1993.

Chapter Thirty-one
1. Don Stefano Gobbi, O*ur Lady Speaks to Her Beloved Priests* (St. Francis, Maine: National Headquarters of the Marian Movement of Priests in the United States of America, 1988) pp. 251-252
2. Ibid., pp. 565-566.
3. Ibid., pp. 683-684.
4. Ibid., pp. 720-722.
5. Ibid., pp. 840-842.

Chapter Thirty-two
1. Janice T. Connell, T*he Visions of the Children* (New York: St. Martin's Press, 1992), p. 109.

2. Joseph A. Pelletier, A.A, T*he Queen of Peace Visits Medjugorge* (Worcester, Massachusetts: Assumption Publications, 1985). p. 205.
3. Fr. Rene Laurentin & Ljudevit Rupcic, I*s the Virgin Mary Appearing in Medjugorje?* (Milford, Ohio: The Riehle Foundation, 1988), p. 120.
4. ——, A *Man Called Jozo* (Milford, Ohio: The Riehle Foundation, 1989).

Chapter Thirty-three
1. Gobbi, Op. Cit., pp. 681-682.

Chapter Thirty-four
1. ——., J*esus and Mary Speak in Ireland - Messages to Christina Gallagher* (Ireland: 1991) [NO PAGE NUMBER]
2. Thomas W. Petrisko: *The Sorrow, the Sacrifice, and the Triumph, The Apparitions, Visions and Prophecies of Christina Gallagher* (New York: Simon And Schuster, Inc., 1995), pp. 186-188.

Chapter Thirty-five
1. Michael H. Brown, T*he Bridge to Heaven* (Lima, Pennsylvania: Marian Communications, Ltd.), 1993.
2. Sr. Margaret Catherin Sims, C.S.J., A*pparitions in Betania, Venezuela* (South Boston, Massachusetts: Star Litho, Inc., 1992), pp. 82-84.
3. Brown, Op. Cit., pp. 66-67.

Chapter Thirty-six
1. Petrisko, Op. Cit.

Chapter Thirty-seven
1. Fr. Rene Laurentin, A*n Appeal from Mary in Argentina, the Apparitions of San Nicolas*, (Milford, Ohio: Faith Publishing Company, 1990). pp. 77-78.
2. Ibid., p. 82.
3. Ibid., p. 135.
4. Ibid., p. 145.
5. Ibid., p. 194.
6. Ibid., p. 219.
7. Ibid., p. 297.

8. Ibid., p. 304.
9. Ibid., p. 315.
10. Ibid., p. 323.
11. Ibid., p. 356.
12. Ibid., p. 358.
13. Ibid., p. 365.

Chapter Thirty-eight
1. ———., M*essages of Love The Mother of the Savior Speaks to the World from Naju, Korea* (Gesham, Oregon: Mary's Touch By Mail, 1996), p. 45.
2. Ibid., p. 76.
3. Ibid., p. 83.

Chapter Thirty-nine
1. Ibid., pp. 120-123.
2. Ibid., p, 142.
3. Ibid., p. 143-144.
4. M*essages of Love*, Op. Cit.

Chapter Forty-one
1. Josyp Terelya, *The Kingdom of the Spirit.*
2. Gobbi, Op. Cit. pg. 801-804.

Chapter Forty-two
1. Vincent P. Miceli S.J., *The Antichrist* (Harrison, New York: Roman Catholic Books, 1981), pp. 201-202.
2. *The Life of Catherine Emmerich* - Vol. II p. 194.
3. Rev. Randall Paine, O.R.C. H*is Time is Short: The Devil and His Agenda* (St. Paul Minnesota, The Leaflet Missal Company, 1989), pp. 54-55.

Chapter Forty-three
1. St. Alphonsus Liguori, *The Holy Eucharist* (Staten Island, New York: Alba House, 1994), p. 7.
2. Miceli, Op. Cit., p. 276.
3. Liguori, Op. Cit. pp. 6-9.
4. Ibid., p. 7.
5. Rev. P. Huchede, H*istory of Antichrist* (Rockford, Illinois: TAN Books and Publishers, Inc.), 1981.

Chapter Forty-three
1. Rev. Eugene M. Brown, D*reams, Visions & Prophecies of Don Bosco* (New Rochelle, New York: Don Bosco Publications, 1986), pp. 105-108.
2. Ibid., pp. 106-108.
3. Ibid., pp. 106-108.
4. Gobbi, Op. Cit., p. 893.

Chapter Forty-four
1. Francis Johnston, F*atima: The Great Sign* (Rockford, Illinois: TAN Books and Publishers, Inc., 1981), p. 99.

Chapter Forty-five
1. Professor Courtney Bartholomew, A *Scientist Research Mary The Ark the Covenant*, (Asbury, New Jersey: 101 Foundation, 1996), pp. 116-117.
2. Ibid., p. 117.
3. Martin Lucia, "Fire from Heaven" in I*mmaculata* (Libertyville, Ilinois: Immaculata), p. 3.

Chapter Forty-eight
1. Gobbi, Op. Cit. pp. 508-513.

Epilogue
1. _____, *Messages of Love, The Mother of the Savior Speaks to the World From Naju, Korea*, (Gesham, Oregon: Mary's Touch by Mail, 1996, pp. 235-237.

BIBLIOGRAPHY

Agreda. Venerable Mary of. *The Mystical City of God*. Rockford, Illinois: TAN Books and Publishers, Inc., 1978.

——. *Akita International Marian Convention*. Metro Manila, Philippines: Two Hearts Media Organization, Inc., 1993.

Alacoque, St. Margaret Mary. *The Autobiography of Saint Margaret Mary*. Rockford, Illinois: TAN Books and Publishers, Inc., 1986

——. *Apparition of the Blessed Virgin on the Mountain of LaSalette the 19th of September, 1846*. Berlin, New Jersey: Gregorian Press (no date)

Alonso, J.M. and B. Billet, B. Borinskoy, R. Laurentin. *True and False Apparitions in the Church* (2nd Ed.) St. Laurent, Montreal: Editions, Belarmine. (no date)

——. *A Man Called Jozo*. Milford, Ohio: The Riehle Foundation, 1989.

Ball, Ann. *Modern Saints*. Rockford, Illinois: TAN Books and Publishers, 1983.

Bartholomew, Professor Courtney. *A Scientist Research Mary The Ark of the Covenant*. Asbury, New Jersey: The 101 Foundation, 1995.

Beebe, Father Phillip, C.P. *The Warning*. Asbury, New Jersey: 101 Foundation, 1986.

Belloc. Hillaire, *The Great Heresies*. Rockford, Illinois: TAN Books and Publishers, Inc., 1991.

Birch, Desmond, *Trial Tribulation and Triumph,* Santa Barbara, California: Queenship Publishing Co., 1996.

Bokenkotter, Thomas. *A Concise History of the Catholic Church*. New York: Doubleday, 1979.

Bonin, Jeanne Savard, *A Stigmatist Marie-Rose Ferron,* Montreal, Canada: Editions Paulines, 1988.

Brown, Rev. Eugene M. (ed.). *Dreams, Visions & Prophecies of Don Bosco.* New Rochelle, New York: Don Bosco Publications, 1986.

Brown, Michael H. *The Bridge to Heaven.* Lima, Pennsylvania: Marian Communications, Ltd., 1993.

Brown, Raphael. *Saints Who Saw Mary.* Rockford, Illinois: TAN Books and Publishers, Inc., 1955.

Brown, Raphael. *The Life of Mary as Seen By the Mystics.* Rockford, Illinois: TAN Books and Publishers, Inc., 1995.

Bunson, Matthew. *Our Sunday Visitor's Encyclopedia of Catholic History.* Huntington, Indiana: Our Sunday Visitor, Inc., 1995.

Carroll, Rev. Msgr. Richard L. *The Remnant Church.* Chelsea, Michigan: Book Crafters, 1993.

Carter, Rev. Edward, S.J. *Mother at Our Side.* Milford, Ohio: Faith Publishing Company, 1993.

Christiani, Msgr. Leon. *St. Bernard of Clairvaux.* Boston, Massachusetts: St. Paul Editions, 1993.

Connell, Janice T. *The Visions of the Children.* New York: St. Martin's Press, 1992.

Cruz, Joan Carroll. *Miraculous Images of Our Lady.* Rockford, Illinois: TAN Books and Publishers, Inc., 1993.

Cruz, Joan Carroll. *Eucharistic Miracles.* Rockford, Illinois: TAN Books and Publishers, Inc., 1987.

Delaney, John J. *Pocket Dictionary of Saints.* New York: Doubleday Dell Publishing Group, Inc., 1980.

Delaney, John J. (ed.). *A Woman Clothed with the Sun.* New York: Image-Doubleday, 1990.

de la Touche, Mother Louise Margaret. *The Book of Infinite Love.* Rockford, Illinois: TAN Books and Publishers, Inc., 1979.

de Montfort, Saint Louis. *The Secret of the Rosary*. Bay Shore, New York: Montfort Publications, 1984.

di Maria, S. *The Most Holy Virgin at San Damiano*. Hauteville, Switaerland: Editions du Parvis.

Faricy, Robert, S.J. and Lucy Rooney, S.N.D. *Mary Queen of Peace Is the Mother of God Appearing in Medjugorje?* New York: Alba House-Veritas Publications, 1984.

Flynn, Ted and Maureen. *The Thunder of Justice*. Sterling, Virginia: MaxKol Communications, Inc., 1993.

Francois, Robert. *O Children Listen to Me*. Lindenhurst, New York: The Workers of Our Lady of Mount Carmel, Inc., 1980.

Freze, Michael, S.F.O. *The Making of Saints*. Huntington, Indiana: Our Sunday Visitor, Inc., 1991.

Fukushima, Francis Mutsuo. *Akita: Mother of God as CoRedemptrix Modern Miracles of Holy Eucharist*. Santa Barbara, California: Queenship Publishing Company, 1994.

Giese, Rev. Vincent. *John Henry Newman Heart to Heart*. New Rochelle, New York: New City Press, 1993.

Gobbi, Don Stefano. *Our Lady Speaks to Her Beloved Priests*. St. Francis, Maine: National Headquarters of the Marian Movement of Priests in the United States of America, 1988.

———. *God is Father* (pamphlet - no publisher or date given)

Gottemoller, Father Bartholomew, O.C.S.O. *Words of Love*. Rockford, Illinois: TAN Books and Publishers, 1985.

Grenier, Brian. *Understanding the Sunday Eucharist*. Staten Island, New York: Alba House, 1990.

Haffert, John M. *Her Own Words to a Nuclear Age*. Asbury, New Jersey: Lay Apostolate Foundation, 1993.

Haffert, John M. *Sign of Her Heart*. Washington, New Jersey: Ave Maria Institute, 1971.

Haffert, John M. *The Meaning of Akita*. Asbury, New Jersey: 101 Foundation, Inc. 1989.

Haffert, John M. *The World's Greatest Secret*. Washington, New Jersey: A.M.I. Press, 1967.

Haffert, John M. *To Prevent This*. Manila, Philippines: Two Hearts Media, Inc. (Printed in U.S. by 101 Foundation, Asbury, New Jersey, 1993).

Herbert, Martin. *"Miracle of the Eucharistic Real Presence"* in *Immaculata*. Libertyville, Illinois: Immaculata (no date).

Higginson, Theresa. *Messages of Our Lord to Theresa Higginson*. (pamphlet - no publisher or date given).

Huchede, Rev. P. *History of Antichrist*. Rockford, Illinois: TAN Books and Publishers, Inc., 1974.

Jahenny, Marie-Julie. *Prophecies of LaFraudais of Marie Julie Jahenny*. (texts related and presented by Pierre Roberdel) Montsurs, France: Editions Resiac, 1977.

Jerimias, Joachim. *The Eucharistic Words of Jesus*. Philadelphia, Pennsylvania: Trinity Press International, 1990.

———. *Jesus Calls Us* (Appearances and Messages from 1945-1973 to Seeress Julia). Germany: Neugra- Druck GmbH, 1985.

John Paul II, Pope. *Crossing the Threshold of Hope*. New York: Alfred A. Knopf, 1994.

John Paul II, Pope. *Dives in Misericordia*. Encyclical Letter published in U.S.A. - Boston, Massachusetts: St. Paul Editions (no date).

Johnston, Francis. *Alexandrena The Agony and The Glory*. Rockford, Illinois: TAN Books and Publishers, Inc., 1979.

Johnston, Francis. *Fatima: The Great Sign*. Rockford, Illinois: TAN Books and Publishers, Inc., 1981.

Johnston, Francis. *The Wonder of Guadalupe*. Rockford, Illinois: TAN Books and Publishers, 1981.

Kodell, Jerome, *The Eucharist in the New Testament*. Collegeville, Minnesota: The Liturgical Press, 1988.

Kosicki, Rev. George W. C.S.B. *The Living Eucharist Countersign to our Age and Answer to Crisis.* Milford, Ohio: Faith Publishing Company, 1991.

Kosicki, Rev. George W. C.S.B. *Now is the Time for Mercy.* Stockbridge, Massachusetts: Marian Helpers, 1991.

Kramer, Rev. Herman Bernard. *The Book of Destiny.* Rockford, Illinois: TAN Books and Publishers, Inc., 1955.

Kunzli, Josef (ed.). *Eucharistic Experiences* (mystical visions and messages of Ida Peerdman received curing Holy Mass from 1970 to 1984). Santa Barbara, California: Queenship Publishing Company, 1996.

Kunzli, Josef. *The Message of The Lady of All Nations.* Santa Barbara, California: Queenship Publishing Company, 1996.

Laffineur, Fr. Matiene and M.T. Le Pelletier. *Star on the Mountain.* Lindenhurst, New York: Our Lady of Mount Carmel de Garabandal, Inc., 1969.

Laurentin, Fr. Rene. *An Appeal from Mary in Argentina The Apparitions of San Nicolas.* Milford, Ohio: Faith Publishing Company, 1990

Laux, Rev. John, M.A. *Church History A Complete History of the Catholic Church to the Present Day.* Rockford, Illinois: TAN Books and Publishers, Inc., 1989.

Liguori, St. Alphonsis. *The Holy Eucharist.* Staten Island, New York: Alba House, 1994.

Liseux, Saint Therese of. *The Autobiography of Saint Therese of Liseux.* New York: Image Books-Doubleday, 1989.

——. *Little Nellie of Holy God.* (pamphlet) Long Beach Dalifornia: Litho Tech Impressions, 1993.

Lord, Bob and Penny. *This Is My Body, This Is my Blood - Miracles of the Eucharist.* Lord: Journeys of Faith, 1986.

Lord, Bob and Penny. *This Is My Body, This Is My Blood - Miracles of the Eucharist Book II.* Lord: Journeys of Faith, 1994.

Lucia, Fr. Martin, "Fire from Heaven", in *Immaculata.* Libertyville, Illinois: Immaculata (no date).

Meagher, Father James L., D.D. *How Christ Said the First Mass*. Rockford, Illinois: TAN Books and Publishers, 1975.

Mansour, Claire and Dr. Antoine. *Our Lady of Soufanieh*. Beverly Hills, California: Mansour, 1991.

Marguerite, *Message of Merciful Love* to Little Souls. San Rafael, California: POPE Publications, 1975.

——. *Messages of Love The Mother of the Savior Speaks to the World from Naju, Korea*. Gesham, Oregon: Mary's Touch By Mail, 1996.

Mitchell, Nathan, osb. *Cult in Controversy - The Worship of Eucharist Outside of Mass*. New York: Pueblo Publishing Company, Inc., 1982.

Menendez, Sister Josefa, *The Way of Divine Love*. Rockford, Illinois: TAN Books and Publishers, Inc., 1972.

Miceli, Vincent P., S.J. *The Antichrist*. Harrison, New York: Roman Catholic Books, 1981.

O'Carroll, Michael, Cssp. *Medjugorje Facts, Documents, Theology*. Dublin, Ireland: Veritas, 1986.

Publican, the. *Miracle of Damascus*. Glendale, California: The Messengers of Unity, 1989.

Montague, George T., S.M. *The Apocalypse*. Ann Arbor, Michigan: Servant Publications, 1992.

Muller, Fr. Michael, C.S.S.R. *The Blessed Eucharist Our Greatest Treasure*. Rockford, Illinois: TAN Books and Publishers, Inc., 1973.

Natalia, Sr. Maria. *The Victorious Queen of the World*. (the spiritual diary of a contemporary mystic, Sr. Natalia of Hungary) Mountain View, California: Queen Publishing, 1993.

Odell, Catherine M. *Those Who Saw Her The Apparitions of Mary*. Huntington, Indiana: Our Sunday Visitor, Inc. 1986.

O'Hare, Msgr. Patrick F. LL.D. *The Facts About Luther*. Rockford, Illinois: TAN Books and Publishers, Inc., 1987.

O'Reilly, Father A.J., D.D. *The Martyrs of the Coliseum*. Rockford, Illinois: TAN Books and Publishers, Inc., 1885.

——. *Our Lady of the Eucharist* (pamphlet). Washington, New Jersey: World Apostolate of Fatima (no date).

Petrisko, Thomas W. *Call of the Ages.* Santa Barbara, California: Queenship Publishing Company, 1995.

Petrisko, Thomas W. (editor) *Our Lady Queen of Peace* - Special Edition I. Pittsburgh, Pennsylvania: Pittsburgh Center for Peace, Inc., 1991.

Petrisko, Thomas W. (editor) *Our Lady Queen of Peace* - Special Edition II. Pittsburgh, Pennsylvania: Pittsburgh Center for peace, Inc., 1992.

Petrisko, Thomas W. (editor) *Our Lady Queen of Peace* - Special Edition III. Pittsburgh, Pennsylvania: Pittsburgh Center for Peace, Inc., 1995.

Petrisko, Thomas W. *The Sorrow, The Sacrifice, and the Triumph, The Apparitions, Visions and Prophecies of Christina Gallagher.* New York: Simon and Schuster, Inc. 1995.

Pius V, Pope. *The Catechism of the Council of Trent.* Rockford, Illinois: TAN Books and Publishers, Inc., 1982.

Pius XII, Pope. *"Mystici Corporis" - Encyclical Letter of His Holiness.* Boston, Massachusetts: St. Paul Editions (no date).

Power, David N. *The Eucharistic Mystery.* New York: Crossroad Publishing Company, 1994.

Ratzinger, Joseph Cardinal with Vittorio Messori. *The Ratzinger Report.* San Francisco, California: Ignatius Press, 1985. Roberdel, Pierre. T*he Prophecies of La Fraudais.* Montsurs, France: Editions Resiac, 1977.

Rengers, Christopher, OFM, Cap. *Mary of the Americas Our Lady of Guadalupe.* New York: Alba House, 1989.

Reuter, Fr. Frederick A. *Moments Divine Before the Blessed Sacrament.* Rockford, Illinois: TAN Books and Publishers, Inc., 1922.

Sales, Lorenzo, I.M.C. *Jesus Appeals to the World.* Staten Island, New York: Alba House, 1955.

Schreck, Alan. *The Compact History of the Catholic Church.* Ann Arbor, Michigan: Servant Books, 1987.

Schmoger, Very Rev. Carl E., C.SS.R. *The Life of Anne Catherine Emmerich - Volume 2*. Rockford, Illinois: TAN Books and Publishers, Inc., 1976.

Sharkey, Don. *The Woman Shall Conquer*. Libertyville, Illinois: Prow Books/Franciscan Marytown Press, 1976.

Sims, Sr. Margaret Catherine, C.S.J. *Apparitions in Betania, Venezuela*. South Boston, Massachusetts: Star Litho, Inc., 1992.

Spechbecker, Franz. *Novena to the Rosa Mystica Novena* (booklet). Asbury, New Jersey: 101 Foundation, Inc. 1996.

Stravinkas, Reverend Peter M.J., Ph.D., S.T.L. (editor) *Our Sunday Visitor's Catholic Encyclopedia*. Huntington, Indiana: Our Sunday Visitor, Inc., 1965.

Terelya, Josyp. *In the Kingdom of the Spirit*. Pueblo, Colorado: Abba House, 1995.

——., "Tertio Millenio Adveniente" in *Inside the Vatican*. New Hope Kentucky: Martin de Porres Lay Dominican Community Print shop, December, 1994.

——., *The Flame of Love of the Immaculate Heart of Mary* (The spiritual diary of a Third Order Carmelite, a widow with six children. 1913-1985) Mountain View, California: Two Hearts Books and Publishers, 1990.

——. *The Miracle in Naju, Korea — Heaven Speaks to the World*. Gresham, Oregon: Mary's Touch By Mail, 1992.

——. *The New American Bible*. Witchita, Kansas: Catholic Bible Publishers, 1984-85 Edition.

Van Den Broek, Rev., Silvere O.F.M. *The Spiritual Legacy of Sister Mary of the Holy Trinity*. Rockford, Illinois: TAN Books and Publishers, Inc., 1981.

Vann, Father Joseph, O.F.M. (editor) *Lives of Saints*. New York: John J. Crawley & Co. Inc., 1954.

Vogel, Aldabert Albert. *Theresa Newman Mystic and Stigmatist*. Rockford, Illinois: TAN Books and Publishers, Inc., 1987.

Williams, Thomas David. *The Textural Concordance of Holy Scriptures*. Rockford, Illinois: TAN Books and Publishers, 1985.

ABOUT THE COVER

"Mary is entitled to be called Mother of the Holy Eucharist and that title tells us all the wonder of Mary's love for us."

—*St. Louis de Montfont*

The Mother of the Holy Eucharist monstrance seen on the cover was created by Gerry and Joe Simboli. Made of mahogany, it stands 3 ft. tall. The Blessed Mother's hands gently encompass a golden luna where Jesus is the focus of attention. She holds her Son over her heart. Thirty five of these monstrances have been created and are used for adoration around the world. As Rouhault de Fleury said: "The Saviour shines in the midst of her breast like the Eucharist with all the veils torn away." Jesus lives in her. Jesus is her life and she is the Word-carrier, she serves as His monstrance.

For more information about the Mother of the Holy Eucharist monstrance please contact:

Simboli Design
Box 26
Cheyney, PA 19319
(610) 399-0156

Visit your local bookstore for other great titles from:
QUEENSHIP PUBLISHING

Not byFaith Alone
by Robert Sungenis
ISBN # 1-57918-008-6

Journeys Home
by Marcus Grodi
ISBN # 1-57918-001-9

A Journey Through Life
The Autobiography of Fr. Luke Zimmer
ISBN #1-882972-83-X

Mary: Coredemptrix, Mediatrix, Advocate
Theological Foundations II
edited by Dr. Mark Miravelle
ISBN #1-882972-92-9

Trial, Tribulation and Triumph
Before, During and After Antichrist
by Desmond A. Birch
ISBN #1-882972-73-2

Jesus, Peter and the Keys
A Scriptural Handbook on the Papacy
by Scott Butler, Norman Dahlgren and David Hess
ISBN #1-882972-54-6

Marian Apparitions Today
Why So Many?
by Fr. Edward O'Connor
ISBN #1-882972-71-6

Mary: God's Supreme Masterpiece
by Fr. Bartholomew Gottemoller
ISBN #1-882972-64-3